CRISES AT WORK

Understanding Work and Employment Relations

Series Editors: **Andy Hodder**, University of Birmingham and **Stephen Mustchin**, University of Manchester

---

Published in association with the British Universities Industrial Relations Association (BUIRA), books in this series critically engage with issues of work and employment in their wider socio-economic context.

Find out more about the new and forthcoming titles in the series:

bristoluniversitypress.co.uk/
understanding-work-and-employment-relations

CRISES AT WORK

Economy, Climate and Pandemic

Steve Williams and Mark Erickson

First published in Great Britain in 2026 by

Bristol University Press
University of Bristol
1–9 Old Park Hill
Bristol
BS2 8BB
UK
t: +44 (0)117 374 6645
e: bup-info@bristol.ac.uk

Details of international sales and distribution partners are available at bristoluniversitypress.co.uk

© Bristol University Press 2026

British Library Cataloguing in Publication Data
A catalogue record for this book is available from the British Library

ISBN 978-1-5292-2490-0 hardcover
ISBN 978-1-5292-2491-7 paperback
ISBN 978-1-5292-2492-4 ePub
ISBN 978-1-5292-2493-1 ePdf

The right of Steve Williams and Mark Erickson to be identified as authors of this work has been asserted by them in accordance with the Copyright, Designs and Patents Act 1988.

All rights reserved: no part of this publication may be reproduced, stored in a retrieval system, or transmitted in any form or by any means, electronic, mechanical, photocopying, recording, or otherwise without the prior permission of Bristol University Press.

Every reasonable effort has been made to obtain permission to reproduce copyrighted material. If, however, anyone knows of an oversight, please contact the publisher.

The statements and opinions contained within this publication are solely those of the authors and not of the University of Bristol or Bristol University Press. The University of Bristol and Bristol University Press disclaim responsibility for any injury to persons or property resulting from any material published in this publication.

Bristol University Press works to counter discrimination on grounds of gender, race, disability, age and sexuality.

Cover design: Nicky Borowiec
Front cover image: Adobe Stock/Shanti

Bristol University Press' authorised representative in the European Union is: Easy Access System Europe, Mustamäe tee 50, 10621 Tallinn, Estonia, Email: gpsr.requests@easproject.com

Contents

Series Editors' Preface: Understanding Work and Employment Relations		vi
List of Figures		viii
List of Abbreviations		ix
Acknowledgements		x
Prologue: The 'Polycrisis'		xi
1	Introducing the Crisis of Work	1
2	Theorizing Crises	21
3	Labour Markets in Crisis	35
4	Employment Relations in Crisis	55
5	Equalities in Crisis	77
6	Trade Unions in Crisis	101
7	Crises at Work: Broader Dimensions	121
8	Crises at Work: Implications and Responses	145
9	Beyond Crisis?	169
References		183
Index		232

Series Editors' Preface: Understanding Work and Employment Relations

Andy Hodder and Stephen Mustchin

We are very pleased to introduce the latest volume in this book series, Understanding Work and Employment Relations. *Crises at Work*, authored by Steve Williams and Mark Erickson, is the fifth text to be published in the series.

This series has been designed as a space for both monographs and edited volumes to highlight the latest research and commentary in the academic field of employment relations. The series is associated with the British Universities Industrial Relations Association (BUIRA), which marked 70 years of existence in 2020. The series seeks to draw on the expertise of the membership of BUIRA and contributions to its annual conference, as well as employment relations academics from around the world. Employment relations is a mature field of study and continues to be of relevance to academic and practitioner audiences alike. BUIRA recognizes the broad nature of the field of employment relations and acknowledges that the field of study is constantly developing and evolving. BUIRA regards employment relations to be the study of the relation, control and governance of work and the employment relationship. It is the study of rules (both formal and informal) regarding job regulation and the 'reward–effort bargain'. These issues remain relevant today, in an era where the standard employment relationship has become increasingly fragmented due to employers' pursuit of labour flexibility and in which we see the continued expansion of the gig or platform economy. Employment relations – and adjacent research areas including human resource management (HRM) and the sociology of work – is taught widely in universities around the world, most commonly in business and management schools and departments. The field of study is multidisciplinary, encompassing law, politics, history, geography, sociology and economics. HRM has a tendency to focus uncritically on management objectives, without exploring issues of work and employment in their wider socio-economic context and has its disciplinary roots in psychology, whereas employment relations retains a strong critical social science tradition. As scholars in this area, we feel there is a need for regular, up-to-date, research-focused books that reflect current work in the field and go further than standard introductory texts. Through this book series, we aim to take an interdisciplinary approach to understanding work and employment relations, and we welcome proposals from academics across this range of disciplines. We also welcome ideas and proposals from a broad range of international and comparative perspectives in order to reflect the increasingly diverse and internationalized nature of the field both in the UK and globally.

Crises at Work makes an incisive contribution to debates around the changing world of work. The authors argue persuasively that changes to work and employment need to be understood in the context of three interrelated crises: economic crisis, the crisis of the COVID-19 pandemic and its long aftermath and the climate emergency. All too often, the changing nature of work and employment is reduced to what goes on within organizations, industries or employment relationships without enough acknowledgement of the wider forces influencing and shaping the evolving nature of how work is organized and experienced. This book avoids this trap by providing a sophisticated analysis of crises in labour markets, employment relations, equalities and trade unions, before considering the wider dimensions of crises that have significant implications for work. By deepening our understanding of this 'polycrisis', the book helps us to frame and interpret the ongoing changes affecting the nature of work.

We hope you enjoy reading this book. If you would like to discuss a proposal of your own, then email the series editors. We look forward to hearing from you.

List of Figures

2.1	Core elements of social structure	28
2.2	Contextualized model of capitalism–work relationship	29
7.1	UK annual GDP growth (%), 2003–22	122
7.2	Quarterly change (%) in UK real average weekly earnings, 2020–23	131

List of Abbreviations

AI	artificial intelligence
CEO	Chief Executive Officer
CJRS	Coronavirus Job Retention Scheme
CoP	Conference of the parties
CWU	Care Workers' Union
EM	electronic monitoring
ETUC	European Trade Union Confederation
EU	European Union
GDP	gross domestic product
GND	Green New Deal
HE	higher education
HRM	human resource management
ILO	International Labour Organization
ITUC	International Trade Union Confederation
JSO	Just Stop Oil
LA	local authority
LGBTQ	Lesbian, gay, bisexual, transgender, queer
LWF	Living Wage Foundation
MP	Member of Parliament
NHS	National Health Service
NPM	New Public Management
OECD	Organisation for Economic Co-operation and Development
ONS	Office for National Statistics
PPE	personal protective equipment
RCN	Royal College of Nursing
RMT	Rail, Maritime and Transport Union
TUC	Trades Union Congress
UAW	United Automobile Workers
UCU	University and College Union
UN	United Nations
WGA	Writers Guild of America
WBG	Women's Budget Group
XR	Extinction Rebellion

Acknowledgements

We appreciate the support and forbearance of Paul Stevens, Ellen Pearce and Isobel Green of Bristol University Press during the writing of this book. We also thank the reviewers for their feedback on a draft version of the manuscript and the series editors, Andy Hodder and Stephen Mustchin, for their helpful and constructive comments. We acknowledge the contribution made by Harriet Bradley to earlier versions of some of the chapters. Mark Erickson thanks Sara Bragg and Milica Erickson-Bragg. Steve Williams thanks Gabriela Nacu of the University of Portsmouth for covering some of his work and enabling him to complete the book, and Anna for her continued support.

Prologue: The 'Polycrisis'

We are surrounded by crises and have lived with, and in, crisis for a long time. The legacy of the multiple crises of the Cold War still haunts our geopolitical landscape; in the UK, our National Health Service is 'in crisis'; we are told we are facing a 'crisis of immigration'; we experience mental health crises; there is a 'homelessness crisis'; the global financial system went into crisis in 2007–8. We could go on. However, we need a sense of perspective and proportion to understand our crisis-ridden world if we are to find ways out of crisis. While there are many ways to conceptualize crisis, and to view crises across a historical perspective, in our current situation the crises we face, be they 'natural' or caused by humans, have a common cause in the fundamental operation and antagonisms of capitalism.

In this book, we argue that the changing world of work must be understood in the context of three crises: the economy, the COVID-19 pandemic and the climate emergency. These three crises are interrelated and have considerable consequences for people's lives. We argue that these three crises combine to form a 'polycrisis' (see Tooze, 2021) which has far-reaching consequences for the world of work and employment. There is a synergy at play here: the polycrisis emerges from the fundamental antagonisms of capitalism and affects work; work is the fundamental generator of the profits of the capitalist system that we are embedded within.

While any crisis may have localized effects on economic relations, two of the major crises discussed in this book – the COVID-19 pandemic and the climate emergency – and their global reach offer the probability of major long-term disruptions to the economy, the third crisis that we explore here. We will view this contemporary conjuncture through the lens of work and employment, and we suggest that work itself is in a state of crisis, a consequence of the economic, epidemiological and environmental crises which themselves are a consequence of the fundamental antagonisms of capitalism.

There is, clearly, much that is badly wrong with work (Pettinger, 2019), not least because of the cocktail of crises we describe in this book. Accounts have proliferated of the miserable state of much contemporary paid work and its harmful consequences for individuals and societies (see for example Horgan,

2021). Indeed, the 'brutality' of work seems to have been exacerbated by the COVID-19 pandemic (Jaffe, 2021). However, we will argue that the ongoing 'race to the bottom' of global international competition, along with processes of automation and digitization, was already causing major disruption to work and employment relations, especially in Global North countries such as the UK.

Moreover, the callous treatment of many workers in the Global South, some of whom make products for hugely successful retail brands, is increasingly documented (Chan et al, 2020). For many countries of the Global South, the legacies of colonialism are still being played out in the operations of the global capitalist system, and the consequences of this for work, employment and everyday life in those societies can be very harsh. In the Global North, the harmful consequences of the shrinking number of 'good' jobs, especially in the US and the UK, have become more widely understood (Blanchflower, 2019). Economic change and deindustrialization have changed work and workforces (Bradley et al, 2000), hollowing out established communities and undermining the social democratic political tradition. As changes to the global economy develop, far too many jobs provide workers with low pay, insecurity and minimal autonomy (Bloodworth, 2018). The UK was fast becoming a country marked by low-paid, insecure jobs and the growth of a precarious workforce even before the COVID-19 pandemic struck. Greater automation, and the prospect of a 'world without work', based on the claim that artificial intelligence tools will increasingly displace human labour (Susskind, 2020), further contribute to a sense that work is in crisis.

As we discuss in subsequent chapters, this crisis of work can be viewed in terms of a lengthy process of deterioration, caused by the application of neoliberal values as globalization increased in intensity (Beynon, 2019). The key turning point for this is often seen to be the 1980s, with the adoptionof Reaganomics in the US and the Thatcherite privatizations in the UK. Sociologist Guy Standing (2011) dates the rise of the global 'precariat' from that era, though we should also note that Harry Braverman's highly influential account of the 'degradation of work' was published in 1974 (Braverman, 1974). However, the 1980s saw an intensification of this trend.

From the 1980s onwards, neoliberal capitalism, marked by the dominance of the free market and the dismantling of hindrances to its operation (deregulation), the privatization of formerly public provision and the erosion of the welfare state, has increasingly been characterized by financialization, especially in the US and the UK. In financialized systems, profits are derived mainly from speculative deals on stocks and shares (shareholder capitalism) and from rents rather than productive activity, and if speculation goes wrong, as happened with the 2007–8 crash, the system is vulnerable. As radical economist Grace Blakeley notes, financialization 'is a process in which the logic of finance – that is, of lending, speculating and investing – penetrates all areas of economic activity to the benefit of a small financial elite and the detriment of working people' (Blakeley, 2020: 168).

As sociologists, we are concerned with both continuities and changes. A question explored in this book will be whether the current constellation of crises and their challenges will simply accelerate the deterioration of work or begin to reverse it, as the impacts of the neoliberal era of capitalism are increasingly challenged. There is already evidence that both the environmental and pandemic experiences are creating new forms of antagonism, such as conflict over health and well-being, which are explored in subsequent chapters. How will these inform the crisis of work?

The remainder of the book is structured as follows. Chapter 1 advances our main argument, explaining how the current crisis *of* work has been produced by three crises which are *at* work – intensified neoliberalization and its consequences, the experience of the COVID-19 pandemic and the escalating climate emergency. In Chapter 2 – 'Theorizing Crises' – we argue that under capitalism a permanent tendency towards crisis exists, exacerbated under neoliberal capitalist conditions, which engender other crises, particularly epidemiological crises – of which the COVID-19 pandemic is a striking example – and an escalating climate crisis. The crisis *of* work, and the interlinked crises *at* work which influence it, are underpinned by a profound 'real' crisis – the fundamental antagonisms produced by a system of neoliberal capitalism, under which work, the self and the environment are degraded and which creates instability and turbulence.

In Chapter 3, we explore the contemporary crisis in labour markets, a function of capitalist dynamics that neoliberalism aggravated and the experience of COVID-19 not only illuminated but also reinforced. The rise of the platform economy and digital modes of intermediation has driven increased precarity to be sure. But the growth of low-paid, casualized forms of 'flexible' labour is a more general and relatively long-term phenomenon, contributing to increased labour market divisions. We show how the 2007–8 global financial crisis, austerity and the experience of the COVID-19 pandemic exacerbated divisions and inequalities, influencing the crisis of work.

In Chapter 4, our attention turns to the field of employment relations – the nature of the relationship between employers and workers and how this relationship is managed – and how they have contributed to the contemporary crisis of work. Under conditions of intensified neoliberal capitalism, financialization imperatives, automation and labour commodification have generated a disconnect between managerial demands for efficiency and workers' aspirations for decent work and to feel valued. The chapter shows how the experience of the COVID-19 pandemic exacerbated the antagonism arising from this. It also demonstrates that efforts to manage employment relations in a more sustainable way, for the purpose of addressing the climate crisis and promoting decent work, are largely ineffective because of the primacy accorded to corporate interests.

Chapter 5 is devoted to social inequalities in work and employment, focusing on the antagonisms generated by divisions centred upon class, gender, ethnicity and age in particular. The chapter explores how inequalities and divisions have been affected by neoliberal capitalism and reflects on the implications of the COVID-19 pandemic. In many ways, divisions have been worsening, contributing to a crisis of multiple inequalities, with important implications for how we understand the contemporary crisis of work.

Chapter 6 focuses on trade unions, organizations which have been prone to crisis themselves, especially given the decline in their membership. The chapter explores the efforts of unions to recover from decline, and even revitalize themselves, and thus transcend the crisis of trade unionism. It points to how the experience of COVID-19 provided unions with opportunities to demonstrate their relevance, based on their contribution to supporting, representing and bargaining on behalf of workers. The chapter also explores the key role trade unions play in efforts to tackle the climate crisis through a 'just transition' to a net-zero world by ensuring that workers themselves can have their interests represented and be active participants in the economic and industrial changes necessary to address the climate emergency.

In Chapter 7, we explore the broader economic and political dimensions of the crisis of work. The chapter starts by covering the economic and labour market aspects of the crisis of work, with particular reference to the experience of the UK. It explains how low economic growth, supply-side constraints and labour shortages, weak productivity, the unhealthy and uncaring nature of the economy, stagnant wages, cost-of-living difficulties and squeezed living standards are both a function of, and in turn themselves exacerbate, a contemporary crisis of work which stems from the dominance of a neoliberal, financialized economic model. The chapter also considers the crisis-ridden nature of contemporary politics and how it intersects with the troublesome nature of contemporary work. A more volatile and turbulent political environment has arisen, not just restricted to the UK, one where support for traditional left-of-centre social democratic parties has waned. Moreover, 'populist' far-right politics has increasingly thrived in settings where, because of neoliberalization, working people feel more insecure and threatened.

Chapter 8 focuses on the prospects for transcending the crisis of work in settings where neoliberalism is under challenge. For one thing, greater state intervention to stimulate economic growth, provide working people with more security and tackle the climate emergency might suggest that neoliberalism itself is in crisis. More important, though, are the implications arising from an upsurge in strikes and labour conflict and growing environmental and climate mobilization, which, even if not concerned with directly challenging neoliberal capitalism, are nevertheless testimony to the contention it generates. Based on all this, the final part of the book – Chapter 9 – offers some reflections on how the crises of work, and their effects, can be mitigated.

1

Introducing the Crisis of Work

Introduction: The crisis of work in perspective

In writing about work, and the crisis of work, we must of course establish what we mean by 'work'. In previous books, we offered a history of the varied sociological definitions of work, noted that there has been a long-term trend in the social sciences to equate work with paid employment – thus ignoring the enormous contribution that unpaid work makes to our socio-economic landscape – and pointed to how work and employment contribute to identities, both individual and collective (Bradley et al, 2000; Erickson et al, 2009; Williams et al, 2013). While the focus of this book is on paid work, involving jobs people undertake in return for wages or salaries, the importance of unpaid household and caring tasks, often carried out by women, should not be overlooked. Perhaps most importantly, there are notable connections between unpaid domestic work and paid employment. People in part-time jobs – primarily women – often value the opportunity to combine paid work with unpaid household responsibilities, not just childcare tasks but also caring for older family members (Rubery et al, 2016). Another complicating factor is that work which is unpaid household labour when undertaken by a family member – domestic cleaning for example – becomes paid employment when a cleaner is hired from outside the family and rewarded with a wage. In distinguishing between paid and unpaid work, then, it is the social relations that structure the work and how it is undertaken, rather than the specific nature of the work tasks themselves, that are important (Budd, 2011).

In capitalist societies, paid work fulfils some important economic functions. The employment relationship, in which a worker takes up employment with an employer in return for a wage or salary, provides the employer with a resource which, managed appropriately, can be used to realize added value from the tasks undertaken. Paid employment of this kind also provides workers with an income, necessary for their subsistence. Importantly, though, work matters, not just on account of its economic value – both for employers and workers, in different ways – but also for myriad other social and psychological reasons, including identity formation and the development of citizenship (Budd, 2011). Paid work can be a source of dignity – giving people a stake in society and a sense they are engaged in something intrinsically worthy – and not just a source of economic reward in the form of a wage or salary (Cruddas, 2021).

Unsurprisingly, given work's importance – to people, economies and societies – it has long been the subject of considerable attention. Indeed, there is a longstanding tradition of historical and sociological studies which – implicitly or explicitly – communicate the idea of work being in crisis. During the early 19th century, for example, the process of industrialization in England, particularly the development of new production methods which threatened the jobs and livelihoods of the existing (largely male) workforce, was accompanied by major disruption in the form of protests, riots and machine breaking (Thompson, 1968). By the first decades of the 20th century, the principal manifestation of crisis, particularly for elites, came from the development of a mass organized labour movement which threatened to advance working people's interests through disruptive strikes on a large scale in major industries such as coal mining and transport (Clegg et al, 1964). The 1930s saw the crisis of work take the form of a period of mass unemployment in the period known as the 'Great Depression', particularly in the US (Garraty, 1976).

While the Second World War and post-war economic recovery mitigated the unemployment crisis, at least temporarily, during the 1970s the focus of attention turned to the degradation of industrial work under full employment conditions (see Braverman, 1974; Nichols and Beynon, 1977; Pollert, 1981). A crisis of work was manifest not so much in the lack of opportunities for paid employment but more in the alienating nature of many jobs themselves, and their effects, a theme which is also apparent in more recent accounts of factory work in parts of the Global South, particularly China (Chan et al, 2020).

In the Global North, the return of mass unemployment in the 1980s and ongoing processes of employment liberalization and flexibilization during the 1980s and 1990s, linked to emergent globalization, generated a new sense of work being in crisis, one manifest in greater employment insecurity (Elliott and Atkinson, 1999; Heery and Salmon, 2000). Declining trade union membership, an outcome of government efforts to weaken the power of organized labour, gave employers much greater control over work and employment relations and diminished protections for workers (Baccaro and Howell, 2017) – leading to a rise in work pressures (Schor, 1993; Green, 2001). The first book we were jointly involved in – *Myths at Work* (2000) – explores these and other issues relating to work and employment at the end of the 20th century, a period when the implications of globalization had started to attract more interest (Bradley et al, 2000).

Contemporary crises of work

Work, then, often seems to have been in crisis, of one kind or another. Since the 2010s, though, two apparent crises have become especially prominent. First, for some the principal contemporary crisis of work is that of greater automation, particularly the increasing use of robotics, artificial intelligence (AI) and algorithmic 'platform' technologies. This is claimed to have the potential to displace existing jobs on a mass scale (Ford, 2015). There is a long tradition of writing concerned with the supposedly diminished standing of paid work, linked to the greater role of non-work activities as sources of social identification, meaning and action (Gorz, 1994). However, claims about the 'end' of work and the necessity of adapting to a 'post-work' environment have become more prevalent given the potentially profound consequences of automation for employment, including predictions of mass unemployment and underemployment. The desirability of a guaranteed income of some kind, to be supplied by the state, has been canvassed as a key policy response to the likely diminished role of paid work as a source of subsistence (Srnicek and Williams, 2015; Susskind, 2020).

Clearly, the implications of greater automation for work must be taken seriously. Yet much mainstream, and even some critical, writing on this topic is marked by a 'vague futurism' which fetishizes technology and assumes automation is an unproblematic process (Pettinger, 2019: 146). Predictions of the diminished relevance of work, or more accurately paid employment, arising from new technology have been made many times before without coming to fruition, not least because technological innovation creates new jobs or complements, and changes, existing roles. There were very few software engineers in the 1960s and 1970s, for example. This time, however, things are purportedly different because more and more tasks can now be undertaken by machines, creating a 'world with less work' (Susskind, 2020: 127). Moreover, the COVID-19 pandemic forced people to use online services to a greater degree, with significant effects on the occupational structure (fewer high street retail jobs and more van drivers, for example).

Yet the claim that automation is likely to make human labour redundant (see, for example, Susskind, 2020) should be treated with skepticism. Prophecies of the 'end of work' have a long pedigree and should be treated cautiously and engaged with critically (Granter, 2009). Such claims pay little heed to the issues, challenges and obstacles that characterize technological innovation in practice and the complex ways it affects work, workers and the relationship between workers and employers (Pettinger, 2019). One particular problem concerns the tendency of 'end of work' conjecturing to neglect the interests and actions of those most affected by change at work – workers themselves (Strangleman, 2007). In some cases, automation has diminished in significance because it is cheaper for employers to use human labour, particularly in environments where workers have few employment rights and protections and thus are highly vulnerable. The rise of hand car washes is perhaps the most notable example of this (Clark and Colling, 2018). Much of the work carried out in the platform or 'gig' economy – think about parcel deliveries and driving services – would have been possible without the development of online labour platforms, and the smartphone apps used to access them, but not so efficiently or on such a large scale.

The example of the platform economy illustrates how the key issue is not so much that automation displaces jobs but rather that technological innovation degrades work and contributes to the greater commodification of labour. What do we mean by the concept of 'commodification'? It is generally recognized that in attempting to secure productive effort from workers, employers cannot treat labour purely as a 'commodity', something that can be straightforwardly and unproblematically bought and sold in the labour market. This is because labour is embodied in human beings – workers who have their own agency (Polanyi, 1957) and have expectations of how they should be treated – with fairness, dignity and respect for example. Yet the experience of the platform economy demonstrates how new technology has been used to facilitate an approach to work where people are contracted, and remunerated, for undertaking one-off tasks, determined by automated systems, and lack employment rights and protections as a consequence. The term 'labour commodification' thus refers to the tendency of organizations, in pursuit of greater efficiency and flexibility, to operate more transactional, market-based forms of work and employment relationships, leaving workers disempowered and subjugated.

Platforms use algorithms to monitor the activities of platform workers constantly, for the purpose of exercising strict control over their work (Prassl, 2018). Algorithmic management techniques have expanded beyond the platform economy and have become more widely used by employers in general as a means of intensifying managerial control over workers (Delfanti, 2020; Kellogg et al, 2020). The COVID-19 pandemic led to a dramatic rise in telework, which allows greater surveillance of individual workers (Hern, 2020). When it comes to automation, then, the key problem for work is not job displacement on a mass scale but rather the implications for job quality in environments where employers enjoy considerable power to direct and manage the activities of workers without challenge. The rise of generative forms of AI, of which ChatGPT is the most well known, has rekindled concerns about the potentially job-destroying effects of automation, especially for sales and administrative roles. Yet by stimulating productivity improvements, AI could generate new jobs and increase wages – assuming that workers are organized sufficiently strongly to benefit. Perhaps the biggest concern with technologies such as ChatGPT, though, is the extent to which they can be used to advance labour commodification, with automation deployed not as a means of replacing workers but as a way of degrading their employment and devaluing what they do (Greenhouse, 2023a).

This is relevant to the second kind of crisis relating to work, namely the seemingly growing paucity of 'good' (or 'decent') jobs, a crisis which the 2007–8 financial crisis and subsequent economic recession seem to have intensified (Blanchflower, 2019). One prominent manifestation of this theme concerns the claim that too much contemporary work lacks meaningfulness. This is central to Graeber's (2018) 'bullshit jobs' thesis, with a 'bullshit job' defined as a 'form of paid employment that is so completely pointless, unnecessary or even pernicious that even the employee cannot justify its existence even though, as part of the conditions of employment, the employee feels obliged to pretend that this is not the case' (Graeber, 2018: 9–10). The growing prevalence of 'bullshit jobs' can be attributed to the tendency for organizations to use productivity improvements as a means of funding unnecessary administrative and management roles (Graeber, 2018: 176–7). While a clearly provocative and radical approach, the 'bullshit jobs' thesis is rather unconvincing. The data on which it is based are of dubious validity; and, anyway, the proportion of workers who perceive their jobs as not being useful has been declining. Perhaps the key problem with the 'bullshit jobs' approach, though, is its focus on job tasks, and some individuals' subjective perception of those tasks, rather than the relationship that exists between workers and their employers and how this relationship is managed (Soffia et al, 2022).

While the 'bullshit jobs' thesis is flawed, it does nevertheless speak to a concern that something is badly wrong with contemporary work and employment, in particular a claimed dearth of 'good' (or 'decent') jobs (Srnicek and Williams, 2015; Blanchflower, 2019). Economies in the Global North have failed to generate sufficient numbers of jobs which are secure, well paid and provide opportunities for progression, particularly since the 2007–8 global financial crisis. The consequences include a proliferation of underemployment, excessive employment insecurity and precarity and ongoing wage stagnation (Kalleberg, 2018; Blanchflower, 2019). The shortage of good jobs is particularly evident in the Global South, in a context of rapid population growth and a young age profile, where informal work – that which is undertaken in an unregulated manner, often ad hoc, without a formal employment contract, in poor conditions and without employment or social protection, generally for extremely low pay – predominates. Informal employment accounts for 85.8 per cent of all employment in Africa (ILO, 2018c; Hammer and Ness, 2021).

Crises *at* work and the crisis *of* work

Despite its importance, the paucity of 'good' jobs, while making a notable contribution, is not on its own sufficient to constitute the contemporary crisis of work, given its magnitude. Instead, our approach highlights the ways in which three crises which are *at* work – the consequences of intensified neoliberalization, the challenges arising from the COVID-19 pandemic and the effects of the climate emergency – have contributed to a profound contemporary crisis *of* work. Our conceptualization is based on Colin Hay's (1999: 324) distinction between 'failure' and 'crisis': while the former can be viewed as an 'accumulation or condensation of contradictions', the latter refers to a 'moment of decisive intervention during which these contradictions are identified'. The term 'crisis', then, can be applied to situations where 'failure is identified and widely perceived, a condition in which systemic failure has become politically and ideationally mediated' (Hay, 1999: 324).

A 'crisis' is therefore not just a time of disruption, nor 'merely a moment of rupture', but, more significantly, 'a moment of decisive intervention' in response to perceived failure (Hay, 1999: 336). What we take from this is the imperative to understand 'crisis', when applied to the field of work, as involving a 'moment of thorough-going transformation' (Hay, 1999: 323) – the crisis explored in this book applies to more than just the problems of contemporary work, their ill-effects and their contradictions, profound and important as they are, and instead focuses upon the imperatives for a 'decisive intervention' that have arisen, the conditions which have influenced this 'intervention' and their consequences.

As an economic system, capitalism is structurally prone to periodic crises. The 'moment of decisive intervention' we identify, though, one that constitutes the current crisis of work, concerns the antagonism that has arisen between the degradation, in the sense of a process of worsening, of work and employment under conditions of intensified neoliberal capitalism – in the context of both the COVID-19 pandemic and escalating climate emergency – and workers' aspirations for decent work and to have their labour valued. The legitimacy of work and employment has thus diminished as a consequence, particularly in societies where people's values and identities are increasingly shaped by other activities, for example in consumption relations, where individuals enjoy greater apparent sovereignty.

For Edwards (1986: 58), work and employment relationships, not necessarily just under capitalism, are founded upon a 'structured antagonism', not only because of their indeterminacy but also due to the tension between the imperative for cooperation and the potential for conflict that exists. We use the concept of 'antagonism' in a broader sense, though, one that recognizes the dynamics of the labour process while also extending beyond the workplace to incorporate a concern with state, economy and society. While acknowledging the project of neoliberal capitalism as an integral dimension of the crisis of work, particularly in the aftermath of the 2007–8 global financial crisis, we also appreciate the importance of efforts by state and societal actors – governments, trade unions and non-governmental organizations for example – to restrain, or even challenge, a neoliberal-inspired process of commodification and flexibilization, efforts which have become more pronounced.

COVID-19 has both illuminated and amplified this antagonism not only by exposing and exacerbating the process of degradation but also by reinforcing existing pressures to re-regulate work and employment relationships, whether because of the activities of organized labour, through a process of institution building or from a more interventionist role on the part of the state. Moreover, the escalating climate emergency both reflects and exposes the failings of neoliberal capitalism, and the degraded model of work and employment which it has produced; it demands a focus, broadly conceived, on sustainability, for the purpose of reconciling a decent work agenda with sustainable economic development, as an effective response to the climate crisis. This, however, will challenge existing consumption relations in their increased centrality, creating new antagonisms and conflicts.

Implicit in all this, and often explicit too, is an apparent crisis of neoliberal globalization. We covered the importance of globalization, as a process of greater worldwide interconnectedness and as a neoliberal project, based on advancing the power of corporations, promoting greater employment flexibility and weakening organized labour, in a previous book – *Globalization and Work* (Williams et al, 2013). In doing so, we highlighted the complex ways in which work and employment were affected by globalization and also the important challenges to neoliberal globalization that influenced the dynamics of work and employment relations in a more globalized setting. As will become clear throughout this book, the contemporary crisis of work is, to a large extent, a consequence of the intensified neoliberalization associated with the project of globalization. At the same time, though, this crisis is also an expression of the growing challenges to neo-liberal globalization, as the antagonisms it has generated have been accentuated by the COVID-19 pandemic, and also because of the imperative for a more sustainable model of work and employment given the mounting climate emergency. For example, the stark necessity of reducing carbon emissions poses a threat to the ubiquity of air travel – for moving commodities and people, for both leisure and business purposes.

Our approach offers a response to the objection that there is insufficient justification for claiming that work is in crisis, given the evidence that most people are satisfied with their jobs: indeed, they generally like and often value their jobs – given how much time people spend engaged in paid work, it would be odd if they did not – while also 'feeling burdened and oppressed by them' (Simms, 2019: 10). Likewise, 'having a bad job doesn't mean you don't value work' (Cruddas, 2021: 100). Work, and people's experience of work, their engagement with work and their relationship with work, are complex and even contradictory. Social relations at work, including the quality and style of management, have a notable influence on people's working lives and how they are experienced (Pass, 2017). It is precisely for these reasons that the crisis of work we explore in this book is so important.

The crisis of intensified neoliberalization

One key element of our approach concerns the intensified process of neoliberalization, especially evident since the 2007–8 global financial crisis and subsequent 'Great Recession', and its implications for work and employment. Neoliberalism has been defined as a 'a theory of political economic practices that proposes that human well-being can best be advanced by liberating individual entrepreneurial freedoms and skills within an institutional framework characterized by strong private property rights, free markets and free trade' (Harvey, 2005: 2). Since the 1970s, neoliberal ideology has underpinned efforts by governments and global institutions to advance marketization and deregulation, often by exploiting natural crises and disasters and using them as a pretext for economic reforms that would otherwise have been rejected (Klein, 2008). As this implies, integral to neoliberalism is the role that strong states play in advancing market relations and suppressing challenges to marketization, for the purpose of transforming society by normalizing the primacy of markets, competition and enterprise (Davies, 2018).

In the field of work and employment relations, neoliberal ideology has influenced efforts by governments to weaken regulatory mechanisms, such as employment protection laws and collective bargaining arrangements, for the purpose of enhancing employers' control over workers and facilitating greater flexibility (Baccaro and Howell, 2017). A clear trend of greater neoliberalization can be observed, characterized by increased employer discretion and the subjugation of organized labour, especially in Western Europe, albeit one that is uneven and far from uniform, with its trajectory varying from country to country (Thelen, 2014; Baccaro and Howell, 2017). Neoliberal globalization is dependent upon extended, cross-border supply chains that help to obscure poor labour conditions (LeBaron, 2020).

The 2007–8 global financial crisis, prompted by the collapse of the subprime mortgage market in the US and resulting in the collapse of several major financial institutions, initially seemed to portend the end of the neoliberal era. The underlying causes of the crisis involved the unsustainable growth of market-based finance, characterized by opaque and complex financial instruments, on a global scale (Tooze, 2018). Yet in the aftermath of the crisis, and the resultant economic recession, neoliberalism not only survived but also prospered, as leading policy makers in governments and international institutions used the magnitude of the crisis as a pretext for intensifying neoliberalization (Crouch, 2011; Mirowski, 2013).

One aspect of this involved a predilection for fiscal austerity measures – tax rises and cuts in public expenditure – complemented by a monetary policy programme of quantitative easing, the consequence of which was to enrich generally wealthy asset holders while particularly disadvantaging users of public services, recipients of welfare support and public sector workers (Blyth, 2015; Baines and Cunningham, 2020). In the UK, this took the form of a package of economic policy measures named as 'austerity' by the then Conservative prime minister David Cameron and his chancellor, George Osborne. Far from stimulating a sustained economic recovery, the emphasis on austerity in the UK made a notable contribution to a prolonged period of low economic growth and wage stagnation (Wren-Lewis, 2018). The emphasis on austerity was not just restricted to the UK; many other European countries quickly discarded fiscal stimulus packages they had enacted in the immediate aftermath of the 2007–8 global financial crisis in favour of austerity measures (Heyes and Lewis, 2015).

A second key manifestation of the intensified neoliberalization of the 2010s concerned the greater emphasis accorded to promoting labour market deregulation and privileging employers' flexibility (Meardi, 2014). The period following the 2007–8 global financial crisis also saw governments in Europe, including France, Italy, Spain and Greece, enact neoliberal labour market reforms, designed to advance flexibilization by weakening trade unions and collective bargaining and diluting workers' rights and protections (Heyes and Lewis, 2015; Lehndorff, 2015).

Globally, increased labour market and employment flexibility is a prominent manifestation of marketization in employment relations (Greer and Doellgast, 2017). In the United States and other parts of the Global North, neoliberalization and marketization have propelled the greater use of short-term, temporary and other forms of flexible employment, where work is often low paid and precarious, with workers left in poor-quality and more insecure jobs (Kalleberg, 2011, 2018). Flexibilization has burgeoned elsewhere, too. In Asia, for example, increased flexibilization is associated with the more extensive use of workers on temporary, short-term contracts, who lack security and protection (Barnes, 2018; Chan et al, 2020; Kalleberg et al, 2021). The rapid growth of platform work arrangements, whereby workers are hired to undertake specific tasks, or 'gigs', accessed through smartphone apps, such as providing a ride or delivering food to someone's home, has, in propagating increased flexibilization, engendered greater precarity and encouraged the commodification of labour (Prassl, 2018). In the Global South, the nature of platform work, its commodifying tendencies and the insecurity it produces exacerbates informalization (Sharma, 2022), given that workers lack access to formal employment protections.

Evidently, flexibilization in work and employment relations is a general, global trend. It reflects a dominant neoliberal ideology which privileges the interests of employers and their demands for efficiency and flexibility while emphasizing the importance of restricting the power and activities of trade unions and weakening employment rights and protections (Baccaro and Howell, 2017). At the same time, though, institutional differences between countries mean that neoliberalization, and the processes of flexibilization and commodification which accompany it, operate in varied ways and trajectories, according to the national setting. For example, coordinated market economies like Germany operate stronger regulatory arrangements and systems of worker protection than liberal market economies such as the UK and US (OECD, 2020a), moderating processes of flexibilization and commodification in some important ways.

One integral dimension of neoliberalism in general is the predominance of finance capital. The intensified neoliberalization of the 2010s in the UK was a function of the emphasis placed on restoring the financialized growth model, fuelled largely by expanding private debt, which had briefly been jeopardized in the aftermath of the global financial crisis (Lavery, 2019). A general process of financialization can be observed, based on the increased prominence of, and privilege accorded to, finance capital, particularly in liberal market economies such as the UK and US (Applebaum and Batt, 2014). Pressure from financial investors for short-term returns means that firms come to focus on generating value by means of corporate restructuring initiatives and 'financial engineering' – mergers, acquisitions, asset disposal, murky accounting practices – rather than by product innovation or improvements in service quality (Thompson, 2013; Batt, 2018). Labour is treated as a commodity, the cost of which should be minimized for the purpose of realizing short-term value by means of measures designed to secure efficiency savings, such as lay-offs and outsourcing initiatives (Batt, 2018).

There are some important consequences of the rise of 'investor capitalism' and the emphasis accorded to minimizing labour costs. One is the greater pressure managers come under to exercise close control over workers and their performance standards (Dundon and Rafferty, 2018). Another concerns the impact on working conditions. In the UK's highly financialized residential care sector, for example, the imperative to cut labour costs bears particularly heavily on low-paid staff, mainly women, often from minoritized ethnic communities, whose terms and conditions of employment have deteriorated because of cost-cutting measures (Horton, 2022).

The phenomenon of financialization exemplifies neoliberalism's predominance, particularly in liberal market economies such as the

UK, which, during the 2010s, experienced a process of intensified neoliberalization. However, sustained economic growth in the aftermath of the 2007–8 global financial crisis and subsequent economic recession was notable for its absence. According to Blanchflower (2019: 79), the 'UK's recovery was the third slowest peacetime recovery in six hundred years' and the most sluggish since 1720. Efforts to restore a financialized growth model stimulated asset-based inflation, not only increasing inequality but also by impeding economic growth and creating considerable political instability and turbulence (Lavery, 2019; Hopkin, 2020).

The process of intensified neoliberalization in the aftermath of the global financial crisis and subsequent economic recession had some profoundly adverse consequences for work and employment. One was the aforementioned paucity of 'good' jobs (Blanchflower, 2019). In much of Western Europe, this was manifest in high levels of unemployment, particularly youth unemployment (Vaughan-Whitehead, 2015). In the liberal market economies of the US and UK, the dearth of good jobs was evident not so much in the headline unemployment figures – during the 2010s, the official rate of UK unemployment fell to its lowest level since the 1970s – but in the phenomenon of 'underemployment' (Blanchflower, 2019; Baines and Cunningham, 2020). The UK saw the growing use of so-called 'zero-hours contracts', a casual form of employment that does not guarantee any minimum hours of work, with workers expected to be available for work and only paid for the hours that they do work (Koumenta and Williams, 2019) – see Chapter 3.

Casualization was also driven by the greater use of bogus self-employment arrangements – so-called 'gig' work – not only by new online platforms such as Uber and Deliveroo (Bloodworth, 2018; Prassl, 2018) but also more widely, in sectors such as parcel delivery, a notable manifestation of growing 'uncertain work' (Heyes et al, 2018; Moore and Newsome, 2018). One estimate from 2020 suggested that around 3.75 million workers in the UK were falsely self-employed – a majority of the 5.2 million total reported in self-employment (Harvey, 2020). The growth of more insecure and precarious forms of employment is an international phenomenon, especially in the advanced economies of the Global North, a function of greater neoliberalization and the promotion of more flexible labour markets (Kalleberg, 2018; Baines and Cunningham, 2020). This trend inspired Standing to develop the idea of the 'precariat', or, as he terms it, the 'new dangerous class'. Standing describes the precariat as a worldwide phenomenon, constituted of people whose relation to employment is episodic, fragmented and insecure (Standing, 2011). While many former members of the old working classes have fallen into it through the loss of stable jobs, the precariat also includes highly skilled and qualified people, such as the army of casual university teachers.

The dearth of good jobs and the growing precarity and commodification arising from intensified neoliberalization have particularly affected workers who were already disadvantaged to a disproportionate extent, exacerbating inequality in employment (Baines and Cunningham, 2020; Horgan, 2021). Too many people in the UK, especially young workers, women workers, workers from minoritized ethnic communities and those from poorer backgrounds, find it extremely hard to progress out of low-paid, poor-quality work (SMC, 2019) because of a 'class ceiling' that impedes upward social mobility (Friedman and Laurison, 2020) – see Chapter 5. Work's increased casualization and commodification is one factor that contributed to the prolonged period of wage stagnation that marked the 2010s (Blanchflower, 2019). Another was the diminished and 'hollowed out' (Tooze, 2021) position of organized labour, a reflection of the 'breaking of union power' (Holgate, 2021a: 10) that occurred during the 1980s, an integral feature of the neoliberal assault on the trade unions – see Chapter 6.

COVID-19: re-regulatory pressures and the crisis of work

During the early 2020s, the effects of one crisis at work – intensified neoliberalization – were exacerbated by another, the COVID-19 pandemic. In the UK, the impact of this epidemiological crisis exposed the fragile state of public services, especially health and social care, which a decade of austerity had left poorly prepared for the challenge of responding to the pandemic (Bettington, 2021; Calvert and Arbuthnott, 2021). COVID-19 aggravated the effects of intensified neoliberalization in a number of important respects, particularly by creating an environment in which precarity thrived, heightening pre-existing inequalities and exacerbating social divisions (Davies et al, 2022; Macartney et al, 2022). Key workers, such as frontline service workers who were required to attend their normal workplace, saw their health and safety compromised (James, 2021; Cai et al, 2022). Those obliged to work from home because of COVID-19 restrictions often experienced greater work pressures arising from employers' expectations that workers be more assiduous at demonstrating their online presence (Hadjisolomou et al, 2022) and the greater spill-over of work activities into their home and family lives (Hodder, 2020).

As already mentioned, the current crisis of work is a consequence of the antagonism that has arisen between the degradation of work and employment relations under conditions of intensified neoliberalization and the aspirations of workers for decent work and to have their labour valued. Clearly, the COVID-19 pandemic has both illuminated and amplified this antagonism, exacerbating pre-existing re-regulatory pressures, prompting the state to adopt a more interventionist role and stimulating greater labour activism. By the latter part of the 2010s – before COVID-19 arose – signs that the legitimacy of neoliberalization was becoming increasingly imperilled had become evident, a consequence of the growing imperative to tackle the profound, adverse consequences for work and employment, particularly concerns over job insecurity, low pay and in-work poverty (Brown and Wright, 2018; Taylor, 2019).

The COVID-19 pandemic accentuated pressures for re-regulation, so that workers' interests can be better served. The greater focus on the prospects for a four-day working week exemplifies the increasing importance being attached to ways of improving the quality of people's working lives, with the pandemic, and its effects, having played a major part in stimulating ideas of how work could be better (Coote et al, 2020). Some are sceptical about the prospects for a four-day work week, especially given productivity concerns (CIPD, 2022). However, trials undertaken among UK firms suggest that reducing the working week can improve workers' well-being without compromising business efficiency (Stewart, 2023).

All this implies there is greater potential for a more activist state and an interventionist government approach, focused on enhancing labour standards and protecting workers' interests rather than privileging employers' flexibility. As has long been recognized, neoliberal projects are rarely laissez-faire in orientation but instead rely on the coercive power of states to enforce marketization, privatization and liberalization, particularly when it comes to subjugating organized labour (Gamble, 1988; Howell, 2005; Šumonja, 2021). Businesses are frequently the recipients of generous amounts of state largesse in the form of tax benefits, subsidies and other rewards which, taken together, can be understood as 'corporate welfare' regimes (Farnsworth, 2012). State intervention can help to facilitate greater neoliberalization by mitigating some of its adverse consequences for the purpose of enhancing employers' flexibility and keeping organized labour in check (Howell, 2016).

Nevertheless, as well as advancing measures designed to facilitate capital accumulation, state actors must also be concerned with moderating the adverse effects of the inevitable instabilities that arise, through appropriate legitimation strategies (Jessop, 2014; Lavery, 2019). Quite evidently, intensified neoliberalization generated considerable instability and disruption, particularly in the labour market, work and employment; importantly, though, the 'interventionist turn' that developed towards the end of the 2010s, and was amplified by the experience of COVID-19, implies more of a concern not with facilitating greater liberalization, by mitigating some of its adverse consequences (Howell, 2016), but rather signalling a possible retreat from it. This shift in approach can be attributed to growing demands for a more active and interventionist government role in tackling the problems caused by excessive neoliberalization, not least the adverse consequences of austerity, and providing working people with greater protection (Richards, 2018; Lavery, 2019).

Indeed, since early 2020 the necessity of responding effectively to COVID-19 has required massive state intervention, often on a scale unprecedented in peacetime circumstances, to organize test and trace arrangements, vaccination programmes and job/income support schemes for those not able to work because of the pandemic, among other things (Šumonja, 2021). Governments around the world intervened to protect the jobs and incomes of people unable to work because of restrictions imposed on the economy to restrict the spread of infection. In some countries, such as Germany, this involved using and updating existing support mechanisms. Elsewhere, governments had to design and implement job retention arrangements from scratch (OECD, 2020b). While the UK's Coronavirus Job Retention Scheme was only a temporary measure, the significance of this 'furlough' arrangement was that, as a manifestation of state intervention, it contravened the market-based approach to restructuring, one emphasizing redundancies, that has long prevailed in the UK (Stuart et al, 2021) – see Chapter 4. There has clearly been a shift in political positioning, one that preceded the COVID-19 pandemic but was accentuated by it, away from market liberalism and towards a more interventionist role for the state, not least because the effects of intensified neoliberalization and neoliberal austerity have stimulated greater demands for labour market support and protection at work.

The challenge to neoliberalization extends beyond the state and the interventionist role played by governments. When thinking about re-regulatory pressures, it is important to recognize that the most important mechanism for ensuring that workers' aspirations for decent work are realized and that their labour is valued is the trade union movement. As we have seen, neoliberalization is associated with the weakening, indeed breaking, of organized labour; and some employers used the COVID-19 pandemic as a pretext for further challenges to unions, especially in the US. Importantly, though, trade unions have been engaged in a process of renewal, one that involves greater efforts to organize and mobilize workers (see Chapters 6 and 8), including those in the platform economy, challenging the kind of commodification and casualization of employment all too common under conditions of intensified neoliberalization (Cant, 2020; Holgate, 2021a). Moreover, the experience of COVID-19 galvanized union activism, especially in the US. During 2021 and 2022, a major wave of labour strikes over wages, working conditions and workplace health and safety occurred, with unions making advances in firms such as Amazon and Starbucks (Sainato, 2022).

The climate emergency and the crisis of work

While we were writing this book in 2023, news broke that July 2023 was expected to be the hottest ever month experienced on earth, a testament to the effect of global warming and a stark manifestation of the escalating climate emergency (Thompson, 2023). The ruinous environmental impact of an economic growth model which is highly dependent upon intensive agricultural production and mass industrial production methods, powered by hydrocarbons extracted from the earth – fossil fuels such as coal, petroleum and gas – has become increasingly difficult to ignore, especially the polluting and global warming effects. While the global warming phenomenon had long been understood by scientists, it was only during the late 1980s that the concept of climate change, and its adverse consequences, attracted the attention of policy makers (Klein, 2014).

As a manifestation of environmental crisis, the concept of climate change, or rather the 'climate emergency' as it is increasingly labelled, refers to the rapid warming of the planet caused by the excessive growth of carbon in the atmosphere. The effects of the climate emergency are already being felt: for example, the erosion of the Antarctic ice shelves and the melting of glaciers; rising sea levels, posing an existential risk to low-lying parts of the world, such as some Pacific islands; more extreme weather events; and the increased prevalence of wildfires in places such as California on the West Coast of the US and parts of Australia. In 2023, Canada was afflicted by hundreds of wildfires, the number and intensity of which were aggravated by the climate emergency, resulting in very poor air quality and harmful particle pollution throughout large parts of North America (Milman et al, 2023). The same year saw major fires erupt around the Mediterranean, including in Greece and Italy, sparked by exceptionally high summer temperatures linked to planetary warming.

Importantly, environmental degradation in general, and anthropocentric (human-generated) global warming in particular, are products of capitalism, and the imperative to commodify, and thus extract value from, the natural world, in a similar way to how it treats workers (Saltmarsh, 2021). Neoliberalism, and the primacy accorded to 'market fundamentalism' which characterizes it, may not have caused the climate emergency, but, as a dominant ideology, one that privileges the interests of corporations, it has certainly contributed to it and stymied the actions required to tackle it effectively (Klein, 2014; Saltmarsh, 2021; Buller, 2022b).

There are clearly important connections between environmental crisis, especially the climate emergency, and the crisis of work. According to Horgan (2021: 113), work 'is a central institution through which capitalism is lived. It is the site and process of value extraction, and this process leaves its mark in the natural world just as much as it does on individual people.' Neoliberalism, especially in its intensified form, exploits and degrades the environment, damaging the climate, for the purpose of value extraction, just as it exploits and degrades human labour (Klein, 2019; Saltmarsh, 2021). Work, as it is currently arranged, contributes to the climate crisis: we work too much, often in energy-inefficient or polluting industries and organizations. Too many jobs are organized and undertaken in ways that are both environmentally and socially unsustainable (Klein, 2019). The climate emergency has exposed and illuminated the degrading effects of neoliberal capitalism, not just in respect of the environment but also with regard to work and employment. A focus on greater sustainability demands effective action to tackle the climate crisis, something which involves an emphasis on creating good jobs and promoting decent work. In addition, environmental degradation is linked to epidemiological crisis: diminished biodiversity through deforestation provides animals such as bats, which host diseases that can be harmful to humans, with greater opportunities to thrive, increasing the risk of future pandemics (Tollefson, 2020).

Destruction of the environment and decreasing biodiversity is heightened by the breakout of armed conflicts, such as those in Yemen, Afghanistan, Ukraine and Palestine which also lead to displacement of populations deprived of the economic means of survival and seeking work elsewhere: wars involving advanced missile technology and heavy tank and artillery use are highly destructive of agricultural infrastructure and wildlife and involve intensive use of fossil fuels, limiting the impacts of international actions to curb environmental pollution. US military activity, given its global scale and complexity, makes a major contribution to increasing carbon emissions (Belcher et al, 2020).

International efforts to address the climate emergency are coordinated by the United Nations. Established in 1988, the Intergovernmental Panel on Climate Change provides expert and authoritative scientific information about climate change and its impacts. The UN's Framework Convention on Climate Change took effect in 1994; 198 countries had ratified the Convention by 2022. It oversees annual 'Conferences of the Parties' (CoPs) which seek to negotiate international agreements on securing progress towards decarbonization and reducing the pace of global warming. The 2015 Paris Agreement, for example, included an objective to keep the global average temperature rise to below 2°C, though even a 1.5°C rise is potentially catastrophic. Individual governments agree to action consistent with what they signed up to in the CoPs. For example, the UK government's 'Net Zero Strategy' is based on the target of ensuring that, by 2050, the amount of carbon emissions added to the atmosphere is the same as, or less than, the amount being removed (HM Government, 2021).

Government and intergovernmental efforts to tackle the climate crisis, though, are generally rather weak and limited. The 2015 Paris Agreement, for example, does not compel countries to take meaningful action to limit emissions. Too much of an emphasis is placed on voluntary and market-based solutions to global warming – such as the use of carbon trading schemes and offsetting arrangements – which, while comfortable for corporations, do little to address the underlying causes of the climate emergency and may indeed make things worse (Klein, 2014; Saltmarsh, 2021; Buller, 2022b). Growing climate activism, exemplified by the activities of the Extinction Rebellion movement, which was established in 2018, is a consequence of the frustration many people feel with sluggish and limited official efforts to respond to global warming – see Chapter 8.

Clearly, a more radical and transformative approach is needed to tackle climate change, one with profound implications for work. The concept of the Green New Deal (GND) originated in the US but has since influenced the approach of many in the UK (Pettifor, 2019). It incorporates a concern with promoting wide-ranging social and economic, as well as environmental, changes in order to deal with the climate emergency effectively. These include greater public ownership, investment in sustainable housing and transport and the democratization of decision making so that people are empowered to take appropriate action in their communities. Central to the GND is the concept of 'justice' – not only that the process of decarbonization, and the economic restructuring it portends, should ensure that workers are treated fairly and have their issues and concerns addressed but also, more importantly, that workers themselves should be actively involved in efforts to develop a new, sustainable economic model and the good, 'green' jobs that are integral to it (Klein, 2019). For Saltmarsh (2021: 100), there needs to be a 'powerful trade union movement leading the struggle for a Green New Deal so that workers are the protagonists, not victims, of economic transition'.

A 'just transition' to a new economic model is required, one that not only privileges environmental and climate sustainability but also emphasizes the centrality of good jobs to securing sustainability and the importance of involving workers themselves, and upholding their interests, in the process of change (Saltmarsh, 2021). According to Klein (2019: 167), an 'alternative' economic model is required, comprising 'integrated solutions' which can 'radically bring down emissions while creating huge numbers of good, unionized jobs and delivering meaningful justice to those who have been most abused and excluded under the current extractive economy'. This is a crucial issue: currently, attempts to switch to greener and cleaner sources of energy production in the UK have raised opposition from some trade unions, concerned at the loss of numerous existing jobs (see Chapter 6). Changes of this kind are tricky and challenging and may require a more interventionist state approach, as discussed in previous sections.

Crises foretold, crises connected

Our three major crises are interlinked in terms of their effects upon one another but also in terms of their underlying causes: the operation of a capitalist – especially neoliberal capitalist – global economy is an additional feature that these three crises share. They have been foretold for many decades, have received considerable academic, public and political discussion and have a considerable societal presence in the form of cultural productions. Despite this, our three crises have elicited little or no preventative measures from state and other institutional actors for many decades. The crises of work we have outlined here have been part of a general public discourse regarding the degeneration of work and the future of work since at least the 1950s. Automation, alienation and meaningless polarization between skilled and unskilled workers, and between owners and employees, have been described in many academic accounts, notably Blauner (1964) and Braverman (1974), and have been a consistent trope in cultural productions since the 1950s – for example Kurt Vonnegut's dystopian novel *Player Piano* (Vonnegut, 1952). Bodies such as the World Health Organization had been warning of likely catastrophic pandemics since the early 2000s; indeed, we had two 'dry runs' for a global pandemic with the SARS outbreak of 2002–4 and then the MERS outbreak of 2012, neither of which prompted many governments to take significant precautions in the form of, say, stockpiling appropriate personal protective equipment. Finally, regarding the climate crisis, we can trace the dire warning of an impending climate emergency back to the 1957s, when no less a person than Edward Teller, often dubbed the 'father of the hydrogen bomb', told the American Chemical Society in 1957 that if we continue to burn coal and oil at the current rate the polar ice caps will melt (Bell, 2021: 261). By the 1980s, so much scientific evidence had been amassed, and so many briefings given to senior politicians and civil servants, that it is simply not credible to claim that world leaders, and fossil fuel companies, did not know what was happening. Given that, the question we need to ask is *why* these multiple, evidenced and credible warnings were ignored by those in power?

Critical social theory can help us here. Many commentators, from Karl Marx onwards, have noted that capitalism is an economic model that cannot be sustained indefinitely, and that capitalism contains the seeds of its own demise. Perhaps the most lucid and prescient contemporary commentator on 'the end of capitalism' is Wolfgang Streeck. Streeck's melancholy realism is based on a recent historical analysis of capitalism which, he believes, is disintegrating from the inside: the 'three apocalyptic horsemen of contemporary capitalism – stagnation, debt, inequality – are continuing to devastate the economic and political landscape' (Streeck, 2016: 18). In short, capitalism has ceased to be an economic regime that can underwrite a stable society. The symptoms of this are legion, but Streeck focuses on the irrationality of the 'senseless' production of money to stimulate growth and the coming apart of the modern state system (Streeck, 2016: 35). For Streeck, these promote an increase of entropy in societies, and the consequences, for people living in democratic capitalist societies at least, are felt at the level of social life. Neoliberalism engenders, indeed promotes, individualism, and 'social life in an age of entropy is by necessity individualistic' (Streeck, 2016: 41). Streeck (2016: 45) argues that we are in a post-capitalist interregnum that is dependent upon individuals as consumers adhering to a culture of competitive hedonism. Streeck's account of capitalism is a purely internal one which ignores the external increases in entropy in the form of nature 'biting back' through pandemics and climate change. However, his point is still valid regarding the failure and irrationality of continued capitalist production and economics.

As to what will emerge at the end of this interregnum, Streeck is by turns pessimistic and melancholic. The resolution of the crisis of democratic capitalism could be the Hayekian triumph of capitalism freed from any democratic control (capitalism without democracy) or it could be democracy without capitalism, where democratic institutions repair the damage wrought on the institutions of social justice that we are losing, or have lost (Streeck, 2017: 173–5). Unfortunately, it is the first path that Streeck considers the most likely. Either way, contemporary capitalism has entered a period of 'deep indeterminacy' (Streeck, 2016: 12), a period when unexpected things can happen at any time, and it is difficult to predict these or even agree what the outcome of events will be.

Conclusion

We have used this chapter to explain how the current crisis *of* work has been produced by three crises which are *at* work – intensified neoliberalization and its consequences, the experience of the COVID-19 pandemic and the escalating climate emergency. The mutability of neoliberalism has been emphasized by some who highlight its capacity to evolve and exist in varied forms, particularly its adaptability to an era of greater political authoritarianism and state intervention (Peck and Theodore, 2019; Callison and Manfredi, 2020; Šumonja, 2021). For others, though, the era of neoliberalization seems to be on the wane, being supplanted by an emerging economic and political paradigm that privileges state intervention, economic protection and popular control over liberal markets, corporate interests and employers' flexibility (Gerbaudo, 2021).

Notwithstanding these different interpretations, the important thing is that there is a rupture evident, even a potential 'moment of thorough-going transformation' (Hay, 1999: 323), one that is responsible for the contemporary crisis of work. It has found expression in the form of the antagonism that exists between the degradation of work due to intensified neoliberalization and workers' aspirations for good jobs and for their labour to be valued. This antagonism has been aggravated by the epidemiological crisis and the escalating climate crisis respectively. The experience of the COVID-19 pandemic exposed, and exacerbated, the difficulties many workers experience, such as excessively precarious employment, while also contributing to greater government activism and boosting re-regulatory pressures concerned with protecting workers. Tackling the climate emergency effectively demands a 'just transition', one which privileges good jobs and sustainable work, upholds workers' interests and actively involves workers themselves in the process. The rest of this book examines key aspects of the contemporary crisis of work in greater detail, considers the implications of this crisis, assesses responses to the crisis and reflects on how the crisis can be surmounted.

2

Theorizing Crises

Introduction

> Capitalism is not compatible with the future, so we've abolished the future.
>
> Graffiti on wall in Brighton, 2023

The material we present in this book supports and illustrates our core argument: that capitalism has a permanent tendency towards crisis, that this has engendered other crises – notably epidemiological crises and the escalating climate crisis – and that while capitalism remains the global economy's primary mode of operation, these crises will continue and will worsen. The crisis of capitalism is visible across societies, communities and cultures, but our focus on work is quite deliberate: work is at the centre of the operation of capitalism; indeed, it is the thing that generates the profits of capitalism that maintain its momentum and purpose. At the outset, we need to identify what we mean by 'crisis' and, specifically, if we think that a crisis is an extraordinary event, something that marks a turning point or is an emergency, whether it is possible to be in a permanent state of crisis.

The permanent tendency to crisis

Hay notes that while the concept of crisis is ubiquitous in political discourse from the 18th century to the present day, it is a concept that has received little analytical attention, remaining diffuse and underdeveloped (Hay, 1999). Hay attempts to rectify this, at least for political theory, by describing 'crisis' as 'a moment of decisive intervention in the process of institutional change' (1999: 320). Placing the state at the centre of any particular crisis is, for Hay, an important move, and we may want to follow aspects of this definition in considering our three crises; after all, in the UK the state is the actor with the most power – economic, military, symbolic – and the most agency. Hay uses this definition of state intervention at a crucial moment to understand the UK, and other, government responses to the 2007–9 'debt crisis' (Hay 2013), and it is clear that without this dramatic state intervention global banking systems would have collapsed.

The 2007–8 global financial crisis was the deepest financial crisis since the Great Depression of the 1930s (Vermeiren, 2021: 1), plunging capitalism into chaos across the globe. Initially seen by many on the left as the possibility for a complete change in how economies operated, it soon turned into a victory for finance capital as central banks and governments poured money into shoring up capitalist institutions and the whole capitalist system itself. This crisis is still with us in the form of ongoing austerity measures, massive government debt, low growth and high inflation. While the sudden emergence of the COVID-19 pandemic obscured some aspects of the financial crisis – as well as the damaging consequences of Brexit – the consequences of the 2007–8 financial crash persist. Streeck notes that this financial crisis was the consequence of three preceding crises that had faced capitalism in rich democratic countries (Streeck, 2017: 6). These were a banking crisis, where banks extended too much credit that suddenly turned bad; a crisis of public finances, where governments faced very heavy debt burdens which reduced their possibilities for public spending; and a crisis of the 'real' economy manifested in high unemployment and low growth or even stagnation (Streeck, 2017: 8–9). These crises are closely interlinked, through access to money and/or credit, and reinforce one another. Capitalism is permanently prone towards crisis, but the confluence of these three crises that culminated in the 2007–8 global financial crisis was unprecedented.

However, while the global financial crisis can be construed and understood in this way, we must recognize that crises take on many different forms, last for considerably different lengths of time, can be concrete or diffuse (as, indeed, Hay [1999] notes) and can even be, oxymoronically, 'permanent'. The global financial crisis emerged from a capitalist economic system that is always prone to crisis, a crisis that dates back decades and is underlying the other crises we discuss in this book. This tendency to crisis is a chronic condition that is progressively deteriorating as capital seeks new ways to shore up its legitimacy and its structures in the face of economic polarization, financialization leading to market volatility and a disconnect from democratic institutions that could provide some restraint over it (Streeck, 2017: xxxvii).

In what ways is this an ongoing crisis? We can see a crisis as being a situation that emerges due to fundamental tensions, or fundamental antagonisms. Capitalism is based on fundamental tensions between interest groups in opposition to one another. The antagonism between the owners of capital and those who work to serve capital is a permanent feature of capitalism and has been for centuries. We can look at the history of capitalist societies to see that this antagonism has been managed to try to ensure social cohesion and a fairly stable social order. Capitalism relies on a form of reciprocity where owners of capital accumulate further capital by providing subsistence, and above, to workers. 'Capitalism is about the expansion of expandable capital in the form of private property; this entails a danger of a withdrawal of cooperation by those who are needed for accumulation but will not own what is accumulated' (Streeck, 2017: xix). Fairness, or the lack of fairness, is thus at the heart of capitalism and capitalist social relations; capitalist societies must find ways of mediating this unfairness and of legitimating the sociopolitical system. Since the global financial crisis, we have seen attempts to do this become more implausible as austerity, infrastructure decline, polarization, and government corruption have all increased. The underlying antagonism at the heart of capitalism engenders ongoing crises that can only expand as capitalism's contradictions increase and play out.

The concept of antagonism is central to our understanding of crisis. At the heart of each of our current crises, we can see significant antagonisms at play: between workers and owners, between government and society, between nature and the economy, between health and global capital. Antagonisms are the common factor to the crises that beset us.

Three types of crises

A crisis is a situation that affects an individual, a household, a community, a society, or all of these together. A crisis arises when a core antagonism becomes irresolvable and starts to have a destabilizing and direct effect on people's lived experiences. We can identify three different types of crises that beset contemporary societies. These operate at different 'levels' and are perceptible in different ways. However, all contain a common feature: at their heart is a profound antagonism that is currently unresolved.

Empirical crises

Empirical crises are visible to all members of society and often have a significant presence in media discourse. Current examples (writing in 2023) would be the cost-of-living crisis, the National Health Service (NHS) crisis, the Ukraine crisis. These crises are clearly based on core antagonisms – respectively the antagonism between income and expenditure for individuals and households, the antagonism between what the NHS requires in terms of resources and what governments are prepared to provide and the antagonism between the Ukrainian and Russian states. These crises are visible, in plain view, and are often also experiential: people are 'living through' the cost-of-living crisis, for example. However, and importantly, we can also discern underlying crises, ones that are not necessarily easily perceptible but which we can, using a critical sociological approach, discern and analyse. The actual crises are precursors and contributors to the empirical crises that we see.

Actual crises

Actual crises are taking place and are causal factors in the empirical crises that we live through. Actual crises take place regardless of our knowledge of them but can be perceived using critical social analysis. In terms of the fundamental crises we are concerned with in this book, the climate crisis and the pandemic are actual crises; we can also, with Habermas (1975) and Streeck (2017), identify a legitimation crisis facing contemporary democracies.

The climate crisis, founded on an antagonism between the continuing expansion of extractivist capitalism and nature, was only identified through the diligent and long-term work of a large and disparate group of science workers. Combining sea temperature records, sea-level records, ice-core analyses and contemporary atmospheric measurements, climate scientists realized the connection between CO_2 levels in the atmosphere and the temperature of the surface of our planet and deduced that rising CO_2 levels were causing the planet to heat up, with inevitably disastrous consequences. Our empirical crisis is extreme weather, which many communities around the globe experience on a regular basis. Beneath the empirical crisis is the actual crisis of climate change.

Similarly, we have all been through an empirical crisis of COVID-19, caused by an antagonism between a virus and human immune systems (among other things). However, the actual crisis of the pandemic is based on a more fundamental antagonism between the expansion of globalized capital and nature, forcing populations to move into new areas or expanding from existing areas into previously unspoilt areas and dramatically increasing the possibility of xenotransmission of diseases from non-humans to humans.

Periodic empirical crises regarding democratic process and structures permeate recent history, but underlying these is the actual crisis of contemporary democracy, formulated by Habermas as a 'legitimation crisis' and by Streeck as 'the crisis of democratic capitalism'. Here we can see a turning away from democratic structures and a belief in democracy in favour of apathy, disaffection or extremist views and political actions. The core of this actual crisis is an antagonism between the imperatives of a capitalist economy (generating more profit through exploitation of workers and the environment) and the imperatives of a democratic society (allowing people's voices and needs to be heard and responded to).

The real crisis

Beneath all of the crises, empirical and actual, that we encounter we can find the 'real' crisis: the crisis of capitalism. The fundamental antagonism at the heart of capitalism has been described in a range of different ways by different commentators, but it is centred on two things. The first is that capitalism is inimical to what it means to be a human being, as Marx noted in his early writings (Marx, 1975), and that the economic organization of capitalism is in opposition to the need for human societies to progress (Marx, 1954 [1867]). The human condition is to cooperate and to work collectively to achieve subsistence and beyond (a good recent example is the emergence of mutual aid initiatives in the COVID-19 pandemic [Mould et al, 2022]), but the operation of capitalism atomizes individuals and enforces competition at all levels of society. Marx's analysis of human history showed societies in constant movement, but the economic organization of capitalism works against human progress, and we are beginning to see this very clearly as climate catastrophe and environmental destruction loom on the horizon. Capitalism is preventing human societies progressing to adapt to climate change and to have a less destructive impact on the environment.

The second is that capitalism's fundamental mechanism is accumulation of surplus value, and that capitalism has to constantly expand to generate further surplus value. Marx describes this in *Capital* (1954 [1867]) but suggests that the process – what we can term 'infinite accumulation' – will lead to the concentration of wealth in the hands of a very small group of capitalists such that the rest of the population would rise up against this situation of gross injustice. This clearly has not happened, nor, as Thomas Piketty notes (2014), is it likely to happen. We are in a situation where capital does need to expand continuously, but the exhaustion of a market or resource, and concentration of capital, is followed by new markets or resources emerging and a diversification of ownership of infrastructure. This process is of course vastly damaging to the planet and its human and non-human populations, but it is a process that continues with its own momentum.

Yet it is very clear to us that there is something very badly wrong with capitalism, something quite fundamental that imperils us all and threatens the way we organize our societies. Piketty's analysis is that the fundamental way that capitalism works, the way that capitalism has worked in the past (here he means in the mid-20th century), has come unstuck. Capitalism, as Marx and many others noted, relies on growth: it has to keep expanding and moving. However, as Piketty points out,

> [w]hen the rate of return on capital exceeds the rate of growth of output and income, as it did in the nineteenth century and seems quite likely to do again in the twenty-first, capitalism automatically generates arbitrary and unsustainable inequalities that undermine the meritocratic values on which democratic societies are based. (Piketty, 2014: 1)

In other words, those who own capital will make more money from simply owning that capital than they will from growing an enterprise, and this situation will become entrenched as money is inherited by following generations. Where in previous periods, notably in the three decades following the Second World War, we saw some convergence in populations as redistribution of wealth and wage increases were happening, now the tendency in society is towards divergence: the rich will diverge more and more from those without their wealth. This is a consequence of the core antagonism between the rate of return on capital and the rate of growth of output and income.

Using analysis of income and wealth and output and growth figures from industrial societies, Piketty shows that this trend is shared across many societies. The rate of return on capital is significantly higher than the economy's rate of growth. He goes on to sum up the current situation with a simple formula:

> The inequality r > g [where r = private rate of return on capital and g = rate of growth of income and output] implies that wealth accumulated in the past grows more rapidly than output and wages. This inequality expresses a fundamental logical contradiction. The entrepreneur inevitably becomes a rentier, more and more dominant over those who own nothing but their labor. Once constituted, capital reproduces itself faster than output increases. The past devours the future. (Piketty, 2014: 571)

This situation of structural and persistent inequality lies underneath our actual crises, such as that of the legitimation of democracy and empirical crises of the cost of living, fuel and food poverty, NHS degradation and so on. We are seeing a huge growth in wealth compared to income (indeed, incomes are shrinking as inflation rises), and this will be reinforced as this gap is passed on to future generations. This is quite different from the situation in most industrial societies following the Second World War, where subsequent generations experienced a higher standard of living than their predecessors. This fundamental crisis will drive actual and empirical crises: actual crises as people lose their faith in the way the political system can protect and benefit them and our faith in democracy seeps away; empirical crises as the cost of living increases and immiserates large portions of society and the super wealthy consume more and more resources, releasing more and more CO_2 and exacerbating the climate crisis.

Crisis and social structure

Sociology provides us with a useful set of tools for understanding the workings of society, at all its levels. In particular, sociology shows us the relationships between different parts of the social structure, how they affect one another and how these social structures and their interrelationships have consequences for society as a whole, but also for communities and individuals. As we consider the crises currently besetting our society, with a particular focus on work and employment, it is clear that some parts of the social structure will be more pertinent to our studies. Further, when we look at these different elements of society, we can see that they are organized in quite specific arrangements where more 'fundamental' parts of society have effects on other elements.

At the core of our society is the economy, the fundamental means for distributing income, wealth and commodities. As we have already seen, our capitalist economy contains some fundamental antagonisms which prescribe its character and preclude certain outcomes for our society while enhancing others. The state facilitates the operation of the economy through macro-economic policies but also through its ideational orientation. We can, in many ways, see that the economy has 'captured' the state, with state economic policies clearly favouring the expansion of capital finance at the expense of the improvement of society for all, a point made some time ago by critical theorist Habermas in *Legitimation Crisis* (Habermas, 1975). The state has changed its imperatives, away from a form of corporatism towards a full-blown neoliberalism that promotes individualism, rolls back state intervention into public life and promotes privatization. The low-tax, low-wage, low-regulation neoliberal agenda has enormous consequences for work and employment, and far beyond.

Given the state's centrality to the lives and experiences of the population, we can see that the sociocultural becomes riven with tensions and antagonisms. As we noted earlier, the fundamental crisis of capitalism directly leads to the diminution of belief in the possibilities of the state improving lives, and this crisis for democracy, witnessed by declining voting figures and party membership, leads us to the rise of populist political agendas. The fragmented and increasingly insecure world that the self inhabits itself becomes riven with internal antagonisms, and we have seen a very dramatic rise in mental health problems across the population but particularly among young people. The sociocultural world we inhabit exhibits the antagonisms between production and consumption, between the needs of the self and the needs of the individual and between the demands of work and the care of the self (Sloterdijk, 2014).

Our current mode of governance, though neoliberal in character, is based on principles of participatory democracy, and this operates at local, regional and national levels to deliver the 'executive' of the state; this leads to our societal self-description as being a 'democracy'. However, our democracy and economy are now inextricably linked in a shared crisis, a linkage that has increased as the state has become more interventionist in the economy as neoliberalism has become entrenched – as predicted by Gamble (1988). Both of these – state and economy – are in opposition to the needs and interests

Figure 2.1: Core elements of social structure

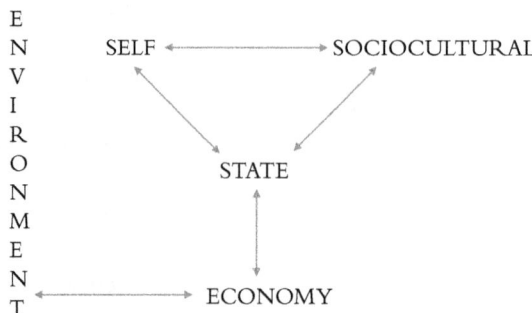

of the self and the needs of society. We can represent this core situation in diagram form (see Figure 2.1).

The economy is in direct relationship with both the environment – where, for example, capitalist extractivism has a significant damaging effect – and the state, which is both affected by the operation of the economy and facilitates the operation of the economy. The three-way relationship between the self, the sociocultural and the state points to the significant influence that the state and the sociocultural have on each other (for example, through state media production and cultural influence on the political), the input of the individual into the state in the form of legitimation and the individual's reliance on the state. Finally, we can see the relationship between the self and the sociocultural, again a reciprocal relationship of influence and support.

This rather stark model gives us a general framework by which we can identify in more detail the effects these spheres of society are having upon one another, by what means and how this has a bearing on the world of work and employment. A more complex diagram illustrates the relationships between capitalism and the world of work that we focus on in this book (see Figure 2.2).

Labour – the work of individuals and communities – is in a reciprocal relationship with the self and with the sociocultural, both sites where work is given meaning. We will investigate this in more depth in subsequent chapters. However, we are focusing in this book on the relationship between neoliberal capitalism and labour, an antagonistic relationship where the needs and imperatives of capitalism dominate the needs and imperatives of workers. This dominance of capitalism is facilitated by the state through its increasing interventions in the economy in the form of economic policies (for example, tax cuts, deregulation, quantitative easing) and employment policies (anti-trade union legislation, deregulation and degradation of work). It is the state in tandem with capital that provides the ideological steering for the economy.

Figure 2.2: Contextualized model of capitalism–work relationship

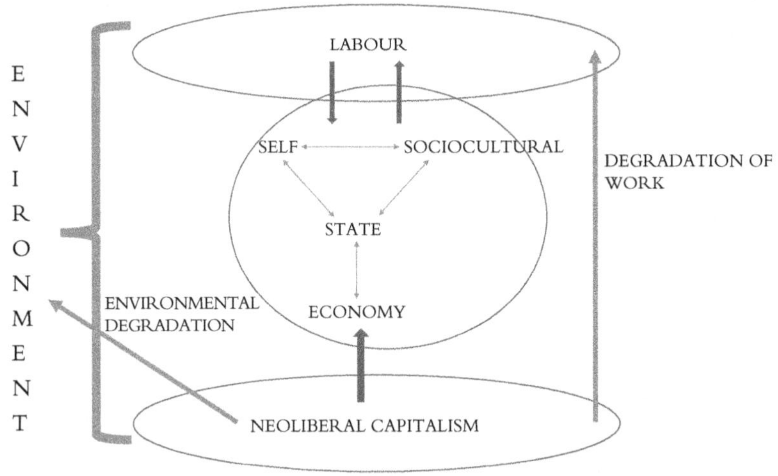

[Diagram: A cylindrical environment labeled "ENVIRONMENT" contains an inner oval with LABOUR at top, SELF ↔ SOCIOCULTURAL in the middle, STATE below, and ECONOMY at the bottom. NEOLIBERAL CAPITALISM sits in an oval at the base, feeding into the ECONOMY. Arrows point outward to DEGRADATION OF WORK (right) and ENVIRONMENTAL DEGRADATION (left).]

In this diagram, we can also see that capitalism and the labour of individuals is located within the environment. The environment that contains us is being actively degraded by the operation of neoliberal capitalism, as is the work that individuals undertake. The removal of neoliberal capitalism would have significant effects for both work/labour and the environment. How could this come about? Streeck's pessimism regarding this is persuasive but perhaps not conclusive. We can envisage scenarios where the harmful effects of neoliberal capitalism can be mitigated and the prospects for the environment and for work are improved.

Here we propose a possible corrective model, where through a combination of activism and regulation the tide of neoliberal capitalism can be held back and then reversed. Central to this model is an active re-engagement with democratic politics and an identification of societal needs above the imperatives of capitalism. This needs to happen at three levels.

At the first level, the voices of people and communities affected by the empirical crises that beset us need to be heard. We can identify the marginalization of these voices at local, national and global levels. For example: locally, communities degraded by the cost-of-living crisis and the driving down of wages and benefits in real terms, and the intensification and commodification of work; nationally, public sector institutions and workers, from nurses to university lecturers, facing privatizations, wage cuts and work intensification; globally, climate crisis-affected communities being denied aid by the polluters who degraded their environment, and migrants facing hostility and violence from countries that have exploited them and their labour across centuries of colonialism. Resistance and activism at this level, and united action at this level, can oppose the degradation of the self, society and environment such that we can move to more decent ways of living together, both materially and psychologically, and more decent ways of working.

Efforts at this level to bring about positive change are predicated on the availability of institutions, channels and spaces where activities for change can be discussed and take place. We will discuss the crisis of democracy in more detail in Chapters 7 and 8; for now, it will suffice to note that democratization of, ironically, democracy is needed to allow the imperatives of society and selves to be heard. Authoritarian and populist regimes are restricting rights of protest, including in the UK, but significant protest movements, often supported by trade unions, are actively opposing this. The long-term trend of the erosion of the power of the public sphere and the colonization of the public sphere by the imperatives of capitalism has been discussed and analysed in depth over many decades (Habermas, 1984, 1987). This relentless process has been accelerated under neoliberal capitalism, and we can clearly see the autonomy and legitimacy of public institutions, notably universities, being crushed by ideologically driven privatization and commodification processes (Gill, 2009; Erickson et al, 2021; Fleming, 2021). Revitalization of the public sphere and the re-activation of political engagement from selves and social groups is the only way to reverse this trend such that the imperatives of society gain primacy and oppose the degradation of the public sphere and social life in general. It is this underlying structure of institutions and spaces where society can debate with itself and find better ways forward that can support the first level of active change needed.

It is also where society can try to amend and restrain the economic motor that is driving the crises that beset us. Underlying the crises we face is the capitalist economic system, now dominant across the globe and relentless in its pursuit of expansion and profit at, seemingly, any cost to the environment and people. Active engagement with politics and political action at the level of everyday life, and through a revitalized democracy and public sphere, can lead us to reversing the trend of recent decades and having less capitalism, rather than more, dominating public discussions and emergent economic interventions. Only less capitalism can resolve the current and future crises that we face. Crucially, only less capitalism can halt and hopefully reverse the degradation of the environment.

Central to this corrective model is still the relationship of state–self–sociocultural, but one where we move away from an economically dominated state controlling the other two actors to a reversed situation, where active citizens in a sociocultural sphere can have agency with respect to the state and direct its imperatives. Underlying this is a necessary change in how work and labour are distributed, managed, rewarded and enacted, and we will explore these in more depth in subsequent chapters. One of the most important elements in addressing the crises we face is to understand the roots of these crises and to challenge the dominant narratives we tell ourselves about how we got to our current situation.

History

The historical roots of our current crises are very deep, predating the consolidation of capitalism in the Global North. Although we can see capitalism consolidating through the 19th century in Western Europe and North America, this rested on colonialist expansion at that time and in the preceding two centuries and on an extractivist programme that underpinned colonialism. Extractivism as a concept 'refers to a complex of self-reinforcing practices, mentalities, and power differentials underwriting and rationalizing socio-ecologically destructive modes of organizing life through subjugation, depletion, and non-reciprocity. Extractivism depends on processes of centralization and monopolization, is premised on capital accumulation, and includes diverse sector-specific development and resistance dynamics' (Chagnon et al, 2022: 763). As Chagnon et al (2022: 761) note, extractivism has long been associated with capitalist processes and 'has recently been characterized as a fundamental expression of global capitalism, particularly in its manifestations across the rural realities of the Global South'. Capitalism in the 19th and well into the 20th century depended on colonialism and the extractivist exploitation of indigenous and trafficked peoples beyond Europe's boundaries. This exploitation abroad allowed the rapid expansion of manufacturing at home as profits from the colonies were ploughed into domestic enterprises.

Piketty's analysis of the relationship between foreign capital and national capital in Britain and France from the 18th century to the present shows just how important and enabling being a colonial power was:

> Between 1880 and 1914, both countries received significantly more in goods and services from the rest of the world than they exported themselves (their trade deficits averaged 1–2 percent of national income throughout this period). This posed no problem, because their income from foreign assets totalled more than 5 percent of national income. Their balance of payments was thus strongly positive, which enabled them to increase their holdings of foreign assets year after year. In other words, the rest of the world worked to increase consumption by the colonial powers and at the same time became more and more indebted to those powers. This may seem shocking. But it is essential to realize that the goal of accumulating assets abroad by way of commercial surpluses and colonial appropriations was precisely to be in a position later to run trade deficits. There would be no interest in running trade surpluses forever. The advantage of owning things is that one can

continue to consume and accumulate without having to work, or at any rate continue to consume and accumulate more than one could produce on one's own. The same was true on an international scale in the age of colonialism. (Piketty, 2014: 121)

The post-Second World War economic collapse, a result of three devastating decades that included world wars and economic depression, and the decolonization movements of the 1950s and 1960s, served to make the vast stocks of foreign assets evaporate, though from the 1970s these have risen again largely through the globalization of the late 20th and early 21st centuries.

Colonialism and extractivism financed the expansion of capitalism in Britain, particularly manufacturing capitalism, in the 19th and early 20th centuries. As the old empires declined, new finance, particularly foreign capital, was needed to replace the old and thus maintain expansion and profits. Globalization, particularly the use of foreign direct investment in the late 20th century, fuelled this need for capital, but the consequences have been significant in terms of the climate emergency and also the current, and possible future, epidemiological crises we face.

The connection between globalization and pandemics has been recognized for a long time (the Black Death arrived by ship in Europe in 1347; cholera spread from the Ganges delta; and the seventh cholera pandemic – which is ongoing – started in 1961 and took the disease to every continent). However, it is the increasingly networked status of contemporary globalized capitalist economies and increased international travel that meant the COVID-19 pandemic spread so widely and quickly. Comparing the medieval plague, the 1957–58 influenza pandemic and the ongoing COVID-19 pandemic, Antràs et al (2023: 940) show that 'the speed of diffusion of each disease increases with measures of international trade links'. Travel between countries transmits disease, and international trade stimulates travel between countries (Antràs et al, 2023: 978). The COVID-19 pandemic originated in Wuhan, China, with cases first being noticed in late December 2019, clustered around a seafood and wet animal wholesale market; the market was closed on 1 January 2020 (Pennington, 2022: 32). The first case in Europe arose after a Chinese woman, who had recently visited her parents in Wuhan, gave a training session to her colleagues at Webasto, a car parts supplier, in Stockdorf, Germany, on 21 January 2020 (Boseley, 2020). Interestingly, this first human-to-human transmission in Europe came from someone who was exhibiting no symptoms, yet the European Centre for Disease Prevention and Control said: "A single detected case in Europe does not change the overall picture for Europe, nor does it change the assessment that there is currently a moderate likelihood of importation of cases" (Boseley, 2020).

As the philosopher Srećko Horvat points out, the COVID-19 pandemic has been characterized by a very strong push by governments and corporations to return us to 'normality': '[A]s much as we needed science and medicine, the decision on how to deal with this eschatological threat was first and foremost a political decision to do with the economy and the capitalist notion of "progress"' (Horvat, 2021: 25).

Are we arguing that globalization was a bad thing, that we would be better off had we stayed, in Peter Sloterdijk's somewhat pejorative phrase, in the 'provincial, plant-like mode for being humans' (2014: 163)? No, that would be absurd. As Immanuel Wallerstein notes, '[i]t was to Europe's credit that it was done, since without the thrust of the sixteenth century the modern world would not have been born and, for all its cruelties, it was better that it was born than that it had not been' (Wallerstein, 1989: 327). But we must recognize the many negative, and multiplying, impacts of accelerated globalization that the world is now facing, particularly the exponential rise in transport and travel carbon emissions. While we can see that there are many advantages to an integrated global system, we must, with Wallerstein, recognize that this advantages the wealthy nations over poor nations and prioritizes the values of Global North societies over Global South societies (Wallerstein, 2006: 28).

Conclusion

We have seen how the three crises we are focusing on are interlinked and all underpinned by the 'real' crisis that we face: the fundamental antagonisms of capitalism, which drive instability, degradation – of work, self, the environment – and push a relentless drive to further inequality. As Mike Savage notes (Savage 2021), we are in a new 'inequality paradigm', which started after the 2007–8 global financial crash. This new paradigm is taking us to levels of inequality last seen in Britain in the Edwardian era. Savage's (2021) work is based on the analysis of Piketty, who, as we have seen in this chapter, shows that the top fraction of society – dubbed by many the '1 per cent' – control the vast majority of wealth in our society and ensure it is retained by them through the expedient of investing in finance and property (thus lowering rates of economic growth) and leaving their heirs to inherit this, thus perpetuating the system. This is a central antagonism in capitalism, one that, ironically, reveals capitalism not to be a dynamic motor for change but a motor for stagnation, degradation and inertia. Work in this model of capitalism faces continuous deterioration as growth stalls and profits for companies must be maintained through driving down costs.

The crisis of work is a consequence of the antagonism between the deterioration of work and employment under neoliberal capitalism and the aspirations of workers for decent work and to have their labour valued. By 'deterioration', we mean that working conditions have been degraded, the status of many occupations has been diminished through deskilling and pay and rewards in general have decreased in relative (and in some cases absolute) terms. The legitimacy of work and employment has as a consequence diminished, particularly in societies where people's values are increasingly shaped by other activities, for example in consumption relations, where they enjoy apparently greater sovereignty. COVID-19 has both illuminated and amplified the aforementioned antagonism as well as exacerbating existing re-regulatory pressures (for example, institution building and labour activism) and prompting a more interventionist role for the state. The climate emergency reflects and exposes the failings of neoliberal capitalism and the deteriorated model of work and employment which it has produced; it demands a focus, broadly conceived, on sustainability, reconciling a decent work agenda with sustainable economic development as an effective response to climate change.

Central to opposing the deterioration of work, the self, society and the environment is finding ways to oppose and restrain capitalism. This can happen at the level of the empirical crises we face: through local and community action on environmental damage, through trade union action against deterioration of work. However, it is at the level of the more fundamental crises we face, that of the crisis facing our democracy and democratic institutions, that change is also needed, and such change to oppose the degradation of public institutions and spaces will ensure that we have mechanisms and opportunities to challenge the empirical crises we face.

Finally, and most importantly, we must address the real crisis head on and challenge the model of capitalism, and its support from states, that is underpinning the other crises we face and is destabilizing our world through its fundamental antagonisms.

3

Labour Markets in Crisis

Introduction: what are labour markets, and why are they in crisis?

The commonly used term 'labour market' is an example of what Gibson-Graham (1996, 2006) and Pettinger (2019) describe as a 'capitalocentric' concept, meaning one that implies the ubiquity, universalism and inevitability of capitalist economic systems. A labour 'market' is one in which an individual's capacity to work (labour power, as mentioned in Chapter 2) is bought and sold as a commodity, and the term connotes physical sites of hiring and firing, or even slave 'markets'. In the current context, labour markets are not physical but abstract: they are the patterns of employment opportunities through which individuals find jobs or occupations.

We speak of labour *markets* in the plural because these arrangements are geographically specific and diverse. In the UK, the local labour market in largely rural Cornwall is vastly more limited than that in London. In general, working-class people, especially youths, tend to seek employment in local labour markets, while middle-class people may access local, national or, more recently, as part of the mechanics of globalization, international labour markets. Ironically, the most underprivileged and desperate jobseekers, migrants and refugees, are also likely to seek work internationally, often ending in informal roles and treated as 'illegal' by the authorities.

This is the first of the chapters in which we explore in more detail how the crises of work and of neoliberal capitalism, discussed in Chapters 1 and 2, are playing out in various aspects of working life. We assert that labour markets are in crisis due to the disruptions and changes inherent in the dynamics of capitalism, especially in the current neoliberal phase. While in the UK in the post-war decades, centred on industrial forms of production, labour markets remained relatively stable, as the economy shifted to its post-industrial service-based forms in the late 1970s and 1980s, the occupational structures and the supply of labour fell out of kilter, causing unemployment to rise in former industrial areas such as South Wales and North East England.

Governments campaigned to match 'the workers without jobs with the jobs without workers', and the Conservative Employment Secretary, Norman Tebbit, was famously credited with telling the unemployed to "get on your bike" to find work in 1981, although in fact he was referring to his father's tactics in the 1930s. However, the costs, economic and personal, of moving to the more buoyant labour markets in the South were prohibitive, and areas marked by long-term unemployment evolved.

The current post-COVID pandemic situation, however, offers an apparently far deeper crisis, one also influenced by the rapid digitalization of sectors of the economy. In the UK, the combination of deaths of key workers during the height of the pandemic and the loss of migrant labour as a result of Brexit, especially from Eastern Europe, has led to shortages of employees in a number of areas, including lorry drivers, fruit pickers, ancillary workers in the National Health Service (NHS) and service staff in the hospitality industries, shortages still making themselves felt.

In this chapter, we show how the spread of precarious labour, growing digitalization and the platform economy have promoted such ruptures, destabilizing established labour markets. We then explore the critical aspects of specific labour markets, where we contrast two examples. The first, the academic labour market, describes the working conditions and labour market dynamics of the section of the UK labour force with the highest level of formal academic qualifications. The second looks at labour market dynamics and working conditions for workers in social care, some of the lowest-paid workers, often with the lowest formal academic qualifications, in the UK labour force. First, though, we take a brief look at how sociologists and political economists have conceptualized labour markets before turning our attention to the role played by platform work in promoting precarity.

Divided labour markets and social divisions

Analysis of labour markets has been strongly influenced by the work of Max Weber, who saw markets as differentiated by levels of skill (Weber, 1922). Weber specifically links this to theorizing of class divisions, and this trend has continued in later analyses.

In the 1970s and 1980s, social scientists spoke of 'dual labour markets', following the influential work of American economists Doeringer and Piore (1971). They argued that the labour market was segmented into primary and secondary sectors. The primary sector was characterized by secure, well-paid, pensionable jobs with promotion chances, often linked to internal labour markets within companies. By contrast, secondary jobs were insecure, often part time or temporary, so that labour could be taken on and laid off according to the demands of the economy. Such work was low paid, often designated as 'unskilled' and lacked the perks and promotion chances of the primary sector. Such jobs were often filled by women, migrant workers and young entrants to the labour market (Barron and Norris, 1976; Ashton and Maguire, 1984). The link to class is more implicit, but it is clear that middle-class occupations would offer primary conditions, although blue-collar men might also find work in the primary sector.

Outside these two sectors was another group, the unemployed or people permanently disengaged from employment. Marxists conceptualize this group as 'surplus labour' or the 'reserve army of labour' in that they constitute a pool which can be drawn on in times of economic expansion (Green, 1991). They serve another, more subtle purpose, as a disciplinary force: workers accept bad pay and conditions for fear of becoming part of the unemployed 'lumpenproletariat'. To make this work, benefits and welfare payments are kept beneath wage levels, a trend especially evident in the UK and US, ostensibly with a view to encouraging those without work to enter the labour force, though there is very little evidence to support this strategy. The structural nature of unemployment on a global level is highlighted by the International Labour Organization (ILO, 2013, 2017), which reports that the proportion of jobless has been increasing internationally since the global financial crisis of 2007–8, rising from 170 million in 2007 to 201 million in 2017. Young people aged between 15 and 24 constitute around half of this global phenomenon, especially in the Middle East, Africa and Asia. Thus, we can speak of a global reserve army of labour (Foster et al, 2011).

With deindustrialization and the growth and expansion of neoliberalism and globalization, this segmentation or bifurcation of the labour market became increasingly more marked, and the boundaries between the secondary sector and the surplus labour population became more permeable. Through the last four decades, we have witnessed the rise of precarity: the loss of secure jobs for life, along with a deterioration in working conditions and pay. According to Herod and Lambert (2016), precarious work displays four common characteristics: it is low paid; it lacks legal protection (for example against instant dismissal); it is unregulated, meaning employers can basically do what they wish; and, most significantly, it lacks any kind of safety net against destitution. Consequently, precarious workers often have to take on two or three kinds of work to survive.

Based on this labour market change, Standing (2011) argued that from the mid-1980s a new class developed: the precariat. This international phenomenon referred to people whose relation to the labour market was tenuous and insecure, leading to a marginal and insecure relation to employment. Many had informal work; others moved in and out of jobs on temporary contracts.

According to Philip Jones (2021), in the decade after the global financial crisis of 2007–8 and the following 'Great Recession', informal work constituted 68 per cent of the labour market in the Asia and Pacific region and 84 per cent in Africa. Recent research in the UK has revealed that there are around 1 million unregistered, and therefore considered 'illegal', immigrants living off occasional work or employed in covert factories where they are paid below the minimum wage (Anand, 2022).

In the post-pandemic era, where COVID is seen as endemic, precarity has become increasingly widespread, not just among less-qualified workers. Young law graduates are employed on temporary contracts as paralegals in the banking and finance sector; 46 per cent of UK universities employ teaching staff on zero-hours contracts (where employers do not guarantee work, but workers must be available when required by employers), and the University and College Union (UCU) estimates that nearly half the university workforce is on casualized contracts (UCU, 2023). While some of these non-standard contracts are voluntary – young adults may combine a 'gig' job with postgraduate study – a lot are not. The current state of the Global North labour market is summed up by Koch et al (2021: 30): 'The labour market has been polarizing in high-income countries over the last two decades, with mid-skill and mid-pay jobs declining, while at the other end of the spectrum high-skill and low-skill jobs are both increasing.'

It is important, however, not to portray labour markets as static. They are constantly changing as the occupational structure alters, resulting from economic, social and political shifts in a society. So far, we have mainly considered the impact of neoliberalism and deindustrialization in the countries of the Global North, notably the US and UK. We also need to consider what impact the climate emergency might have on the occupational structure and thence on labour markets. The impact in the UK so far has not been massive, though even here some changes are noticeable. New jobs have been created in the development of green energy sources, such as wind farm installation (though turbines are created elsewhere and imported), the development of heat pump systems and the production of solar panels (Friends of the Earth, 2021). The setting up of solar panel farms is one of the changes ongoing in Britain's agricultural sector, alongside the investment in new crops, such as soya, in line with the drive to cultivate more plant-based foods to replace consumption of meat (Murray, 2021). There are also new jobs in conservation and rewilding, although some of this work is on a voluntary basis and if rewarded is not very well paid. There are, however, increasing numbers of training schemes for young people in horticulture, arboriculture and forestry, jobs offering interesting careers for the younger generations as well as being beneficial to the planet (Friends of the Earth, 2021).

At the same time, in many areas of manual work or low-level service work, disgruntled by precarity, increasing workloads and pay levels inadequate to deal with the current cost-of-living crisis, people are either quitting their jobs or turning to industrial action (see Chapter 8). Here we see the sociopsychological side of the 'crisis of work' explored by Jesse Potter, who identifies this as 'a greater destabilization of the self–work relationship' (2015: 117). Potter studied middle-class professionals who had become disillusioned with their work and transitioned into new occupations providing greater satisfaction. However, arguably this kind of rupture within prevailing work conditions has now spread among the working class. In August 2022, Mick Lynch, General Secretary of the Rail, Maritime and Transport union, proclaimed "the working class is back" and "we refuse to be poor anymore" (Sleigh, 2022).

But change is never easy, and the switch to a Green New Deal would create antagonisms, as existing jobs are threatened, for example in the fossil fuel industries, arms manufacture or automobile production. In many cases, unions, which might otherwise have been sympathetic to radical changes, fight to retain skilled jobs in these areas. Moreover, jobs in the 'ecological sector' are often poorly paid and lack union coverage (Vachon, 2021) – see Chapter 6. This is why some argue that increasing the sustainability of economies must be based on decent jobs and a 'just transition', including support for Global South countries whose contribution to environmental degradation is less than those of more advanced economies (ILO, 2015; Gueye, 2022). The struggles around the 'just transition' are fully explored in Chapter 6.

At the moment, though, UK labour markets are characterized by increasing precarity, especially for new entrants, by low pay and, perhaps most frighteningly, by digitalization. The hi-tech giants, Amazon, Microsoft, Google and Apple, seem keen on replacing human labour with robots and bots (Beynon, 2019); while in the UK the railway companies seek to do away with ticket offices and guards on trains (although largely unsuccessfully so far) in order to cut labour costs and increase shareholder profits. Many travellers already buy e-tickets online. Welcome to the platform economy and the rise of artificial intelligence (AI).

Precarity, digitalization and the platform economy

Precarious contracts

In 2001, Nancy DiTomaso wrote a prophetic piece entitled 'The loose coupling of jobs and subcontracting of everyone' (DiTomaso, 2001). At the time, this seemed a tad exaggerated, but in fact the trend has continued apace in the 21st century. In the platform economy, firms such as Uber, Just Eat and Deliveroo subcontract tasks ('gigs') to mainly young and/or minoritized employees. The term 'gig economy', coined in America, refers to the practice of hiring people for specific tasks or projects, in the same way that bands are hired for gigs in the music industry.

The visible success of Uber and the food delivery enterprises unfortunately encourages other companies seeking to maximize revenues to adopt 'gig economy' principles. For example, in 2020 the Morrisons supermarket chain decided to scrap 3,000 managerial roles, replacing them with 7,000 new roles paid on hourly rates of £9 (BBC News, 2020b). This is typical of the way secure full-time jobs with reasonable rewards and levels of responsibility are being reconstructed and replaced with low-paid precarious positions, changes justified in terms of the neoliberal icons of flexibility and profitability. Moreover, part-time workers are less likely to join a union.

According to the Labour Force Survey (LFS, 2020), the level of self-employment among men rose from 2,646,512 to 3,317,470 between 2005 and 2019. The highest area of self-employment was construction (880,000), followed by scientific and technical services (421,000) and transport and storage (300,000). Some of this can be categorized as 'pseudo self-employment', as many van drivers, for example, are actually working for companies such as DPD or Yodel. Some 'white van' builders are genuinely running small businesses, but others effectively work for the big companies on a 'gig' basis. In this way, many profitable haulage and construction companies achieve that desired flexibility. Self-employment among women also increased, having been less than a million before 2005 but reaching 1,670,952 by 2019 (LFS, 2020). These women entrepreneurs tend to run genuine small businesses in areas such as childminding, craft products, beauty work or therapies. Self-employment has often been a preferred choice for women raising a family, enabling them to reconcile paid and unpaid work, running their small business from their home.

This tendency to subcontract is also linked to privatization. Large institutions hive off parts of their labour process to other organizations, usually resulting in lower pay and conditions for the workers (Pettinger, 2019: 42). In the UK, the NHS has been outsourcing clinical and non-clinical services for many years: in 2018–19, the private sector won over 51 per cent of the contract awards by number and was granted just over 65 per cent of the total value of awards – amounting to just over £3.2 billion (NHS for Sale, 2019).

Accordingly, the early 21st century saw the multiplication of these new contractual relations: zero-hours contracts, self-employment, pseudo self-employment, the 'gig economy'. This latter term has now been superseded by the notion of 'platform capitalism', which springs especially from the progress of digitalization led by the tech giants, Amazon, Google, Apple and Alibaba. According to Eurofound, platform work is characterized by a relationship between an online platform, a contracted worker and a client (or 'requester') requiring a particular task. Some tasks are carried out in person (Uber and Deliveroo come into this category), while others are online pieces of 'microwork' (P. Jones, 2021). The tasks are designated, contracted, monitored and regulated online.

Digitalization

P. Jones' 2021 book on platform work, *Work without the Worker*, focuses particularly on microwork, small online tasks carried out on online platforms such as Mechanical Turk (owned by Amazon), ClickWorks and the not-for-profit Samasource (now renamed Sama), which provides training and work for refugees. Tasks are carried out chiefly for the digital corporations: examples are the tagging of locations as part of the process of developing military drones or driverless vehicles, a key project of Elon Musk's Tesla, or teaching bots and algorithms to recognize and identify images, be they of cars or cats (or fire hydrants and traffic lights, as you will know from being asked to tag them as part of online CAPTCHA verification). Other common tasks are the translations of text from English to other languages and the weeding out of posts considered to violate the rules of online social media sites like Twitter/X. Many of these tasks are small, so workers have to be perpetually alert for new requests. P. Jones (2021) reports that following the 2007–8 global financial crisis, an estimated 20 million workers are involved in microwork, mostly in the Global South. Platforms apparently target people in refugee camps and other types of displaced workers. P. Jones (2021) also suggests that some 5 per cent of the UK working population may pursue microwork, though mostly in order to top-up insufficient earnings.

Digitalization affects the labour market in other ways. Digital systems are increasingly used both to cut jobs and to control and monitor workers' activity, for example in warehouses, notably those of Amazon, a key player and leader in the field, and the second largest employer in the world after Walmart. Jobs are allocated, timed and logged by computer programs, putting immense physical pressure on the predominantly young employees, often from minoritized communities, who have to run around the vast premises picking items to fulfil orders. Their labour is described in Alessandro Delfanti's powerful study *The Warehouse*:

> Now imagine warehouse workers. They work under physically punishing rhythms, dictated by distant corporate algorithms which organize their labour. A pervasive surveillance system monitors their productivity at every step. The valuable information generated by their labour is captured and monopolized by Amazon's software systems and then fed to the machines that run the warehouse. (Delfanti, 2020: 23)

Another example of digitalization is the ongoing replacement of staffed supermarket tills by automatic tills. Although till work is poorly paid and repetitive, such jobs have been popular with women, as they can arrange shifts compatible with childcare and domestic work, and the shops can be found in most localities, to eliminate travel time and costs. The UK's Office for National Statistics has estimated that around two thirds of cashier jobs are at risk of digital replacement (ONS, 2019). Such ongoing moves to cut labour costs have now been augmented by the post-lockdown labour shortages. Robots and computers, although they may need maintaining, do not catch COVID-19. The pandemic gave a major boost to digitalization and online services.

A low-pay economy

Inevitably, these new, precarious and digitalized jobs are paid less than the full-time jobs they replace. Low pay lies at the heart of the cost-of-living crisis that started in 2022 in the UK. Inflation has outstripped pay levels, as the costs of food, energy and accommodation have soared, partly as a result of Brexit and the war in Ukraine (see Chapter 7) but more fundamentally because of neoliberal financialized capital's voracious demand for increased profits, discussed in previous chapters.

More and more families in the UK are forced to rely on foodbanks. The numbers of rough sleepers in Britain's cities rose in 2022, and rent rises led to further evictions. Mortgages rose by an average £250 a month as banks raised their interest rates. Resulting from all this, an article in the *Guardian* estimated that by 2024, 30 million people in the UK will be living in poverty, with 21 million already living on less than £12,570 a year (Elliott, 2022). This is the combined effect of precarious work, digitalization and excessive profits.

It is important to stress that the current labour market skews pay, with the elite earning huge salaries and investors (often the same people) benefitting. Some examples follow. The Royal Mail made a record £758 million profit in 2021–22, of which £567 million went to shareholders and £2 million to the Chief Executive Officers (CEOs) of its various sectors; the starting salary of a postal worker is £22,425. The wealth of Britain's billionaires increased from £212 billion in 2012 to £653 billion in 2022 – these are the super-rich with their super yachts, multiple luxury dwellings and offshore tax haven holdings, who also saw their wealth grow during the COVID lockdown. The CEOs of major British charities such as Oxfam, Save the Children and the Red Cross all earn six-figure salaries; by contrast, the starting salaries of key workers are increasingly insufficient to maintain family needs: in 2023, the starting salary for a nurse in England was £24,907 and £28,000 for a teacher. These are demanding and increasingly stressful jobs, leading their unions to engage in strike activity between 2022 and 2024 – see Chapter 8. This is the result of labour markets marked by increasingly unequal structures of occupational hierarchy, as will be demonstrated in the two sketches of specific labour markets, academic work and adult social care, that follow.

The academic labour market: casualization and stress

For many university graduates, further study is a way to move towards future stable professional employment. However, if graduates stay at universities and enter the academic labour market, they may find themselves trapped in precarity. Back in the 1990s, a number of seminal, critical texts were published that launched what has come to be called 'Critical University Studies'. Writing about the changes to university governance structures, funding regimes, marketization, new public management (NPM) initiatives and a general ideology of neoliberalism pervading the upper echelons of their respective universities, Bill Readings (1996) and Stanley Aronowitz (1997) provide vivid descriptions of higher education (HE) on the brink of dramatic and disconcerting changes.

Readings shows how the grand narrative of the university is changing, away from describing universities as institutions promoting culture and learning to a discourse of 'excellence'. This stems from the changing role of the nation-state – no longer the primary locus of the reproduction of global capital, it has lost its purchase in an era of multinational companies, transnational capital and globalization (Readings, 1996: 12).

Aronowitz's focus is on his everyday work as an academic at the City University of New York. Aronowitz gives a detailed account of his daily work routine, peppered with interruptions, bureaucratic interventions and meetings; while he may have the 'last good job in America', a job offering some self-managed time for thinking, its conditions are being rapidly eroded.

Both writers are showing, in different ways, how economic, political and sociocultural conditions external to the university impact on how HE is conceptualized, described, organized and, ultimately, delivered by academic workers. The external conditions change the university's internal culture – Readings, for example, notes the 'commodification' of his university, citing the example of his university bookshop now devoting considerable space to selling merchandise with the university logo on it:

> Thus commodified, belonging to the University carries little ideological baggage and requires no reaffirmation through giving, any more than a consumer, having purchased a car, feels the need to make further periodic donations to General Motors in excess of the car loan repayments. That some students do make such gifts is an interesting symptom of an atavistic desire to believe that they did not attend a University of Excellence but instead a University of Culture. (Readings, 1996: 11)

For Aronowitz, it is the intensification of work and imposed conformity to management strictures and curricula norms that best characterizes this external intervention into the university system. Universities have been restructured as businesses along the lines of global capitalism, and most academic workers are

> [i]n less privileged precincts of the academic system. We have witnessed relatively declining salaries and the erosion of our benefits. And like many industrial workers we have been driven into an impossibly defensive posture and are huddled in the cold, awaiting the next blow. We know that full-time lines are being retired with their bearers, that more courses are taught by part-timers at incredibly low pay and few if any benefits. We are aware of the tendency of elite as well as middle-tier universities toward privatization and toward aligning the curriculum with the job market, and we are experiencing the transformation of nearly all the humanities and many social sciences into services for business, computer technology, and other vocational programs. (Aronowitz, 1997: 107–8)

The academic labour market began a process of radical change from this point onwards with increasing use of short-term and temporary contracts, lowering of remuneration for junior academics and lack of job security, leading to housing and food instability.

This deprofessionalization of faculty roles in the US university system has led Kezar and colleagues to describe the current situation as 'the gig academy' (Kezar et al, 2019). They note that this strategy allows senior managers to have much greater control over HE institutions: '[T]he pervasive insecurity foisted on most college employees, regardless of the particular duties they perform, is a key strategy used to regulate the postsecondary workforce writ large' (Kezar at al, 2019: 16).

America was the forerunner of the commodification and commercialization of HE at the behest of neoliberal ideology, but the United Kingdom has followed enthusiastically. The introduction of NPM processes and methods has utterly transformed the UK HE landscape, with dramatic consequences for academic workers and students alike.

Two significant areas of change in UK HE have led to a transformation of working and studying conditions. Successive governments since the 1990s have reduced funding for UK HE and then introduced student fees. The starting point for this was the expansion of the UK HE sector in 1992, when former polytechnics were granted university status. This led to internal markets and increased competition between institutions. Increased marketization (Naidoo, 2008) came with the introduction of tuition fees for undergraduate students in England (the largest part of the UK HE sector) in 2003 (subsequently raised in 2012 and again in 2016). This external push towards marketization and commercialization from successive governments on both sides of the political divide shows the adoption of a neoliberal agenda alongside policies to force UK HE to become more flexible, more competitive and to have greater 'impact', both in terms of supporting and advancing business through innovation and through providing graduates trained on public funds to enter the labour market. The neoliberal emphasis on personal responsibility is visible in an emphasis on quality and labour market supply.

NPM is directly linked to political changes in the UK, US and elsewhere, with a clear shift to the right of the political spectrum and the rise of 'New Right' thinking. NPM was, and still is, presented as a reformist approach to public service delivery, and its narrative includes 'the growth of markets and quasi-markets within public services, empowerment of management, and active performance measurement and management' (Ferlie, 2017: 1). Ferlie notes that the UK adopted NPM at the level of governance in the 1980s, where the governance mode is a 'markets-and-management mix combining more competition among public services agencies with stronger line management within them' (Ferlie, 2017: 1). This governance-level mode was then replicated across public services.

Before the introduction of NPM, UK HE was a largely autonomous realm, but this changed with the rise of neoliberal governance and ideology. Until then, academic management and student education had not been subject to stricter marketization or restricted public capital investment: the sector enjoyed a lengthy period of freedom around learning and application of knowledge, escaping any significant scrutiny by government (Deem, 2004). With NPM, the sector experienced significant changes to both internal governance and external funding regimes. The rhetoric of treating students as 'customers', while still not fully embedded, changed the relations between academic staff and those they were charged with educating. This coincided with the erosion of democratic structures of control and leadership across the UK university sector (Radice, 2013: 410): academic staff in universities lost much of their voice and say in how their institutions were run, and the direction they were taking, a shift from democratic to managerial governance (Erickson et al, 2021). This has led to major changes in how academic staff are doing their work: Gill (2009) notes the emergence of more bureaucratic modes of control and surveillance of academic workers, along with Taylorist modes of academic production, consistent with scientific management principles (Halfmann and Radder, 2015: 77). Heller notes that managerialism creates burdens for academics but with no apparent benefits (Heller, 2022: 6).

The gulf that has opened up between senior university managers and the bulk of a university's staff can be seen most clearly in terms of remuneration and job security. Writing in 2021, Peter Fleming notes that '[n]early half of

Vice Chancellors/Presidents in the UK receive over £300,000 a year, and five are paid £500,000 or more. De Montfort's Vice Chancellor received a 22 per cent salary increase in 2017–18' (Fleming, 2021: 47). In contrast, academic staff pay has declined by 25 per cent between 2009 and 2022. In terms of job security, in UK HE senior managers are all on full-time and permanent contracts, but 41 per cent of teaching-only staff are on hourly paid contracts, and one third of all academics are on fixed-term contracts (UCU, 2021). Job insecurity puts considerable additional pressure on workers, who often feel they need to show their commitment to an institution through presenteeism (Hadjisolomou et al, 2022). Academic staff regularly report working way over their contracted hours, increasing stress and burnout, and taking on unmanageable workloads. Recently recruited hourly paid teaching staff – often recent graduates or even PhD students – must carry out career-building activities as unpaid labour. These burdens are compounded by the entrenched and increasing managerialism and bureaucracy that permeate and direct many aspects of work and research in universities.

Central to the NPM project is assessment and evaluation of change and 'progress' through measurement and metrics, which underpin the Taylorist model. The UK HE sector is beset with metrics at almost every level. Internal metrics in the form of Key Performance Indicators (KPIs) are legion; all academic staff will have come across these, and many have to formally report on and respond to KPIs as part of their work duties. Externally, the Research Excellence Framework, the Teaching Excellence Framework, the Knowledge Exchange Framework and the National Student Survey measure, respectively, research 'quality' and impact, teaching and knowledge exchange 'quality' and student satisfaction with degree delivery and environments. The introduction of these metrics has led to an increasingly harsh and pervasive 'audit culture' (Martell, 2017) and the use of league tables to rank universities; such league tables become tools to force staff to work even harder to improve a wide range of indices. Metric-driven organizational cultures are a major factor in the emergence of 'statactivist' research, where researchers will deliberately collect statistics that can be used to oppose and challenge employers and state institutions. Recent statactivist research, designed to create a 'league table' of universities ranked according to staff appraisal of senior managers, revealed very high levels of staff dissatisfaction with the audit culture, new managerialism, lack of democratic governance and increased bureaucracy putting pressure on already high workloads (Erickson et al, 2021).

This context of increased workloads, audit culture, marketization, job insecurity, loss of democratic governance and an increasing separation of senior managers from the rest of the staff of an institution provides the backdrop for the crisis in UK HE caused by the COVID-19 pandemic. Staff faced the rapid and very disruptive imposition of online provision of learning. The pandemic and its attendant lockdowns rapidly and dramatically changed how university staff taught, researched and interacted with students and colleagues, and these changes to work and interaction patterns are still influential (Erickson et al, 2023).

However, in addition to changing and intensifying work patterns, the COVID-19 pandemic also engendered significant psychological changes and harm for university staff. In the summer of 2020, following the first wave of the pandemic, the UK government instructed all education institutions to reopen at the start of the autumn term. The reopening was haphazard, causing considerable chaos across the sector, but many universities complied with this edict, telling staff that they must return to face-to-face teaching. The chaotic return to 'business-as-usual' across the UK HE sector led to student protests against lack of access to facilities and resources. In some cases, students returned to campus only to find themselves locked down in student accommodation (BBC News, 2020a). As one Manchester University student put it: 'They brought us here for profit rather than our safety ... We've tried protesting and withholding our rent but the university won't respond to our demands for support' (BBC News, 2020a). Staff delivering face-to-face teaching had to contend with challenges regarding the provision of personal protective equipment, finding adequately ventilated teaching spaces, caring for their own families and friends and coping with health challenges of their own. Many had to make very difficult decisions, often acting against their own moral principles to carry out management instructions. A survey carried out just after this period of reopening found that almost 70 per cent of responding academic staff thought that at work they had acted in ways that made them uneasy; nearly 40 per cent found that their work had made them compromise their own moral judgement (Hanna et al, 2022: 7). Participants in the research considered senior management to bear most responsibility for this (43 per cent), followed by the UK government (25 per cent). The conclusion that these people had suffered a 'moral injury' is based on the work of psychiatrist Jonathan Shay (1994, 2014), who found US combat veterans suffering from forms of psychological trauma caused by being ordered to carry out acts, or to be complicit in acts, that conflicted with their personal moral values. Similarly, academic staff often reported being forced to undertake academic work where they knew it was wrong to do so. Staff felt betrayed by management. For example:

'They have betrayed staff and students – I think this has destroyed any trust staff had in their senior management.' (Male, 64, White, over £60k, full-time, permanent)

'Up until COVID I believed in the community of values espoused by my employer. But now I know it was all rhetoric. A management that seeks to uphold student experience by exposing its teaching staff to a serious virus is morally bankrupt.' (Male, 54, White, over £60k, full-time, permanent) (Hanna et al, 2022: 10)

Participants recognized that universities' senior managers were themselves under pressure to deliver what the UK government was requesting, although many thought their leaders should have done more to resist:

'To say that it has been shambolic would be to praise it too highly. It has revealed precisely the venality, nihilistic cynicism, and basic inhumanity of HE senior management, the lily-liveredness of the VCs (who have done fuck all to put pressure on the government, because they are much more concerned with their own personal ambitions).' (Male, 47, White, £50–59k, full-time, permanent) (Hanna et al, 2022: 10)

The UK HE sector provides us with an object lesson in how NPM and neoliberal orientations can bring about dramatic changes in a labour market, the labour process and the governance of public institutions. Reversing the trend of deprofessionalization and de-democratization (with its attendant delegitimization of the institution) is a difficult task. At the forefront of this are trade unions, which have been waging an almost continuous industrial relations battle with university employers since 2019. In 2020, the UCU, the academic researcher and lecturer union, consolidated its industrial action around four fights: against casualization, increasing workloads, discrimination and for pay increases. This campaign continues in the increasingly divided and bitter industrial relations landscape that now characterizes UK HE.

Adult social care: underfunding and digital control

Adult social care work can be seen as paradigmatic of the conditions within contemporary labour markets: low paid, made precarious by privatization and subjected to digitalized control systems.

At the same time, the need for a skilled and engaged care workforce has never been greater. The UK, like many contemporary societies in the Global North, is currently facing a severe 'crisis of care' (Bunting, 2021; Dowling, 2022). A challenge, too often neglected by policy makers, is to ensure that people who need support from others – children, people with disabilities and older people – receive the care they need to lead dignified lives.

Adult social care, in particular, is a massive and growing industry. It can be linked to the demographic phenomenon of an ageing society (older people living longer, so that their numbers increase in proportion to the working population that must support them). As people live longer, chronic health conditions, including dementia, become more prevalent, so that care work, whether paid (by workers) or unpaid (by family members or friends), is becoming ever more important to societies.

The current crisis of care rests on the disparity between this ever-increasing demand for care and the actual resources available to meet it (Bunting, 2021; Dowling, 2022). Care work is undervalued, not least because of the gendered assumptions that apply to it. Largely performed in the home by women, it is stereotyped as intrinsically feminine and thus commonly presented as 'women's work'; like other work characterized in this way, it has low status and consequently is less well rewarded.

There are about 2 million people employed within the industry, and 82 per cent of the workforce is female. In addition, large numbers of people work as unpaid carers, around 5.5 million according to the Commission on Care (2016). Most of these are women.

Neoliberalism has led to greater privatization and marketization of how social care is organized and delivered (Dowling, 2022; Simmonds, 2022). Before the advent of Thatcherite marketization, local councils offered both domiciliary (in the client's home) and residential care services. But from the 1980s councils started to shed these jobs to cut costs, and the whole adult care sector opened up to private investment and provision, first through the expansion of private care homes that were variable in quality but often expensive and well resourced and subsequently through the outsourcing of council-run domiciliary services, as austerity bit into council budgets.

Consequently, since the 1990s, private sector, for-profit and corporate providers have come to dominate the delivery of social care in the UK, based on the presumption that care is a commodity, something that can be rationalized and quantified and thus provided as a service for a price (Dowling, 2022; Simmonds, 2022). The social care sector has become heavily financialized, with private equity funds and other kinds of financial vehicles using debt-based finance to secure ownership of residential care homes and to benefit from rising property values from which they can realize greater financial value (Horton, 2022). As so often in privatized organizations in financialized capitalism, homes are run for profits, often owned by offshore bodies, and the well-being of both residents and staff is a secondary concern. For example, in one chain of care homes studied by Horton (2022: 152), the private equity firm which had taken over the business made changes to bank holiday payments, resulting in staff losing 'the equivalent of 7.5 days' earnings per year', a 'substantial deterioration' in the terms and conditions of the workforce.

As a result, the care system has become more unstable and turbulent, with some notable insolvencies occurring, the most well known of which was the collapse of the Southern Cross chain, with over 700 sites, in 2011. Financialization has degraded the quality of care provided. Major private chains, such as HC-One, whose majority owner is a US private equity fund, accept tens of millions of pounds of public funds to look after residents in their care homes, many of which are judged 'inadequate' or 'requiring improvement' (Booth and Goodier, 2023a).

Within the residential sector, there is a high level of employment of migrant workers: in 2019, over a fifth were born outside the UK, with 17 per cent from non-EU countries and 6 per cent from EU states (McKinney and Sturge, 2023). This includes men, though women still predominate. This is very demanding and often physically and emotionally draining work, especially with the high numbers of dementia patients and others who are bedbound. While visits to care homes reveal that many carers are committed to their work and creative in addressing problems, it is not for everybody: many homes struggle with high staff turnover and recruitment problems. These were exacerbated during the COVID lockdown when many infected patients were discharged into care homes from hospitals, inevitably spreading the infection among other patients and carers. Deaths were frequent, and many carers were virtually imprisoned in their workplaces. The newly established Care Workers Union (CWU) reports that up to 2021 one third of COVID deaths were in care homes (CWU, 2022).

However, it is the domiciliary care workers who provide the starkest demonstration of the impact of contemporary employment conditions – low paid, precarious and digitalized. Their work has been studied by Lydia Hayes and Sian Moore (Moore and Hayes, 2016; Hayes, 2017; Hayes and Moore, 2017) and Gail Hebson, Jill Rubery and Damian Grimshaw (Hebson et al, 2015; Rubery et al, 2015), whose research is drawn on in the following account.

As mentioned already, the domiciliary workers were formerly employed by local authorities (LAs), which provided secure jobs, reasonable conditions and trade union protection: they were organized, like other public service workers, by UNISON. Due to Conservative austerity policies and cuts to budgets, 97 per cent of domiciliary work has been outsourced to, contracted out to private tenderers, 97 per cent according to Moore and Hayes. As a result of this, the conditions and pay worsened drastically. Most care workers are on zero-hours contracts, as a result of the commissioning system. The women in Hebson's study reported their wages had fallen from £23.40 to £13 per hour in 2008, and a considerable proportion of care workers currently earn less than the living wage (the living wage, calculated on the basis of real living costs, was fixed in September 2022 at £10.90 – £11.95 in London – slightly more than the legal minimum of £10.42). This is the result of the tendering process: the LA will push to lower the bid, the private provider needs to cream some money off as costs and profit, so the downward pressure is considerable. The burden of privatization is borne by individual workers.

In addition to the problems caused by low pay, working conditions have also been affected by the private companies, as a care worker explained to Moore and Hayes:

> 'They said to us, if we went over our time with a service user we wouldn't get paid because that's not the contracted hours. The council won't pay them so the agency won't pay us. So if we did an extra hour, which happened quite often if somebody had a fall or someone wasn't well and you stay on because it's your duty of care, we wouldn't get paid for that.' (Moore and Hayes, 2016: 1)

To add to this exploitative situation, care workers are generally not allowed to claim for the time spent travelling between home visits. There could hardly be a more egregious example of how the neoliberal drive for profits has forced workers to provide free labour while at the same time reducing the quality of service.

This regime is reinforced by the system of electronic monitoring (EM) set up to police the rules on the timing of visits. The rhetoric surrounding the implementation of this digital technology stresses that it is done to ensure safety, quality of work and to maximize efficient bureaucratic logging within the contractual system, but from the care workers' perspective it is simply a way to ensure that much of their labour is unpaid.

Moore and Hayes (2016) explain how the EM system works to tighten management control. Timesheets are replaced by integrated computer-telephone technology to log, analyse, report on and invoice service-user visits. Workers can log in and out of their visits through service-users' telephones, or they can do so by swiping tags on service-users' files on their smart phones. Alternatively, they can be tracked through smart phones via Global Positioning System technology. In this way, discretionary use of time can be eliminated or, if it is given, will be unpaid. Workers interviewed by Hayes and Moore spoke of the pressure this imposed on them. Moreover, they are faced, as employees but also as human subjects, with a choice between a decline in the quality of service they can offer or a sense of 'working for nothing'. Thus, one woman spoke of how the system was bringing an end to what she categorized as "human care", her task now being to "put drugs in you, whip the hoover around quickly and then get out". The work thus becomes more standardized, more technologized, in a similar fashion to the jobs of Amazon's warehouse labourers.

The alternative is for the workers to stick to their old values of high-quality thoughtful care and building real relationships with the elderly folk they look after. In their research, Hebson et al (2015) observed that the women they interviewed spoke of the commitment and satisfaction they experienced in their work. Because of this, they were prepared to do extra little tasks that the clients might require, a bit of shopping, washing up or taking out the bins. Under the old system of LA control, they had the freedom to do this, but now they face the dilemma of losing paid time if they continue these practices. Here, again, we see organizations squeezing unpaid labour out of workers.

Hayes and Moore (2017) conclude that EM is a technological driver for very real degradation. In this way, care is cheapened – they estimate the cost has been halved under the new system – at the expense of the care workers' pay, conditions and autonomy. One reason that underlies all this is that, as emphasized already, these workers are mainly women, and the very real skills they use in their work are deemed to be 'natural' or at the least 'learned in the home' and thus considered worth less – or indeed worthless – compared to technical and predominately 'male' skills.

In sum, funding difficulties and concomitant pressures to reduce costs are responsible for an employment model which is marked by high staff turnover, with care workers enjoying little scope for progression (NAO, 2018; Skills for Care, 2022). Although domiciliary care staff generally report high job satisfaction, with positive engagement in meaningful work (Hebson et al, 2015), a care commissioning model based largely on cost minimization means that employment in social care tends to be characterized by low pay, high work intensity and few benefits (Rubery et al, 2013; Cunningham and James, 2014; Baines and Cunningham, 2015). It is not surprising that quit rates are so high.

The cost-of-living crisis (see Chapter 7) seems to have exacerbated the problem of staff shortages. In 2022–23, some 10 per cent (152,000) of social care positions in England were unfilled; and the annual rate of staff turnover – over 28 per cent – was exceptionally high (Skills for Care, 2023). A key reason why care providers face such profound difficulties in recruiting and retaining staff is the low pay prevalent in the sector, reflecting the lack of adequate funding.

Indeed, in the context of a post-pandemic labour shortage it appears that care workers were being wooed away from care homes. Staff were lost to supermarkets, where pay rates are often higher and the work is less demanding (Booth, 2022b). The CWU reports on a care home near Nottingham whose manager stated that a newly opened Amazon warehouse was offering their care staff 30 per cent more than their current wage. Other companies were offering joining bonuses of up to £1,000. Given the awful experience of the lockdown period, it is unsurprising that three quarters of care home operators reported staff leaving after April 2021, when COVID restrictions began to be eased: interviews revealed motives for quitting were low pay and stress, a familiar story of contemporary work in crisis (CWU, 2022).

There are alternative ways to deliver adult social care if it is fully funded by local and/or central governments. In the Scandinavian countries, such as Denmark and Norway, caring is viewed as a skill for which training and qualifications are offered. In the UK system, the emphasis on cost reduction means there is insufficient consideration given to investing in staff by offering them higher pay and improved access to training and development opportunities, leading to high turnover rates and the undermining of care standards (NAO, 2018). The rates LAs pay to care providers are generally insufficient to cover the latter's costs.

The troublesome features of the social care sector – low pay, intensive work and digitalized control – encapsulate the problems with the more degraded nature of work and employment relations evident under intensified neoliberalism, where minimizing costs and creaming off profits for shareholders are key features. Workers are increasingly viewed as components inputted into a system rather than human beings with skills, experiences and emotions. As Horton puts it, because of the low value accorded to care workers, they 'are treated as if they are disposable and can be easily substituted' (Horton, 2022: 153). Ironically, as we have seen, this is not the case, as human beings can say 'Enough is Enough' and walk out. Without transformative action to improve pay, working conditions and development opportunities for workers in social care, there is little prospect that the care sector can be sufficiently well resourced, especially given that nearly half-a-million new jobs in care could be needed by 2035 to meet the expected rising demand for care services (Skills for Care, 2022).

Conclusion

As we have noted, the emergence of a divided labour market, characterized by security and enormous rewards for an entitled few but by insecurity and low pay for the underprivileged mass, has been a lengthy process, commencing in the 1980s from the era of Thatcher and Reaganomics. The 2007–8 financial crash, subsequent austerity policies and the COVID pandemic have each fostered new waves of inequality, leading to the current crisis of work, manifested in labour market divisions and insecurity. Our two examples of labour markets – academic work and social care work – show remarkable similarities in terms of increased precarity, increased extraction of unpaid labour, stagnant or declining pay and increasing stress and burnout, despite the participants in these labour sectors having very different formal qualifications.

The global nature of neoliberal consumerist capitalism has fostered a 'race to the bottom' as the old economies of the Global North face tough competition from China and South Asian countries. The march of the giant digitalized corporations has been speeded up by the pandemic, driving both goods and services online. The result has been continued pressure on workers to produce more goods and services for less reward to ramp up profits, resulting also, as we have shown, in increased extraction of unpaid labour. Cole describes this extraction of unpaid labour both within the working day and outside paid hours as 'wage theft' (Cole, 2021). A typical example reported in the *Observer* in December 2022 illustrates the processes pushing down on employees: an economic study of wages in the US hotel industry from 2019 found that prices had risen by 16 per cent while wage costs had risen only 5–6 per cent. This was due to proprietors using fewer staff to improve productivity: '[T]his rise in efficiency was being channelled to shareholders, not consumers, who were fed a story that prices needed to rise to cope with rising wage bills' (Inman, 2022). This typifies neoliberal shareholder-oriented economic practice. Moreover, digital and AI technologies are increasingly being used to dehumanize labour. This is why we speak of a crisis of work, and consequently a crisis of labour markets. In the bleak vision of Jones: 'Informal work, underemployment, wage stagnation, jobless recoveries, widespread precarity and a withered worker's movement are some of the many ominous symptoms that reveal a more terminal crisis of employment' (P. Jones, 2021: 26).

Certainly, these are features of the 21st-century UK economy. But such dystopic conditions have now provoked new forms of antagonism, which are explored in other chapters of this book.

4

Employment Relations in Crisis

Introduction

This chapter is concerned with how developments in employment relations, understood as the nature of the relationship between employers and workers, and the contemporary management of employment relations have contributed to the current crisis of work. It demonstrates how intensified neoliberalization, by promoting deregulation, enabling greater managerial control and weakening labour, has contributed to greater employer flexibility, with adverse consequences for workers, particularly in more financialized settings and in a context of greater automation. The crisis of employment relations is thus a product of the increased disconnect between managerial imperatives for short-term efficiency improvements, with the consequence that labour is increasingly treated as a commodity, and workers' aspirations for decent work and to have their labour valued. This has heightened the antagonisms we discuss in Chapters 1 and 2.

This disconnect was particularly evident at the height of the COVID-19 crisis. As the chapter shows, the expectation that the experience of the pandemic would temper the trend of labour commodification, because workers' efforts were better valued and their interests more clearly recognized, was somewhat misplaced. The imperative for short-term efficiency gains meant that employers prioritized managerial control and flexibility objectives, with adverse consequences for workers. There is an increasing recognition of the contribution that a greater focus on sustainability in employment relations can make to improving the quality of people's jobs and addressing environmental degradation, particularly by mitigating the effects of the climate emergency. However, the last part of this chapter shows that efforts to manage employment relations in a sustainable way, in order to tackle the climate crisis and promote decent work, are of very limited effectiveness, not least because of the large extent to which corporate interests are privileged.

Neoliberalization, financialization and labour commodification

As we explain in Chapter 1, the contemporary crisis of work is, in important ways, a function of a long-term process of neoliberalization that commenced in the 1980s. When it comes to employment relations, one of the most notable features of this process concerns the marked increase in employer discretion, particularly in the Global North, arising as a consequence of greater labour market deregulation and the diminished power of the trade unions (Baccaro and Howell, 2017). Importantly, while neoliberalization is a general phenomenon, its trajectory varies from country to country, being uneven and far from uniform (Thelen, 2014; Baccaro and Howell, 2017). While the process of neoliberalization in employment relations was a long-term trend, it was amplified by the 2007–8 global financial crisis and its consequences (Tooze, 2018). In many EU countries, for example, the principal policy response to the financial crisis involved the intensification of neoliberalization, manifest, among other things, in the weakening of employment protection legislation, the undermining of collective bargaining agreements and efforts to reduce the power of trade unions (Heyes and Lewis, 2015; Hermann, 2017). This was a function of a belief that greater wage moderation and employer flexibility were necessary for securing economic recovery.

In respect of the UK, a notable source of the crisis in work is the growing mismatch that exists between workers' expectations of security and protection, as a consequence of the intensified neoliberalization of the 2010s, and policy makers' ideological belief in the desirability of operating a lightly regulated system of employment relations. This is in the context of the imperative to restore the finance-led model which had dominated the UK's economic growth in the period before the global financial crisis, based on the primacy of privately held debt (Lavery, 2019). The predominance of finance capital in economic and social life – captured by the term 'financialization' – has generated profound tensions in the management of employment relations within organizations.

The field of human resource management (HRM) is concerned with the management of people within organizations, particularly how this is undertaken in a way that serves business goals. HRM is often marked by a strong normative belief in the desirability of using sophisticated approaches for managing people at work, for the purpose of securing workers' greater commitment to, and engagement with, organizational goals. This is claimed not only to benefit workers, because the quality of their working lives is enhanced, but also, so it is assumed, their employing organizations, on the basis that commitment-based HRM is associated with improvements in business performance. Overall, though, the relevance of such an approach is highly questionable, not least because the way in which it is applied and used largely neglects the experiences of workers themselves and the – often harmful – consequences of managerial interventions (Godard, 2014; Harney et al, 2018; Kaufman, 2020). Perhaps most importantly, though, the powerful influence of financialization, and the commodification pressures with which it is associated, are major obstacles to the development of commitment-based HRM.

The concept of 'financialization' refers to the ways in which economic and social activities are influenced by, and indeed subservient to, the interests of finance capital (Lapavitsas, 2011). The UK, in particular, is a highly financialized setting. For businesses, revenues and profits are increasingly derived through financial rents, based on the ownership and control of assets (for example, financial assets, land and property, natural resources, digital platforms, intellectual property) rather than by engaging in trade, producing goods or delivering services to customers (Christophers, 2020). Greater pressure comes from shareholders for short-term returns on their financial investment (Thompson, 2013). One important consequence is that under financialization a business is treated as a 'bundle of mobile assets to be bought and sold with the goal of increasing returns – often short or intermediate term – to shareholders. Capital is mobile and should seek out the best deal in the marketplace' (Batt, 2018: 467). Given the immediate focus, there is an emphasis on generating value, not so much from the improvements in production processes or better service quality but rather from financial engineering techniques – mergers, acquisitions, disposals of assets and accounting tricks and so on – in a way that minimizes short-term business costs, delivers swift returns to financial investors and satisfies financial markets (Batt, 2018).

Importantly, the rise to prominence of this model of 'investor capitalism' means that managers enjoy less power and control over their businesses, as the interests of shareholders and investors, often financial institutions and investment vehicles of various types, come to predominate (Dundon and Rafferty, 2018). What does this mean for managing employment relations in organizations though? As we will now show, not only is financialization inconsistent with, and a major impediment to, the realization of commitment-based HRM; it is also a notable driver of labour commodification given the emphasis accorded to securing efficiencies through cost reductions, greater manager-controlled flexibility and intensified control over workers.

Under financialization, there is a greater tendency to treat labour as a commodity, the cost of which must be minimized through lay-offs and downsizing initiatives, with the aim of making short-term efficiency gains rather than as a source of value (Batt, 2018). In highly financialized sectors, such as residential social care, which is dominated by a private equity fund ownership model, cost-cutting pressures are manifest in the efforts that are undertaken to reduce the pay and benefits of the low-paid workforce (Horton, 2022), as Chapter 3 highlights. There is an onus on improving the 'flexibility' of the workforce. In sectors such as retail and hospitality, financial pressures mean that organizations have looked to realize efficiency savings through the use of highly flexible, employer-controlled flexible working-time arrangements (Wood, 2020; Ioannou and Dukes, 2021). Their purpose is twofold. First, to align labour supply as closely as possible with demand for services; and second, to reduce supposedly 'unproductive' time, when a worker is not actively engaged in what the employer regards as legitimate work. One prominent manifestation of employer-controlled working-time flexibility concerns the use of so-called 'zero-hours contracts', the prevalence of which increased in the UK during the 2010s. As stated in Chapter 3, with these kinds of contracts an employer does not provide any specified or guaranteed hours of work, and workers are expected to be available for work and only paid for the hours they do work (Koumenta and Williams, 2019).

In addition to an emphasis on cost cutting and casualization, employment relations under financialized conditions are also characterized by the use of tighter and more rigorous managerial methods for planning, recording and evaluating workers' performance – for the purpose of enhancing efficiency, in an attempt to extract more effort from workers. A greater emphasis is placed on devising and operating techniques whereby managers can 'command and control' workers more readily, based on a 'proliferation' of performance measures (Taylor, 2013; Dundon and Rafferty, 2018). There is widespread evidence, for example, from logistics warehouses, banking and retail, of how new technologies, such as electronic systems for monitoring workers' activities and recording their work tasks, enable managers to exercise tighter control over performance standards (Laaser, 2016; Bloodworth, 2018; Evans and Kitchin, 2018). The firm Prodoscore, for example, provides employers with employee productivity monitoring software which uses an algorithm to calculate an individual worker's daily 'productivity score' and ranks them accordingly (Corbyn, 2022).

Workers in professional occupations can also be exposed to greater performance pressures when working in financialized environments, with adverse consequences. The law firm partners studied by Allan et al (2019) understood how the regime of 'financialized performance management' within which they operated affected their working lives. It manifested itself in a preponderance of financial 'metrics' which the firm used to regulate work activities. The result was a notable degree of insecurity among staff, arising from fears and anxieties they experienced about the potentially adverse consequences for developing their careers, as professionals, should they be deemed as underperforming.

A further consequence of the 'financialized performance management' regime in which the law firm partners worked was the escalating work pressures they experienced (Allan et al, 2019). In the UK, a general trend of work intensification has been evident since the 1980s; it abated somewhat in the second half of the 1990s, before picking up again in the early 2000s (Green, 2001; Green et al, 2022; Creagh, 2023). In the UK private sector, work intensification was severest between 2006 and 2012 – during the global financial crisis and subsequent economic recession – while in the public sector it was most acute between 2012 and 2017, a period when neoliberal austerity was at its height (Green et al, 2022). Technological change, particularly the increased use of digital tools and software designed to improve efficiency, seems to be a notable cause of work intensification, in an environment where work has become more demanding and, because of the weakness of organized labour, resistance to demands from employers to intensify work has been negligible (Green et al, 2022). The increased extent to which people use their personal mobile devices for work purposes can also aggravate work intensification. Greater expectations of connectedness heighten work demands by blurring the boundaries between 'working' and supposedly 'non-working' time (Cavazotte et al, 2014; Dén-Nagy, 2014; Adisa et al, 2022).

The case of Royal Mail in the UK demonstrates how new digital technologies contribute to greater work pressures. The firm was criticized for using monitoring technology in the form of so-called 'postal digital assistants', to track the speed at which postal workers were delivering mail on their rounds. The information from such devices was reportedly then used to manage workers' performance and to discipline any judged to be underperforming, thus pressurizing them to work faster (Sweney, 2023). The greater connectedness that mobile information and communications technologies offer enables workers to operate remotely, including working at home, thus potentially giving them more flexibility in their jobs. At the same time, though, their use can give rise to expectations that workers are 'always on', and thus available for work, exacerbating work pressures and adversely affecting their lives outside work (Creagh, 2023).

There is some good evidence of how financialization imperatives, of the kind integral to neoliberal capitalism, have contributed to greater work pressures, as employers seek to cut costs by reducing the size of their workforces, with increased workloads for those who remain. In the care, retail and telecommunications firms studied by Smith (2016), work intensification arose from budget constraints and reduced staffing levels, in settings where competitive pressures and demands for greater efficiencies were acute. Excessive work pressures are a major cause of work-related ill-health and can be enormously damaging for workers' well-being (Creagh, 2023). In 2021–22, there were 914,000 incidents of work-related stress, depression or anxiety reported in Britain, a half of all cases of work-related ill-health. The main causes of work-related stress include workload pressures, tight deadlines, too much responsibility and a lack of managerial support (HSE, 2022).

From all this, the damaging consequences of financialization for people at work, under conditions of intensified neoliberalization, are clear. There are some broader implications for the management of employment relations. One concerns the difficulty of developing long-term, sustainable and high-trust relations between employers and workers (Dundon, 2019) given the growing disconnect between managers and workers, with the former being increasingly unable to satisfy the latter's expectations of work and how it should be undertaken and rewarded (Thompson, 2013). In the multinational company studied by Cushen and Thompson (2012), for example, widespread and deep-rooted perceptions of insecurity, in a highly financialized context where cost-cutting imperatives threatened redundancies, meant that workers treated managerial efforts to boost their commitment to the organization with barely disguised contempt. Far from facilitating a more benign, high-commitment approach to managing employment relations, HRM functions 'as a servant and propagator of labour commodification' (Butterick and Charlwood, 2021: 849). In other words, the management of employment relations has not only been constrained by financialization pressures, leading to a highly marketized approach which treats workers as if they are commodities, but also, in so doing, has itself facilitated such a process of commodification, with highly adverse consequences, including greater performance pressures, diminished trust and increased inequality (Dundon and Rafferty, 2018; Butterick and Charlwood, 2021).

Automation and labour commodification

The growing automation of the management of employment relations in organizations makes the job of building high-trust, commitment-based relationships between employers and workers even more difficult, exacerbating the already manifest disconnect under conditions of financialization. Managerial efforts to improve efficiency frequently involve using new technologies to specify, monitor and evaluate workers' behaviour and performance, including the application of artificial intelligence (AI) and algorithmic management (AM) techniques to enable greater control over the labour process, amplifying commodification pressures. In Chapter 1, we point to the concerns that have arisen about the potential for automation to displace jobs, increasing the risk of unemployment for workers in more routine types of jobs – concerns that have intensified with the arrival of AI-powered language models such as ChatGPT. The most notable consequence of greater automation is not such a displacement effect, though, but rather how it changes work and the nature of people's jobs, in particular by facilitating greater managerial control and rendering workers more compliant (Adams-Prassl, 2019).

Before proceeding any further, it is important to explain how we are using concepts such as AI and AM. AI can be understood as involving the 'use of digital technology to create systems capable of autonomously performing tasks commonly thought to require human intelligence', tasks that one would normally expect a human being to undertake, such as making decisions or recognizing images (Office for AI, 2019, cited in Charlwood and Guenole, 2022: 731). An algorithm refers to a 'set of rules that a computer applies to make a decision' (TUC, 2021b: 15). The concept of AM was developed to describe how online labour platforms use data, captured through an app, to allocate, price and evaluate workers' labour – in a highly transactional, task-based way – in the 'gig economy' (Prassl, 2018; Duggan et al, 2020). Employers are also making greater use of 'HR analytics' or 'people analytics' techniques, comprising 'statistical tools such as algorithms, big data and A.I. to "measure, report and understand employee performance, aspects of workforce planning, talent management and operational management"' (Collins et al, 2017, cited in IPA, 2020: 4). Some major retailers have developed advanced information management systems to collect, process and evaluate data on a large scale, which are then used for the purpose of managing workers (Evans and Kitchin, 2018).

AM's use as a tool for managing employment relations was pioneered in the platform economy, but AI, AM and analytics technologies have since become more widely used (TUC, 2021b). Wearable electronic devices, in settings such as warehouses and among delivery drivers, enable managers to collect data on workers' activities in real time and monitor their activities, with algorithms used to determine appropriate performance standards and evaluate workers against those standards (Milmo, 2021; Wood, 2021). The COVID-19 pandemic seems to have stimulated greater interest among employers in how AM tools can be used to manage employment relations, largely because they provide managers with opportunities to monitor and exercise surveillance over people working remotely, including at home (Reece, 2022).

From a managerial perspective, the most attractive feature of AI and AM technologies is the contribution they can make to improving efficiency. There are three areas of managing employment relations where efficiency savings are particularly apparent. First, automation can reduce the cost of hiring workers. Firms such as Vodafone have made use of a system pioneered by a company called HireVue, which enables job candidates to be interviewed remotely, 'without a human interviewer, recording the candidates' responses and then using AI to analyse their answers including their vocal and facial cues to give an assessment of whether they should progress to the next stage of the recruitment process' (IPA, 2020: 8). Second, AI tools such as

RotaCloud, a workforce scheduling platform, are used to allocate labour and manage work schedules efficiently, without the intervention of a human supervisor (TUC, 2021b). Third, AI and AM technologies enable a highly efficiency-driven approach to managing workers' performance, based on the collection of data, including in real time, about what workers are doing and evaluating them against what they should be doing, as determined by the algorithm (TUC, 2021b).

There is a case to be made for embracing AI and AM technologies as tools for managing people at work. By realizing efficiencies in the management of employment relations, and undertaking more routine, transactional tasks, they can contribute to the success of organizations and give managers more time to focus on developing relations with workers and measures designed to enhance the experience of work (IPA, 2020; Charlwood and Guenole, 2022). By taking away the direct influence of human beings, automated hiring, scheduling and performance management tools can reduce the potential for illegitimate, and potentially unlawful, bias and discriminatory treatment (IPA, 2020). That said, though, there are widespread concerns that, when used for the purpose of managing employment relations, AI and AM tools are often infused with gender and racial biases that can result in discriminatory outcomes (TUC, 2021b). Increasing automation, particularly the greater use of monitoring and surveillance techniques, raises important ethical issues, such as access to, and control over, employee data and privacy matters.

A further, notable problem with these technologies concerns the large extent to which they are used, in the name of efficiency, for the purpose of intensifying control over workers, adding to their work pressures and commodifying their labour (Adams-Prassl, 2019; Duggan et al, 2020). Automation thus heralds 'a new digital Taylorism ... with its heavy focus on quantification, monitoring, control and efficiency' (IPA, 2020: 23). Importantly, when it comes to managing employment relations, AI and AM technologies are not neutral tools: they are designed, developed and deployed for managerial purposes. To the extent they are used to direct workers' labour, evaluate their performance and, when required, discipline them, 'algorithmic technologies have the potential to transform managerial control in important ways' (Kellogg et al, 2020: 367).

It is clear from all this how automation at work, marked by the greater use of AI and AM tools for the purpose of managing employment relations, has some profoundly adverse consequences for working people, augmenting and reinforcing a process of labour commodification arising from intensified neoliberalization and financialization imperatives. Three qualifications are necessary, however. First, some appreciation of the diversity and variation that potentially exists in how AI and AM tools are designed and used is required. For Charlwood and Guenole (2022), the key challenge for managing employment relations is to ensure that AI is used in a consensual rather than coercive manner, one that recognizes and accommodates workers' interests. Second, following on from this, regulation, including legislation and interventions from trade unions, can help to moderate the commodifying effects of AI and AM tools by restricting management prerogative and ensuring that working people, and their representatives, are involved in the design, development and deployment of new technologies (Aloisi and De Stefano, 2022a). Third, it is important not to assume that workers are powerless in the face of sophisticated AI and AM tools: there is some good evidence of effective worker resistance, on both an individual and collective basis, to algorithmic control imperatives (Kellogg et al, 2020; Wood, 2021). One example of this arises in situations where workers seek to negotiate work tasks and remuneration with clients directly, providing an opportunity to escape from management by algorithm (Kellogg et al, 2020).

COVID-19 and employment relations

How did COVID-19 affect employment relations in the early 2020s? Early in the pandemic, there were expectations that this epidemiological crisis would have the effect of moderating efforts to commodify labour arising from the process of intensified neoliberalization. Governments were required to intervene on an immense scale to protect businesses that would have folded and jobs that would have been lost because of the measures taken to prevent the spread of the coronavirus, particularly the stay-at-home 'lockdown' orders. At the same time, there was a marked appreciation of the important contribution made by those 'key' workers who were still required to attend work as normal because of the importance of their jobs to keeping society functioning – in health, social care, food processing, retail and transport – and the value of their labour. Taken together, this signalled a potential challenge to neoliberalization and a reaction against commodification, contributing to growing re-regulatory pressures in employment relations, given the supposedly greater importance attached to supporting workers and recognizing their contribution.

As a major epidemiological crisis, the emergence and spread of COVID-19 in early 2020 necessitated rapid, large-scale government intervention to avert economic collapse, including support for businesses and measures aimed at protecting people's jobs. One common response was the use of job retention schemes. Such schemes are designed to protect jobs and support workers' incomes in circumstances where, because of a crisis of some kind, employers are required to reduce their business activity or shut down entirely for a temporary period (Stuart et al, 2021). In May 2020, at the peak of the first wave of COVID-19, job retention schemes were used to support some 50 million jobs in the Global North (Scarpetta et al, 2020). Some countries, such as Germany, with its longstanding short-time working scheme – Kurzarbeit – were able to apply pre-existing arrangements to cope with the effects of the pandemic. The UK, though, was not in such a position and was required to quickly establish a new Coronavirus Job Retention Scheme (CJRS), or 'furlough' as it popularly became known.

Introduced in March 2020 by the UK government at the urging, and with the involvement, of the trade unions (Bettington, 2021), the CJRS enabled employers who were obliged to close or reduce their operations because of the pandemic to retain staff, with the state initially funding 80 per cent of the wages of furloughed workers (up to a maximum of £2,500 per month). The furlough scheme, as a state-led measure to facilitate job retention, was highly significant in that it constituted a departure, albeit only temporary, from the market-based paradigm governing restructuring in the UK, one that traditionally favours redundancies (Stuart et al, 2021). By the time it ceased, at the end of September 2021, the CJRS had been used to support 11.7 million jobs in total, at a cost of £69.3 billion, with the peak use having occurred in May 2020, when 8.9 million jobs were supported (Powell et al, 2021).

Internationally there is good evidence that the presence of effective job retention schemes helped to reduce job losses because of the impact of the COVID-19 pandemic (Adams-Prassl et al, 2020; ILO, 2022b). While the design and operation of job retention measures varied considerably across European countries, they nevertheless played a crucial part in preventing mass unemployment from arising, consistent with the presence of a European 'social model', one characterized by protective welfare arrangements and partnerships with trade unions (Ebbinghaus and Lehner, 2022). Countries without such schemes, especially in the Global South, or where schemes operated in a partial, uneven way, such as in the US, saw correspondingly higher rates of job losses and unemployment (ILO, 2021c).

As a novel job retention measure the UK's furlough scheme attracted a considerable amount of attention, including its implications for employment relations (Stuart et al, 2021). Yet the design and operation of the CJRS was flawed in some important respects. For one thing, employers were given far too much latitude in making furlough decisions which meant that workers in non-standard forms of employment – agency workers, self-employed workers and casual workers in general – could be denied payments (Codd and Ferguson, 2020; Ewing and Hendy, 2020).

The pandemic not only disproportionately affected low-paid workers in precarious employment; it also exacerbated the ill-effects of their precarity and insecurity. Because women are more likely to be employed in non-standard jobs than men, and thus less likely to be eligible for furlough payments, one effect of the CJRS was to aggravate gender earnings inequality (House of Commons Women and Equalities Committee, 2021). A further problem with the CJRS was its 'passive' character. While in theory the furlough scheme could have been used to 'build longer-term, potentially more productive relations' between employers and workers, and to promote 'longer-term investment in people', in practice the opportunity to encourage firms to develop a job retention orientation in general was missed (Stuart et al, 2021: 913).

Expectations that the experience of COVID-19 would somehow moderate labour commodification and contribute to re-regulatory pressures in employment relations by ascribing greater value to the labour of workers, especially 'key' workers, do not seem to have been borne out in practice. To illustrate this, look at the widespread disregard for workers' health and well-being that was evident during the pandemic.

Frontline workers in sectors such as food processing were particularly exposed to health risks because of COVID-19, not least because of the unpreparedness and neglect of employers and the pressure put on them to attend unsafe workplaces. Not only did this increase their risk of COVID-19 infection but it also jeopardized the health of others, in the context of weak, indeed often barely evident, regulatory and enforcement arrangements (House of Commons Work and Pensions Committee, 2020; Bettington, 2021; James, 2021). Certain settings – food-processing factories and call centres, for example – were particularly prone to mass coronavirus outbreaks as a consequence of weak infection control measures (Butterick and Charlwood, 2021; Taylor, 2021). Workers in call centres came under intense pressure from employers to attend their normal workplaces, predicated on a 'business-as-usual' rationale, despite the widespread lack of effective social distancing measures and expectations of working in close proximity with others (Taylor, 2021). One year on from the start of the pandemic, COVID-19 exposure at work had caused more than 350 deaths and around 31,000 infections (GMB, 2021).

Even before the pandemic, workers often came under pressure from employers to attend work when they were ill (Taylor, 2013), with the stinginess of the UK's statutory sick pay regime discouraging people from taking sickness absence. In the context of COVID-19, though, workers were reluctant to stay away from work and self-isolate because of COVID-19, or even test themselves for infection, because of the fall in income that would arise from not being able to work (Ewing and Hendy, 2020; Butterick and Charlwood, 2021; Cai et al, 2022). There is evidence from the care sector that in settings where staff received sick pay, there was a lower likelihood of 'cases of coronavirus in residents, compared with those care homes where staff do not receive sick pay' (TUC, 2021a: 8). The UK's system of enforcing workplace health and safety standards proved inadequate to the task of protecting workers during the pandemic. The main regulatory body in the UK – the Health and Safety Executive – is inadequately funded and has insufficient resources to undertake its role effectively in general (James, 2021; Allegretti, 2023b).

A further profound consequence of the pandemic for employment relations was the greater prevalence of working-from-home arrangements because of COVID restrictions. For workers obliged to work from home, often for the first time, there could be some benefits, including greater control over work tasks and activities. Yet in addition to blurring the boundaries between paid work and other activities, working from home was also associated with greater volume and intensity of work, in a context where around two fifths of workers doing so have their work activities and work rate monitored by automated systems (Bettington, 2021; Taylor, 2021; Adisa et al, 2022). Work intensification was a function of people working from home spending longer undertaking work activities, linked to employers' expectations that they should be more assiduous at demonstrating their online availability – a kind of 'virtual presenteeism' (Adisa et al, 2022; Hadjisolomou et al, 2022) – and also the tensions arising from the greater spill over of work activities into home and family life (Hodder, 2020).

A further, unwelcome way in which COVID-19 affected employment relations concerned the greater use of surveillance and monitoring tools at work, especially for people working from home, intensifying managerial control and increasing work pressures. Greater use was made of so-called 'productivity tools' and other digital technologies that can scan emails and computer files, record computer keystrokes, measure how much workers are typing and monitor the activities of remote workers, either by periodically capturing screenshots or through permanent audio and/or video surveillance via webcams (Eurofound, 2020; Jack, 2021; Aloisi and De Stefano, 2022b; TUC, 2022a). The data such tools produce are a valuable resource for managers desirous of finding ways to improve efficiency and raise performance standards (Aloisi and De Stefano, 2022b).

Unscrupulous employers around the world also took advantage of the pandemic to weaken employment standards (Dobbins, 2022a). In the UK, for example, COVID-19 exposed and aggravated the adverse consequences of the liberalized regulatory environment and decollectivized system of employment relations, wherein employers have the whip hand. A particularly notable manifestation of this arose during the pandemic when some firms, such as British Gas and British Airways, deployed so-called 'fire and rehire' tactics. These involve employers dismissing employees and then offering to re-engage them on lower rates of pay and/or worse conditions as a cost-saving measure (ACAS, 2021). Some employers were clearly not shy of using the epidemiological crisis as a pretext to cut costs by eroding the terms and conditions of their staff, taking advantage of a system of employment relations which privileges business flexibility (Ewing and Hendy, 2020).

The behaviour of the ferry firm P&O, which in March 2022 dismissed 786 UK-based employees with no notice, communicating the decision to the workforce by video message, exemplifies how such a system operates to the benefit of unscrupulous employers. The company claimed that terminating the contracts of existing staff and replacing them with agency-supplied labour on lower pay and inferior conditions was essential if the business was to remain viable. The sacked workers were given two weeks to accept the company's offer of compensation.

Responding to angry questions from MPs in a parliamentary hearing, the company's chief executive, Peter Hebblethwaite, admitted P&O had broken employment law by failing to consult with trade unions in advance of the dismissals but made no apology for doing so, on the basis that any such consultation would have made no difference to the firm's decision. P&O's controversial behaviour was widely condemned, including by Conservative government ministers, and it was temporarily forced to suspend sailings on its routes. Yet the company faced no lasting consequences, and the government did nothing meaningful to prevent workers elsewhere from being treated similarly in future (Topham, 2022; Topham, 2023).

The COVID-19 pandemic, as an epidemiological crisis, clearly had some major consequences for employment relations and how they are managed. Much attention has justifiably been focused on how the experience of the pandemic influenced workers' expectations, particularly when it comes to matters such as the organization of working time, based on workers' aspirations for greater temporal and spatial flexibility, with workers appreciative of remote and 'hybrid' forms of working arrangements that suit their lives, and the prospect of being valued more by their employers, especially when their jobs serve a useful social purpose. Yet the experience of the pandemic points to the important ways in which COVID-19 led to a situation in which employers' interests were further privileged in employment relations particularly when it comes to exercising control over workers, securing their flexibility, intensifying their work and – ultimately – efforts to commodify their labour. In this way, the pandemic, contributed to the broader crisis of work by illuminating and, more importantly, amplifying the antagonism that exists between the degradation of employment relations under conditions of intensified neoliberalization and workers' aspirations to be treated with respect and dignity, to have their interests recognized and for their labour to be valued.

Environmental degradation, the climate emergency and employment relations

So far, this chapter has explained how neoliberalization, particularly the intensified neoliberalization arising from the 2007–8 global financial crisis, has been associated with greater efforts by employers to commodify labour, degrading the quality of employment relations. The COVID-19 pandemic exacerbated this process of degradation while also fuelling already evident re-regulatory pressures linked to workers' greater expectations that they should be supported and protected at work, have their labour valued and their interests recognized. Moreover, the environmental crisis in general, and the climate emergency in particular, are intimately connected to the degradation of employment relations under neoliberal capitalism.

The summer of 2022 saw record high temperatures in the UK, reaching 40°C for the first time ever – a stark illustration of the consequences of the climate emergency and how it is causing the planet to heat. Global warming has profound implications for work and employment relations, not least the greater risk posed to workers' health, safety and well-being from heatwaves that are becoming more commonplace and intense (TUC, 2022b). The 2022 summer heatwave in the UK provides a vivid example of how the climate crisis affects working people. This demands a focus, broadly conceived, on managing employment relations in a more sustainable manner, one that both values working people and that responds effectively to the adverse effects of environmental and climate change (Baldry and Hyman, 2022).

The influence of the environment, and environmental factors in general, on work and employment relations has long been understood. One prominent issue relates to the adverse consequences for workers' health and well-being of their ambient environment. The term 'Sick Building Syndrome' (SBS) was originated to capture the phenomenon whereby 'in certain buildings the workers appear to suffer on a frequent, or recurrent, basis from a wide range of symptoms including coughs, wheezing, nose and sinus inflammation, dry skin or rashes, sore eyes, headaches, and general tiredness and lethargy' (Bain et al, 1999: 126). There is some good evidence, from studies of call centres for example, of how substandard heating, ventilation and air-conditioning systems, by producing low air quality, poor air circulation and excessively variable temperatures, damage workers' health and well-being. The difficulties produced by poor ambient environments are exacerbated under employment relations regimes that privilege managerial control, mandate demanding performance targets and restrict workers' autonomy and influence (Taylor et al, 2003).

Given the necessity of shielding workers from heatwaves and ensuring comfortable ambient temperatures, global warming is creating greater demand for air conditioning in workplaces. Too often, though, the way in which air-conditioned workplaces are configured creates serious health difficulties for the people that work in them (Redman et al, 2011). The issue of SBS, then, points to the importance of the connections that exist between the environment, environmental change, the experiences of workers and the management of employment relations. Clearly, there is much that organizations can do to improve the functioning of their heating and ventilation systems. But giving workers greater control over how their jobs are undertaken – so they have greater flexibility when it comes to work schedules and rest breaks for example – would also do much to lessen the ill-effects of SBS.

There are also important connections that exist between environmental degradation, the degradation of employment relations and the commodification of labour, particularly at a global level. As well as being bad for workers, neoliberal capitalism also harms the environment (Baldry and Hyman, 2022). Efforts to promote decent work and high-quality employment relationships are made more difficult because of environmental degradation given its symbiotic relationship with labour exploitation (ILO, 2018b).

One prominent example of this connection concerns the global 'fast fashion' industry. Major mass-market Western brands and retailers compete on cost, sourcing garments from low-cost supplier factories in the Global South, with profoundly serious consequences for both the environment and workers. The way in which the global 'fast fashion' industry operates is terribly damaging for the environment. The cheapness of the goods and the emphasis on disposability encourage wasteful overproduction and overconsumption, with environmental consequences including excessive water consumption and land use, widespread chemical and plastic pollution and scarily high carbon emissions:

> Textile production is a major contributor to climate change. It produces an estimated 1.2 billion tonnes of CO_2 equivalent (CO_2e) per year – more than international flights and maritime shipping combined. It is estimated that across the full lifecycle of clothing globally, the industry has an annual carbon footprint of 3.3 billion tonnes CO_2e. (House of Commons Environmental Audit Committee, 2019: 28)

The global 'fast fashion' industry not only operates in a way that degrades the environment; its low-cost business model also depends upon an exploited and commodified labour force, who typically work in unhealthy and unsafe working conditions for poverty pay. Forced labour and child labour are by no means uncommon (House of Commons Environmental Audit Committee, 2019). The 'fast fashion' sector is perhaps the prime example of an industry that depends for its success on violating environmental and labour standards. In the UK, for example, the online fashion retailer Boohoo is alleged to have sourced products from garment producers based in the East Midlands city of Leicester, where unlawful underpayment of workers and modern slavery practices are rife (Labour Behind the Label, 2020).

But other industries operate in a similar way. In the electronics sector, for example, both environmental degradation and labour abuses are evident at all stages of the production process, from extracting the raw materials in countries with the relevant natural resources to assembling products in supplier factories and then disposing of still usable products when they have supposedly been superseded by newer, more 'trendy' versions (Pellow et al, 2006; Chan et al, 2020). Pollution from hazardous substances, including industrial chemicals, from electronics plants in China not only damages the health of nearby residents but also that of the factory workers themselves (Chan et al, 2020).

All this demonstrates the interconnectedness of environmental issues and employment relations, particularly the symbiotic relationship between the degradation of the environment and the degradation of work under neoliberal capitalism. The escalating climate crisis, and the necessity of responding effectively to it, put a greater onus on the importance of managing employment relations in ways that are both environmentally sustainable and, to the extent that they mitigate labour commodification and promote decent work, socially sustainable too.

For example, there is a growing understanding of the importance of heat stress as an employment relations issue: that it is becoming more prevalent because of global warming, that it poses significant risks to workers' health, safety and well-being and that it can compromise efforts to improve the quality of people's working lives (ILO, 2018a, 2019). Workers in some countries, such as Australia, are particularly affected by the dangers associated with extreme heat and heat stress. Yet they often find it difficult to take effective mitigating action because of how their work is managed. Because of their desire to privilege efficiency and performance improvements, there is a sense that managers are insufficiently accommodating of requests from workers to work at a slower pace or take more breaks because of the conditions:

> Workers whose jobs are externally 'paced' – for example by a tight roster in the case of many homecare workers, or by the speed of machines in the case of manufacturing workers – found it more difficult or impossible to slow down or take additional breaks. Some said they were unable to leave 'their machines', or to take short breaks without stopping production and creating more work for themselves. (Humphrys et al, 2022: 264)

Pressure to keep costs in check means that managers are reluctant to invest in effective heat mitigations, such as more effective climate control systems and the provision of generous water supplies (Humphrys et al, 2022). When it comes to managing employment relations, then, there is clearly a tension between the imperative of responding to the climate crisis effectively, by operating benign working environments, on the one hand, and expectations of efficiency, on the other.

Managing employment relations for sustainability

What can be done to facilitate a sustainable approach to employment relations? The concept of the 'just transition' (see Chapter 1) holds that greater environmental sustainability is contingent upon work and employment relationships also being managed in a sustainable way (Klein, 2019). There is a widespread understanding that 'decent work', in the sense of jobs that respect workers' freedom, welfare and dignity, is integral both to sustainable development in general and to progress towards a decarbonized economy in particular (ILO, 2018b; Baldry and Hyman, 2022). Indeed, one of the UN's Sustainable Development Goals is to 'promote sustained, inclusive and sustainable economic growth, full and productive employment and decent work for all' (United Nations Department of Social and Economic Affairs, no date).

Three broad approaches to managing employment relations for the purpose of enabling greater sustainability can be identified. The first involves efforts to develop 'green' jobs, in the sense of work that mitigates environmental damage and is undertaken in an environmentally sustainable manner (Pettinger, 2017). For Renner et al (2008: 3), 'green' jobs involve work that contributes 'substantially to preserving or restoring environmental quality. Specifically, but not exclusively, this includes jobs that help to protect ecosystems and biodiversity; reduce energy, materials, and water consumption through high efficiency strategies; de-carbonize the economy; and minimize or altogether avoid generation of all forms of waste and pollution.'

An essential facet of 'green' jobs is that they involve 'decent work', 'providing respect for workers' fundamental rights at work, health and safety protection, as well as the means to live with dignity' (ILO, 2012: 134). A 'job that is exploitative, harmful, fails to pay a living wage, and thus condemns workers to a life of poverty can hardly be hailed as green' (Renner et al, 2008: 4). In practice, though, many supposedly 'green' jobs are unhealthy, unsafe and exploitative, often more so than traditional forms of work (ILO, 2012; Pettinger, 2017). The managers in Econie and Dougherty's (2019) study of work in recycling companies, for example, not only wanted workers who would follow standard procedures in a regimented manner but also desired flexibility over how labour was used. In order to realize these objectives, they hired workers through temporary agencies – securing managerial efficiency, but at the expense of greater insecurity for the workforce. Work in Tesla, the world's leading producer of electric vehicles, is far from 'decent'. Manufacturing jobs are arduous, working conditions are exacting and managerial control is exercised in a harsh and highly coercive manner (Minchin, 2021). Workplace injuries are frequent on the shop floor, a consequence of the highly intensive and efficiency-driven approach to managing employment relations and the prevailing culture of overwork in the firm: '"I've seen people pass out, hit the floor like a pancake and smash their face open", summarized worker Jonathan Galescu. "They just send us to work around him while he's still lying on the floor"' (Minchin, 2021: 443). The case of Tesla, a pioneer when it comes to developing environmentally sustainable transport solutions, provides a salutary example of how supposedly 'green' jobs fail to provide work that can in any way be considered 'decent'.

A second approach to managing employment relations to enable greater sustainability involves efforts, particularly by multinational companies, to develop private regulatory arrangements. These commonly take the form of codes of conduct, which specify environmental and labour standards that should apply throughout multinationals' supply chains. Based on a voluntary, corporate social responsibility (CSR) rationale, such private modes of regulation formally lie outside the public regulatory authority of governments (Bartley, 2018; Kuruvilla, 2021) and are predicated on the belief that the development and operation of voluntary, corporate initiatives, sometimes in association with non-governmental organizations, will improve firms' brand image and market reputation, thus increasing their competitive advantage (Locke, 2013; Donaghey and Reinecke, 2018; Altura et al, 2021).

Apple's Supplier Code of Conduct covers matters such as labour and human rights issues, workers' living and working conditions, the 'responsible' sourcing of raw materials that comprise its products and the management of waste and greenhouse gas emissions. Supplier firms 'are required to provide safe working conditions, treat workers with dignity and respect, act fairly and ethically, and use environmentally responsible practices wherever they make products or perform services for Apple' (Apple, 2022: 1). Private regulatory arrangements proliferated during the 1990s and 2000s, a consequence of the development of transnational production networks under globalization and the onus on multinationals to signal that they were responding to the instances of environmental degradation and labour exploitation in their supply chains highlighted by activist campaigns (Bartley, 2018; Kuruvilla, 2021).

Studies evaluating the effects of private regulatory arrangements show that, in general, the voluntary efforts of employers, based on a CSR rationale, have had little positive impact on protecting the environment and combatting labour exploitation (Bartley, 2018; Kuruvilla, 2021; Baldry and Hyman, 2022). The example of corporate approaches to address forced labour and so-called 'modern slavery' – so called because the term itself is highly ambiguous and open to challenge (Kenway, 2021) – is instructive. Through the development of global private governance initiatives – sustainability reporting, social auditing programmes and ethical certification schemes – multinational firms have seemingly led the way when it comes to dealing with labour abuses in their supply chains. Such efforts, though, should generally be seen as 'fairy tales' – stories that are designed to improve firms' corporate image and reputation and avoid having more stringent measures imposed upon them while doing nothing substantive to improve workers' rights and protections (LeBaron, 2020: 35).

Private labour and environmental initiatives tend to be exercises in 'public relations' rather than genuine efforts to improve corporate sustainability (Baldry and Hyman, 2022: 76). This is evident from the experience of the global fashion industry, for example: here, brands and retailers have 'marked their own homework for too long', and 'voluntary corporate social responsibility initiatives have failed significantly to improve pay and working conditions or reduce waste' (House of Commons Environmental Audit Committee, 2019: 3).

The third broad approach to managing employment relations for greater sustainability concerns efforts to develop 'sustainable' or 'green' HRM within organizations. The concept of 'sustainable HRM' refers to the 'adoption of HRM strategies and practices that enable the achievement of financial, social and ecological goals, with an impact inside and outside of the organization and over a long-term time horizon while controlling for unintended side effects and negative feedback' (Ehnert et al, 2016: 90). By operating in a sustainable way, HRM can enable organizations to realize their broader 'corporate sustainability goals' (Mariappanadar, 2019). Integral to this is an understanding that the issue of sustainability is not just something that applies to environmental matters but also concerns the way in which employment relations are managed (Aust et al, 2018).

There has been a notable growth of interest in the concept of 'sustainable HRM' during the 21st century (Ehnert, 2009; Aust et al, 2018; Mariappanadar, 2019; Kramar, 2022). Unlike conventional approaches to HRM, which focus on the link between the management of people at work and the strategic goals and financial performance of organizations, the sustainable version incorporates a concern with the 'human outcomes' of people management activities, the effects they have on individuals and groups within the organization and their 'social outcomes', or how they affect relationships between people at work (Kramar, 2014: 1069–70). This implies a repudiation of short-term, efficiency-driven and cost-minimization approaches to managing employment relations in favour of efforts to enhance workers' well-being and treat them as valuable assets whose long-term development should be optimized (Ehnert et al, 2016; Richards, 2022). 'Sustainable HRM' is thus associated with the provision of opportunities for skills training, the payment to workers of a 'living wage', the operation of safe and healthy working environments and the use of practices that give workers a positive work–life balance. Ultimately, 'sustainable HRM' is predicated on the belief that recognizing, and being responsive to, the interests of workers is not only desirable because it facilitates decent work and high-quality jobs but also because it enables the organization's long-term success (Kramar, 2022).

The concept of 'green HRM' – linked to, but separate from, the field of 'sustainable HRM' – started to attract considerable attention during the 2010s (Renwick et al, 2016; Renwick, 2018; Paulet et al, 2021). It can be defined as 'those parts of sustainable HR management dealing with the needs that relate to environmental sustainability' (Wagner, 2013, cited in Paulet et al, 2021: 444). Integral to 'green HRM' is the emphasis which is placed on managing workers in ways that contribute to improvements in the environmental performance of organizations (Aust Ehnert et al, 2020). This can encompass using recruitment and selection techniques to hire environmentally committed staff, performance and reward arrangements that prioritize relevant environmental outcomes, training and development interventions designed to support environmental activities and systems of employee involvement that enable workers to be better engaged with, and thus be able to contribute to, environmental improvements (Renwick et al, 2008; Harvey et al, 2013; Renwick et al, 2013).

The food service multinational studied by Haddock-Millar et al (2016) used a system of 'green champions' to promote employee engagement with environmental matters and, as a consequence, improve the firm's environmental performance. 'Green HRM' can be good for business: organizations that demonstrate positive environmental credentials will find it easier to attract, engage and retain talented staff (Guerci et al, 2016; Richards, 2022). All this points to the potential direct impact 'green HRM' can have on an organization's environmental activities and outcomes. But an indirect effect is also possible. People who have greater job satisfaction, because they perceive they are managed well, that their interests are recognized and that their contribution is valued, are more likely to engage positively with their employer's environmental agenda (Harvey et al, 2013).

Notwithstanding all this apparent positivity, the concepts of 'sustainable' and 'green' HRM are by no means without problems. There is considerable ambiguity over what they actually mean and how they should be understood (Kramar, 2014; Aust Ehnert et al, 2020). When it comes to organizational practice, there is often a notable degree of variation. See the case of the aforementioned food service multinational, for example, where despite the overall 'commitment to environmental sustainability' that was evident in the firm, the 'positioning and alignment of the environment and HR function' differed between its subsidiaries, as did how these subsidiaries opted to 'engage the workforce in environmental sustainability' (Haddock-Millar et al, 2016: 208). Anyway, the kind of engagement with environmental issues evident in this case may be rather uncommon. There are often limited opportunities for HRM to influence corporate sustainability efforts (Stahl et al, 2020). Too much of a focus on financial imperatives, based on a short-term, efficiency-driven approach to managing employment relations, can also hinder HRM's contribution to realizing greater sustainability (Kramar, 2022).

This points to a broader problem with the notions of 'sustainable' and 'green' HRM, namely the way in which financialization imperatives, of the kind associated with neoliberalization, not just hinder but are also, more fundamentally, antithetical to promoting genuine sustainability when it comes to employment relations (Baldry and Hyman, 2022). Given the large extent to which HRM activities in organizations have been marketized and dominated by the objectives of realizing immediate performance improvements and serving short-term business interests (Dundon and Rafferty, 2018), how feasible, really, is an alternative approach, one concerned with managing employment relations in a long-term, sustainable way? In practice, much so-called 'sustainable' and 'green' HRM is of rather limited effectiveness, often concerned with matters such as promoting alternative travel-to-work schemes which, while useful, are relatively inconsequential. This reflects the more general inadequacy of corporate sustainability approaches when it comes to addressing the scale of the climate emergency and the tendency for businesses to engage in 'greenwashing exercises' – relatively minor and inconsequential activities designed to communicate they are taking environmental issues seriously, not least for reputational purposes, while leaving their business models fundamentally unchanged (Wright and Nyberg, 2017; Cooke et al, 2022).

Workers are often rather sceptical of corporate efforts to engage with environmental issues (Harvey et al, 2013). Getting the support and engagement of workers is central to the effectiveness of 'sustainable' and 'green' HRM policies and practices, particularly where workers themselves are involved in, or can influence, corporate approaches (Haddock-Millar et al, 2016; Markey et al, 2016; Paulet et al, 2021). Yet the dominance of employers' interests means that workers' interests get neglected, tempering the contribution that 'sustainable' and 'green' HRM initiatives can make to greening workplaces and organizations (Richards, 2022). A consequence of this is that workers' support for, and engagement with, corporate environmental activities cannot necessarily be assumed, especially when they are used in ways that augment managerial control, raise performance expectations and add to work pressures. This points to the important extent to which 'sustainable' and 'green' HRM interventions can be contested, potentially producing conflict between workers and employers (Harvey et al, 2013).

Conclusion

This chapter has reviewed developments in employment relations, exploring how employment relations are managed and what they mean how we understand the contemporary crisis of work. Neoliberalization, particularly in the intensified form characteristic of the period following the 2007–8 global financial crisis, fuelled the crisis of work by encouraging greater labour commodification. By enabling greater managerial flexibility and control in employment relations, and with concomitant increases in insecurity and work pressures, processes of financialization and automation have amplified the commodification trend. Developments under COVID-19 – an epidemiological crisis – both illuminated and aggravated the tensions arising from the efforts to commodify labour on the one hand and growing re-regulatory pressures on the other. The experience of the pandemic highlighted how employers' ambitions to exercise greater control over labour and use it more flexibly to improve efficiency came into conflict with workers' aspirations to be treated with respect and dignity and to have their contribution valued.

Given the scale of the mounting climate crisis, there is greater concern being exhibited in how employment relations can be managed in ways that are both socially – in the sense of promoting 'good' jobs and 'decent' work – and environmentally sustainable. However, the issues and challenges arising from 'sustainable' and 'green' HRM approaches reflect a profound difficulty when it comes to business-led efforts to manage employment relations for the purpose of realizing greater social and environmental sustainability. They are too dominated by corporate managerial interests and the imperative to operate within, and be consistent with, a market-led, neoliberal paradigm and are therefore only of limited palliative use at best (Wright and Nyberg, 2017; Baldry and Hyman, 2022). Effective environmental and climate action, consistent with securing a 'just transition', cannot be left to the whims of corporations but rather requires more fundamental change in employment relations, not least the greater participation of workers and trade unions (Klein, 2019), as discussed in Chapter 6.

5

Equalities in Crisis

Introduction

Chapters 3 and 4 focus on two critically important dimensions of contemporary work and employment: the function of labour markets in distributing workers to various roles in organizations and occupational hierarchies, and employment relations, concerning the interplay between workers and employers, including the role of managerial approaches in shaping these relations. Implicit in these chapters, and sometimes also explicit, is an understanding of how capitalism produces inequalities – between managers and employees, for example, or between those in roles at different levels within occupational hierarchies. Such inequalities, we argue, produce antagonisms, especially the classic antagonism between capital and labour, as highlighted in the work of Marx and manifest in class conflict. But workplaces are also the site of many other forms of inequality, and these also generate antagonisms: those arising from the many forms of sociocultural difference, such as gender, ethnicity, nationality, age, sexual orientation and dis/ability. Countries in the Global North have enacted legislation, to varying extents and in different ways, aimed at combatting unfair discrimination at work. In the UK, for example, the Equality Act 2010 consolidated pre-existing legislation prohibiting employment discrimination on the basis of sex, race and other so-called 'protected characteristics' and extended protections elsewhere (for example, gender reassignment). Overwhelmingly, major employing organizations now operate policies focused on promoting equal opportunities and/or facilitating greater diversity and inclusion, not least because of the presumed business benefits that arise from doing so.

As this chapter demonstrates, however, inequalities remain profoundly important in contemporary work and employment, notwithstanding governmental and organizational efforts to address them. We focus, to start with, on a dimension which governments and employers typically overlook, namely the prevalence of disadvantage based on social class and the disparities experienced by people from working-class backgrounds. Underpinned by an intersectional approach, the remainder of the chapter then covers three further social cleavages – relating to gender inequality, racial and ethnic disparities in employment and the parlous position of young people, especially those from working-class backgrounds. The chapter demonstrates that there is a crisis of equalities, as disadvantage at work has been exacerbated under conditions of intensified neoliberalism, a crisis which is responsible for, and has been influenced by, other notable crises – relating to poverty, care, housing and the experience of the COVID-19 pandemic. The resulting antagonisms help to fuel the contemporary crisis of work.

Social class inequality and disadvantage under neoliberalism

During the 1990s and 2000s, it became common to question the relevance of social class (see Pakulski and Waters, 1996), as societies were supposedly becoming more 'meritocratic' and 'classless'. In a climate of greater 'market-driven egalitarianism' (Ashley, 2022: 172), the extent to which people become successful or not should be a matter of their own individual talent, drive and determination rather than their social background. However, the salience of class-based disadvantage, and its influence on contemporary work and employment relations, is stark. Indeed, amid concerns about burgeoning social inequality, during the 2010s and 2020s there has been a resurgence of interest in the persistence of class-based disadvantage and how it adversely affects people from less privileged backgrounds (Savage et al, 2015; Friedman and Laurison, 2020; Ashley, 2022).

The dynamic relationship between work and social class has long been recognized (see Bradley, 1999), particularly how the work that people do contributes to fuelling class-based disadvantage. In particular, too many people, especially young workers, women workers, people from minoritized ethnic communities and those from poorer backgrounds, find it extremely hard to progress out of low-paid, poor-quality work (Friedman and Laurison, 2020). Social class inequality and disadvantage, and their adverse consequences for work and employment, have been amplified under neoliberal conditions – see, for example, the way in which wealth and assets are increasingly hoarded by the already extremely well-off.

The 'return of the rich'

The globalized, neoliberal, heavily financialized economic climate has resulted in the rise of an elite of millionaires and billionaires, playing the world's market, with their superyachts, helicopters and savings held in tax havens. Moreover, the economic disparities of class have been increasing dramatically throughout the periods of austerity, the pandemic and the current confluence of crises. In May 2023, the *Sunday Times* Rich List showed that Britain's 171 billionaires have joint earnings of £684 billion; this while so many citizens were struggling to pay their bills and cope with the 'cost-of-living crisis' – see Chapter 7.

The rise of massive salaries for executives, and of course for the CEOs of giant corporations, is one dimension of what Andrew Sayer (2012), in an insightful critique of neoliberal economies (especially the Anglophone nations), has termed the 'return of the rich'. Sayer argues that much contemporary analysis of class focuses on the contrasts between the working and middle classes but often ignores the upper class or elite. Yet the return of the rich is one of the key factors in the current crisis of work. Sayer speaks of the 'return' of the rich (and the super-rich) because in the early decades of the 20th century some equalization of wealth occurred in the UK, with a fall of the share of earnings of the top 1 per cent from 20 per cent in the 1920s to 6 per cent in the 1970s (Sayer, 2012: 165). But with the advent of neoliberalism the share rose to 15 per cent and has continued to rise ever since. Even amid the global financial crisis of the late 2000s and the COVID-19 pandemic during the early 2020s, the already well-off nonetheless continued to get wealthier.

There is substantial evidence in support of Sayer's argument. Lansley (2022: 235) states that the rich are extractors rather than creators of wealth: landowners, property tycoons and oil barons, for example. Financialization lies at the heart of this – the UK's five major banks have assets of over £5 trillion; similarly, in the US BlackRock, Vanguard and State Street hold massive assets, while in 2020 Apple's market value was over 2 trillion dollars (Lansley, 2022: 235). Moreover, the COVID-19 crisis only served to further enrich the wealthy: the world's billionaires saw their wealth rise by a quarter, and the corporate giants in finance (for example, Goldman Sachs and J.P. Morgan) and the huge tech companies (for example, Amazon and Facebook) all saw their market value rise (Lansley, 2022: 250).

It seems that the crises described in this book simply help the rich to get richer while the poor get poorer. Lansley quotes the *Financial Times*: '[T]his crisis has broadly separated us into the exposed poor and the shielded rich' (Lansley, 2022: 249, quoting Ahuja, 2020). As Mike Savage argues in *The Return of Inequality* (Savage, 2021), for decades the rich have been pulling away from the rest of the world's population, and the super-rich have been pulling away from the rich.

Sayer (2012) asserts that such escalating inequality is a consequence of the rise of unearned as opposed to earned wealth, as Piketty (2014) has also influentially argued. Whereas in the post-war period income came mainly from the production of goods and services, neoliberalism is associated with the greater financialization of capital, as wealth increasingly comes from rents and interest (on land and property) and forms of investment, such as shares and hedge funds. This can be seen, Piketty (2014) states, as 'rentier capitalism' (see Chapter 2 for a fuller discussion of Piketty's arguments). A key factor has been the increased stress put on shareholder value as a criterion for business success: profits are passed to investors rather than ploughed back into improving infrastructure and wages (Sayer, 2012).

The working class and the 'class ceiling' at work

The 'return of the rich' is one notable manifestation of the prevalence of inequality based on social class. The disadvantage experienced by those from working-class families is another. As Friedman and Laurison (2020) explain, the UK is marked by the presence of a powerful 'class ceiling'. What this means is that those 'who start out ahead are the ones most likely to succeed': people from privileged social backgrounds 'are disproportionately getting into the most desirable, high-powered, glamorous, and influential occupations, and those from the working class are too often left – or kept – out' (Friedman and Laurison, 2020: 31). According to the UK's Social Mobility Commission, someone 'from a professional background is over 60% more likely to be in a professional job than someone from a working class background', and people 'from privileged backgrounds are better able to hold on to their position, resulting in fewer opportunities for those at the bottom to move up' (SMC, 2021: 9).

In professions such as law, medicine and accountancy, high-ranking positions at elite firms are predominantly held by people from privileged backgrounds, especially the privately educated (Friedman and Laurison, 2020). Just 7 per cent of children in the UK attend private, fee-paying schools. Yet the top jobs are disproportionately filled by people educated outside the state system – 65 per cent of judges, for example, and 59 per cent of senior civil servants (Sutton Trust, 2019). In some largely graduate occupations, there is a notable underrepresentation of those from working-class backgrounds. Take broadcasting, for example, where nearly two thirds of people in the industry have parents who are professionals, well above the proportion across the economy as a whole (Ofcom, 2022).

Extensive 'opportunity hoarding' activities by those from privileged backgrounds demonstrate the fallacy of arguments that one's work situation is a product of individual merit – a combination of innate talent and hard work – and fuel class-based disadvantage (Elliot Major and Machin, 2020). Parental wealth and networks confer copious advantages. Consider, for example, the role of education, where young people from well-off families can benefit from expensive private schooling and private tuition services in ways their less privileged peers cannot. Graduate career opportunities are often restricted to students from a small number of supposedly 'elite' universities, which are dominated by students from well-off and privately educated backgrounds. Young people from privileged families have greater opportunities to make use of unpaid internship schemes, often a prerequisite for accessing good jobs and careers in sectors such as the fashion and media industries, because they have parental wealth to fall back on and can thus work for free (Friedman and Laurison, 2020).

Corporations are increasingly making use of social mobility programmes to open up access to positions to people from working-class backgrounds. In a study of City of London legal and financial services firms, Louise Ashley demonstrates the positive, even life-changing, effect that such initiatives can have for individuals who would have been unlikely to succeed without them. Yet they do little to alter prevailing, class-based assumptions about the kinds of attributes necessary for entry into, and being successful in, professional working environments. Indeed, the key purpose of such social mobility programmes appears to involve upholding existing elite interests by promoting corporate reputations and maintaining class-based privileges (Ashley, 2022).

Working-class people often treated with derision, and even contempt, by others, as described in Owen Jones' classic study *Chavs: The Demonization of the Working Class*. Jones (2011) explains how the elite view their privileges as the result of merit and hard work, while poor working-class families are seen as lazy and lacking ability. Comments from some Conservative MPs castigating benefit claimants as idle, thriftless and wasting their money on mobile phones and alcohol are typical of this stigmatization. Some of this prejudice can be ascribed to increasing residential class segregation (Savage et al, 2015). A strong account of how polarization then arises is offered by Roberts (2001):

> The confidence of the upper class is also rooted in the closed world that its members inhabit, insulated from challenges to their opinions. They are schooled, work and spend their leisure separately. They have very little contact with the working class, even the workers whom they indirectly employ, their customers or even small shareholders. The media are mostly in upper-class ownership, and the owners are accustomed to seeing their views in print ... Politicians usually listen respectfully to actual or potential investors ... Closed worlds tend to breed closed minds: hence the apparent arrogance of the ruling class. (Roberts, 2001: 189–90)

The dynamic and complex social class structure

In thinking about class-based inequality and disadvantage and how they intersect with the crisis of work, it is important to recognize the complexity of the social class structure. As Savage et al (2015) explain, the classic sociological focus on the relationship between the upper and working classes is outdated. They instead highlight a very different, more complex structure, 'one in which a small, wealthy elite class is pitted against a precariat with few resources, and between these two extremes there exist a patchwork of several other classes' (Savage et al, 2015: 53).

The 'precariat' comprises groups of people who are largely excluded from formal employment and experience profound levels of disadvantage as a consequence – those who are unemployed, reliant on welfare benefits or working in the informal economy. Lisa McKenzie has graphically described the life of struggle and frustration of such people, living in estates stigmatized as 'holding pens for the undeserving poor' (McKenzie, 2012: 129). The lives of people from this type of background are recounted in D. Hunter's (2018) *Chav Solidarity*, a chilling account of childhood experiences of abuse, violence and prostitution. Interestingly, both authors describe life in Nottingham, an East Midlands city which in the post-war decades had been a relatively prosperous place, based on the good jobs available in the hosiery and lace industries. Deindustrialization, though, meant that such employment has largely disappeared, with greater deprivation as a result.

Another profoundly important feature of the UK's class structure is the rise of middle groupings. In *A Nation of Shopkeepers*, Evans (2023) focuses on the petty bourgeoisie, the class of small businesses and the self-employed, placed above Marx's proletariat in the social hierarchy. It embodies a different relation of production from the propertyless manual workers, with 'nothing to sell but their labour'. Marx predicted that with the growth of industrial capital, the petty bourgeoisie would slowly shrink, with its members either falling into the proletariat or expanding their businesses to become part of the bourgeoisie itself. But in fact, as Evans points out, in recent decades this class has massively expanded: by 2020, the number of self-employed in the UK was over 5 million.

As a result of deindustrialization, redundancy and long-term unemployment, former industrial workers were forced to find other ways to earn a living. A classic example is the rise of so-called 'white van man', the numerous self-employed skilled craftsmen in the construction and home maintenance industry. Other examples are musicians and artists, therapists and life coaches, child minders and 'mumpreneurs' – sellers of baby goods and services. Self-employment is highest among those communities often excluded from employment, such as people of Pakistani heritage moving into taxi-driving and takeaway deliveries.

The petty bourgeois class, then, is highly diverse and also encompasses a considerable number of people we might consider to be workers but who have been defined by their employing organizations – online platforms providing gig work opportunities for example – as self-employed. Evans

(2023) argues that the petty bourgeoisie have their own distinctive cultural values: they venerate hard work and are dismissive of those they see as 'shirkers' – the unemployed, benefit claimants and students. Many have become disillusioned with traditional political parties and are attracted to right-wing populist politics, based on the appeal of economic protectionism, nationalism and climate change denial – see Chapter 7.

Two further aspects of the contemporary class structure are worthy of note. First, Evans (2023) identifies a 'new petty bourgeoisie', which we might rather consider to be 'lower-middle class': groups such as nurses, junior teachers, clerical workers and the like. These people are clearly not owners of the means of production, so it is hard to see them as part of the petty bourgeoisie. Second, above the petty bourgeoisie in the occupational structure is a large body of people employed in elite occupations, whom Goldthorpe et al (1980) and Goldthorpe (1982) have described as the 'service class', because they undertake services for the elite and the powerful. These people may be critical of the elite and of the capitalist economy, but they have a stake in the system, which rewards them with good salaries and comparatively secure employment. Following Ehrenreich and Ehrenreich (1977), Evans labels them the 'professional/managerial' class. They are extremely numerous: there are 5.7 million professionals (21 per cent of the workforce) and 3.5 million managers in the UK (Evans, 2023: 142).

Class-based disadvantage – inequality, housing and work

Having emphasized the importance of social class, and highlighted its complex structure and dynamics, what are the implications of class-based disadvantage and how has it amplified the troublesome nature of work under neoliberalism? One problem has been pronounced income inequality. Data from the UK's Office of National Statistics (ONS) highlight the geographic dimensions of income inequality. Of the top 20 areas in the UK with the highest average incomes, 18 are in London, while the 20 poorest neighbourhoods are in Leicester, Derby, Bradford, Leeds and Calderdale. The richest UK neighbourhood is Tower Hill and Wapping South, with average household disposable income of £67,100, while the poorest is St Matthews and Highfields North in Leicester, with only £11,300 (Dubas-Fisher and Clements-Thrower, 2023). Significantly, the latter is an area with a high African-Caribbean population. As we shall discuss in this chapter, Black communities often suffer the most in times of economic depression and scarcity. It is indicative that the next poorest area is Belgrave South, also in Leicester, where there is a concentration of British Asian residents.

The ONS data are from 2018, before the impact of the COVID-19 pandemic had made itself felt, so what is now named the 'cost-of-living crisis' had not yet begun to bite. As we discuss in Chapter 7, the level of in-work poverty has risen acutely due to declining living standards in the UK. Since the early 2010s, the use of food banks offering support to the poorest families – with a high proportion of lone mothers among the recipients – has risen each year. There are now over 2,000 food banks in the UK, more than there are McDonald's outlets. The Trussell Trust, which operates many food banks, reported providing nearly 3 million emergency food handouts in 2022–23 compared to around 300,000 ten years earlier, and just a few tens of thousands a year in the 2000s (Pratt, 2023). While the 'cost-of-living crisis' has aggravated the problem of poverty in the UK, the increasing use of food banks since the 2000s points to the steady rise of class inequality – a consequence of the intensified neoliberalism evident in the aftermath of the 2007–8 global financial crash and subsequent 'Great Recession', particularly the emphasis placed by Conservative-led governments on austerity.

Growing class inequality is something that is clearly manifest in the 'crisis' of housing (Dorling, 2015; Tunstall, 2023), with consequences for the troublesome nature of work, not least because in the UK it is becoming ever more difficult for working people to secure decent accommodation on income derived from employment alone. Neoliberalization and financialization have favoured owners of assets, people who are generally older and wealthier than average. This is a major source of intergenerational inequality, since asset price inflation, especially rising property prices, has outstripped income from employment. Even workers on good salaries, earning well above the average, cannot afford to raise a sufficient deposit to purchase their own home with a mortgage loan without financial support from their parents. In 1997, the sale value of the average home was 3.5 times that of median full-time annual earnings; by 2022, this ratio had soared to 8.3 (ONS, 2023a). The average age at which people buy their own home for the first time has been rising, not least because the typical deposit required has risen markedly in value. Home ownership, especially among younger people, has declined as a consequence, increasingly becoming 'the preserve of the better off' (Judge and Leslie, 2021: 5).

A pronounced housing shortage, in the context of population growth, has inflated property values – to the advantage of rentiers, especially property owners and landlords (Dorling, 2015). The crisis of housing is, to a large extent, a function of social class divisions. A quarter of Britain's richest people have property as their chief asset (Slobodian, 2023: 52). Acquiring property assets has become a popular strategy for the elite to increase their incomes as well as their social power. This is a global phenomenon. Drawing on the work on Fernandez et al (2016), Slobodian (2023: 50) highlights the role of offshore investors: '[I]n 2012, 85% of all high-end residential real estate and 50% in New York was bought by foreign buyers.'

The stock of publicly owned social housing for rent in the UK is far lower than used to be the case because of the 1980s Conservative government's policy of allowing tenants to purchase their homes ('right-to-buy') without councils building new ones. The number of council-owned houses fell by two thirds, from 6.5 million to 2.2 million between 1979 and 2022 (Hanley, 2022). Most former council houses, once inhabited by working-class families, were sold on after their purchase to landlords and property companies and subsequently rented out privately. The 'right-to-buy' policy also led to a steep increase in rural second home ownership as houses that were previously owned by local councils became available for sale on the property market and bought by outsiders, pricing out working-class people (Tyler, 2020). The stock of so-called 'affordable' social housing available for rent, owned by local authorities and housing associations, is inadequate, with a lack of funding having restricted the building of new homes (Jayanetti, 2022). In 2022, some 1.2 million households in England were on waiting lists for social housing (Booth, 2022a).

With demand for social housing outrunning its supply to such a large degree, local authorities tend to privilege the most disadvantaged applicants – those with a large number of young children, for example – leading to the increasing stigmatization of what have come to be seen as 'sink estates', dumping grounds for those with 'social problems' (McKenzie, 2015). While most people in the UK live in good-quality housing (Tunstall, 2023), much existing social housing is poorly maintained and inadequate, with damp and other problems often posing severe risks to residents' health.

In 2022, around 4.4 million UK households rented privately, twice the number during the 2000s (Hanley, 2022). The growth of the private rental sector encapsulates the commodification of housing, with property treated as a commodity, to be bought and sold for the purpose of financial gain rather than a home in which people live (Dorling, 2015). While policy changes have reduced the incentives that drove the growth of the private rental sector, buying up properties, letting them to tenants and, most importantly, benefitting from the rise in value of their assets over time has generally been a worthwhile investment, especially for people with inadequate pension arrangements (Tunstall, 2023).

The growth of a non-productive form of 'rentier capitalism', as described by Piketty (2014), has become a major feature of the UK economy. Indeed, building on Piketty's account of rentierism, Adkins et al (2020: 8) argue that property investment and consequent inflation (with frequent rises in rental costs) have become 'the linchpin of a new logic of inequality'. Coining the term 'asset economy', they suggest that 'the key element shaping inequality is no longer the employment relationship but rather whether one is able to buy assets that appreciate at a faster rate than both inflation and wages' (Adkins et al, 2020: 10). Overall, the expansion of the private rental sector has been advantageous for rentiers – those fortunate enough to have capital to invest in property as assets. However, it is a different picture for the increasing number of – capital-poor – households obliged to take up private tenancies, with a preponderance of short-term lets fuelling housing insecurity and exposure to frequent rent hikes exacerbating cost-of-living difficulties.

There are clearly some important linkages between the troublesome nature of contemporary work and the crisis of housing. As we have already mentioned, even people on good salaries can struggle to secure decent housing, especially on a long-term basis. A lack of real wage growth, during a period when the cost of buying or renting a home has soared, has made housing far less affordable than it once was. For low-paid workers, particularly those in precarious employment, the scale of the housing crisis is even more pronounced. Many have to resort to renting insecure, substandard accommodation in the private sector for which they have to pay over the odds. As Dorling (2015: 23) has commented, precarious 'living is not just about precarious employment; it is also about being precariously housed'. Affordability difficulties mean that many workers resort to staying temporarily with friends – 'sofa-surfing' – or family members. Given that work no longer provides people with the opportunity to escape poverty that it once did, the rise of 'in-work homelessness' is perhaps not as surprising as it may once have been (Jones et al, 2020).

The COVID-19 pandemic and its aftermath highlighted one further important, but hitherto overlooked, aspect of housing inequality, namely the disparities in the space people have available to them and the implications this has for working from home (Tunstall, 2023). Older home owners generally have an excess of space, whereas people who rent their accommodation often lack space, especially if they are sharing a property with others. For the former group, working from home is much more feasible and attractive than it is for the latter.

The crisis of housing illuminates the links between class-based disadvantage and the troublesome nature of contemporary employment, emphasizing the symbiotic relationship between social class and work. Class exercises an important influence on the kinds of jobs people do, the content of those jobs, how the jobs are organized and rewarded and any opportunities such jobs provide for progression. Because of their class position, too many workers are trapped in low-paid, dead-end jobs which offer limited opportunities for advancement and upward social mobility (SMC, 2019). The troublesome nature of much contemporary work is, to a large extent, infused by class divisions. At the same time, work itself upholds and reinforces such divisions, as demonstrated by the evidence from elite occupations, which are disproportionately filled by people from privileged backgrounds.

As an illustration, consider the difficulties and obstacles experienced by working-class women involved in insecure, precarious and low-paid work as home carers (Hayes, 2017). Too many people in such work face insuperable barriers, such as a lack of high-quality skills training opportunities (SMC, 2020), that obstruct their capacity to improve their upward social mobility and transcend the influence of social class. Over two thirds of people from working-class backgrounds believe that the economic system is rigged against them and that wealth accrues to those who are given more opportunities and not because they work harder or are more talented (CLASS, 2022).

There are three further, related points that need emphasizing. The first involves the importance of recognizing the diverse nature of the contemporary working class. What Ainsley (2018: 23) calls the 'new' working class includes people in 'hundreds of different types of jobs in today's economy, employed as cleaners, shop workers, bar tenders, cooks, carers, teaching assistants, secretaries, delivery workers, and so on'. Today's working class is much more diverse than it once was, particularly in respect of gender, race and age (CLASS, 2022).

Following on from this, the second point concerns the importance of taking an intersectional approach to understanding social class. This appreciates the salience of other social characteristics and how these produce distinctive experiences and understandings of class-based disadvantage. Precarity, for example, is often a function of class-, ethnic- (think about the overrepresentation of migrant workers in precarious employment) and gender-based disadvantage.

Arising from all this is a third point. This concerns the potential for workers to develop shared interests and a sense of collective solidarity based on their experiences of class and other divisions at work and in opposition to structures of exploitation and oppression. Social class is not just about categorizing people into hierarchical groups based on their access to material resources; it also has an important relational dimension, as people's shared experiences of disadvantage, arising from the way they are treated by employers and other dominant actors, come to influence their potential for action (Umney, 2018). In this way, then, class politics makes an important contribution to the antagonism that is central to the contemporary crisis of work, including by fomenting activism, as we explore in Chapter 8.

Gender inequality and disadvantage at work

As the issue of social class demonstrates, an intersectional approach is critical to understanding disadvantage, including in the field of work and employment. An intersectional approach holds that specific patterns of inequality are influenced by a complex range of influences derived from people's social characteristics and identities (Crenshaw, 1991). In the rest of this chapter, we consider three further dimensions of disadvantage at work – gender, ethnicity and age – and their implications for the crisis of work. As we will see, there are longstanding disparities in each of these areas. Yet these disparities have been aggravated under conditions of intensified neoliberalization, with the experience of the COVID-19 pandemic exacerbating the resulting antagonisms.

Gender segregation is commonplace in contemporary employment, with women and men clustered in different occupations – think about the preponderance of women in care work for example. In addition to such horizontal segregation, there is also 'a vertical dimension; that is, within any industry, occupation or job, women tend to be in the lower echelons with men clustered near the top of the employment pyramid. Most CEOs and directors are men' (Bradley, 2018: 101–2). This persistence of gender-segregated work in the Global North may seem surprising, given the decades of feminism and organizational development of gender equality policies, along with government backing for gender audits. We may explain this, perhaps, by two interlocking factors: the continued concentration of power and decision making, both political and economic, in the hands of men; and the fact that women enter the labour market on differing terms from men, as Miriam Glucksmann cogently argued in her influential account of the total social organization of labour (Glucksmann, 1995).

Women's labour market participation is shaped and constrained by their reproductive function, which often also leads to them taking responsibility for domestic activities and household maintenance: even childless women are stereotypically considered in terms of such commitments. A research study of women science postdoctoral researchers carried out by Mark Erickson found that almost all of them were asked in job interviews if they intended to have children (Erickson, 2016: 158). Although such questioning by an employer is unlawful in the UK, there is nevertheless an underlying assumption about women's roles and orientations that stokes gender disadvantage. In some occupations, there is a preference for hiring men, since it is assumed that they have fewer restrictions on their time or their spatial mobility; nor do they give birth to children, compelling organizations to pay for maternity leave.

The problems of care work, both paid and unpaid, and its attribution and allocation to women (see Chapter 3) are also an important cause of gender disadvantage at work. Around 5 million people in England and Wales provide some unpaid care to adults, and 1.5 million spend more than 50 hours per week on such activity (Booth, 2023). Doing so impedes their ability to take up and make the most of opportunities for paid work: unpaid carers often have to give up their jobs and struggle financially as a result. Women in paid work are often engaged in a 'double shift', having to fit in unpaid household labour, including caring activities, around the demands of their jobs (Hochschild, 2012). The effort to accommodate the two is the main reason why such a high proportion of part-time jobs are undertaken by women (Rubery et al, 2016).

Neoliberalism has compromised progress in tackling gender inequality and disadvantage. If the later decades of the 20th century had witnessed a slow movement towards equalization, the advent of austerity policies in response to the Great Recession proved a setback to women, especially working-class women, in what the UK's Women's Budget Group (WBG) describe as a 'triple whammy' (WBG, 2020). First, major cuts to public services meant the loss of thousands of secure jobs for women: 80 per cent of National Health Service employees are women, as are 82 per cent of care workers and 76 per cent of teachers (see WBG, 2020). Second, cuts to benefits, rising costs and falling income levels put strains on the consumption patterns of many families, especially those headed by lone parents. Third, services which helped less well-off women to cope with the 'double burden' of work and motherhood, such as Sure Start, were axed or shrunk by Conservative-led governments, while the costs of childcare have risen and continue to do so. The important intersection of gender and ethnicity is illustrated by evidence that minoritized women in the UK were particularly badly affected by the impact of austerity (WBG, 2017).

The WBG (2020, 2022) has undertaken surveys of contemporary gendered employment patterns in the UK. In 2020, the vast majority of employed men (87 per cent) were full-time workers, whereas 37 per cent of women worked part time. Women were close to half (47 per cent) of those with jobs but were still much more likely to be in non-standard forms of employment. They made up 72 per cent of part-time workers and 57 per cent of those who indicated their part-time employment was involuntary. They were the greater proportion of those working in temporary employment and in zero-hours contracts (54 per cent in each case). They also accounted for 69 per cent of low earners (defined as those earning less than 60 per cent of an average weekly full-time wage), a figure that has remained fairly constant since 2011. The WBG also point out that the pay of women of Bangladeshi and Pakistani heritage is lower than that of other minoritized ethnic groups, illustrating how gender and ethnicity intersect to amplify disadvantage.

These problems are further compounded by gender pay inequality. Research by the Living Wage Foundation (LWF) confirms the picture of lower pay for women. The 'real' living wage is taken to be what is needed for a decent standard of living in the UK. In 2023, it was calculated as £10.90 per hour (£11.95 in higher-cost London). By contrast, the official government legal minimum wage was £10.42 per hour, and lower for those under 23 – £10.18 for those aged 21 to 22, £7.49 for those aged 18 to 20 and £5.28 for those aged under 18. According to the LWF, about 2.07 million jobs held by women are paid less than the real living wage, compared with 1.4 million of men's jobs. Moreover, it is very likely that women are among the numbers of workers who are illegally paid less than the government's minimum wage. This may be because they are working within family businesses, in unregulated sweatshops or in sectors such as domiciliary care where underpayment is commonplace. Women are also more likely to be on zero-hours contracts. These insecure contracts make budgeting and timetabling extremely difficult and stressful (Glaze, 2023).

The COVID-19 pandemic further amplified gender inequality and disadvantage at work (ONS, 2020; Reid, 2020). Those in frontline jobs, such as teachers, nurses, retail staff and care workers, faced worsening and in many cases outright dangerous conditions. Workloads were increased to such an extent that many women were unable to tolerate the stress and subsequently quit their jobs. Many low-level jobs in the hospitality sector, another area where women are concentrated, were lost due to business closures. Women barred from work during the period of lockdown bore most of the responsibility for home schooling their children, especially if their partners were key workers; although male partners often helped, the major share of housework and childcare, as ever, fell to women (ONS, 2020).

For poor families in rented accommodation and cramped living spaces, the stresses of coping with children stuck at home were considerable where access to green spaces and play areas was restricted. Lone mothers suffered particularly badly, having to balance earning a living and children's education and welfare (Armstrong, 2020). As Reid (2020: 39) puts it, they had to balance the need to be a 'mother, teacher, cook, cleaner, entertainer, with the need to put food on the table'. The WBG report that while housing costs had risen, frozen Local Housing Allowances meant that many households, especially those headed by a lone woman, would struggle to pay rent (WBG, 2022). Such difficulties arising from the impact of COVID-19 were not, of course, just confined to the UK: women in countries as diverse as Bulgaria and Canada reported similar problems of stress, overwork and worries about children (Langan et al, 2023; Stoilova and Ilieva-Trichova, 2023). A further highly concerning problem in both Bulgaria and the UK was the increased numbers of children suffering from school phobia after lockdown, an issue of major difficulty for single parents, especially mothers.

Although some of these problems were alleviated when the COVID lockdowns ended, many women remained stuck in low-paid and precarious jobs, and some had impaired physical and mental health because of the pandemic. Burki (2020) reports that working mothers in the UK were more likely than others to have lost or quit their jobs. Across the Global South, large numbers of informal economy jobs were lost. In the UK, families were then hit by rising costs, as the combined impacts of the economic repercussions of the pandemic, of Brexit trade deterioration and the effects of climate change on the production of food hit home. As women bear most of the responsibility for domestic work and budgeting, the burden of coping with soaring food prices and the choice between 'heating and eating' fell upon them, and especially, of course, on lone mothers. Concerns about children's welfare create extra stresses, with a soaring mental ill-health crisis among the young, as noted by Reid (2020). In addition, because of the housing crisis, many young graduates are compelled to return to their parental homes, adding to the pressures on food and energy bills (Ingram et al, 2023).

Racial and ethnic disparities

Disparities linked to 'race' and ethnicity are longstanding and deeply embedded features of work and employment in societies such as the UK. We have characterized gender inequalities in the workplace as marked by segregation – women are allowed in, but preferably in different jobs and lower in the organizational hierarchy. In the case of ethnicity, however, disadvantage is often manifest in exclusion, through attempts to keep workplaces all White for example. This pursuit of exclusion can be seen in the ill treatment accorded to undocumented migrant workers, refugees and people seeking asylum, people who are particularly disadvantaged in the labour market.

Despite the provision of anti-discrimination legislation and the development of equality, diversity and inclusion policies, people from minoritized ethnic communities often find it hard to gain access to employment in the UK. Since it can be more straightforward for them to enter certain occupations within their communities, in shops and restaurants for example, this can produce ethnic segregation (Waldinger, 1994; Ruhs and Anderson, 2010). Yet there are marked differences between minoritized ethnic groups in the UK. The economic profiles of British Chinese and Indian citizens are closer to those of the majority population – for example, in their take-up of higher education – while the worst off and most excluded are people from Pakistani, Bangladeshi and Black African-Caribbean backgrounds. It is important to mention that some ethnic groups are too small to show up in national datasets, especially as they are concentrated in particular areas, such as people of Turkish heritage in North London and Somalis in Bristol. People of North African, Lebanese and Palestinian heritage are also overlooked in such quantitative investigations, although details about these groups can be found in detailed survey investigations (Finney et al, 2023).

In their study of intersectionalities, Hall et al (2018) illustrate the situation of the larger minoritized ethnic communities. They report that 50 per cent of Bangladeshi-origin households, 46 per cent of Pakistani-origin households and 40 per cent of Black African-Caribbean-origin households were living in poverty in 2015, compared to only 19 per cent of White households. This may partly be due to the nature of immigration trajectories. In a fascinating study of labour and migration, Kalra (2000) notes that people from the Indian subcontinent and the Caribbean tended to be brought into declining industries, such as textiles and car manufacturing. Thus, they lost what were relatively well-paid jobs and moved into less well-rewarded insecure jobs – moving, as she puts it in the title of her book, from 'textile mills to taxi ranks'. Men of Bangladeshi and Pakistani origin are now heavily concentrated in transport (mainly taxis), retail and restaurant work (see also Khan [2020] for the experience of Brighton, on the south coast of England).

Kalra's study of Oldham, a town in North West England, charts the decline of employment in the textile industries. In 1971, there were 18,234 workers employed in textile manufacture in Oldham, falling to 13,324 in 1981 and 3,254 in 1991 due to the deindustrialization and recession of the 1980s. By 1995, only 1,827 employees remained (Kalra, 2000: 133). As Kalra points out, while White women were compensated by being able to move into service-sector and white-collar work, those from minoritized ethnic communities were largely excluded.

The loss of waged employment pushed many people from minoritized backgrounds into self-employment, especially as taxi-drivers and in various types of retail enterprise, notably 'take-aways': small kebab and chicken shops (Kalra, 2000). Pakistani-origin men have the highest level of self-employment in the UK (23 per cent), followed by those of Bangladeshi origin (18 per cent) and Chinese origin (14 per cent) (Clark and Shankley, 2020: 181). The advantage of these small businesses is that family members can work within them; however, they tend to be precarious and of limited profitability. Many closed down during the pandemic: there were just over 5 million self-employed workers in 2020, but this had fallen to 4.39 million by 2023 (Statista, 2023a).

Survey data not only illustrate how people from minoritized ethnic communities suffer from discrimination and tactics of exclusion but also display the intersections of ethnicity, age and gender (Clark and Shankley, 2020). High levels of economic inactivity and unemployment are particularly manifest among men of Bangladeshi and Black African-Caribbean origin, especially young men, who are particularly likely to be excluded. Their earnings are also much lower, on average, than men of White British origin and those of Indian and Chinese origin. Clark and Shankley (2020: 191) note that people of Pakistani and Bangladeshi origin tend to work in small firms, often minoritized ethnic concerns, and are frequently paid below the legal minimum wage, especially if they are relatives of the owner or unpaid helpers.

Employment levels are strikingly low among Muslim women. While this may be caused by voluntary economic inactivity, in terms of traditional gender roles in the household, it also suggests that exclusion and discrimination may be at play, possibly due to Islamophobia – prejudice against and hostility towards Muslim people – to a certain degree. Analysing data from the British Social Attitudes surveys, Kelley et al (2017) found that people were twice as likely to say they would be concerned if a family member married someone who was a Muslim than if the marriage was to someone from an Asian background in general. The intersection of ethnicity and gender is particularly evident when we look at pay. Men of Bangladeshi origin experience clear disadvantage in this respect, earning on average less than all women in general; but the situation for women of Bangladeshi origin is by far the worst (Clark and Shankley, 2020).

Workers from minoritized communities are widely discriminated against by employers. Experimental studies, involving fake job applications from matched pairs of White and non-White workers, demonstrate employers' preferences for the former (Heath and Li, 2018). Minoritized women encounter particular obstacles. They experience multiple disadvantages framed by sexism, racism and class prejudice. A study by Hall et al (2018) found that discrimination and bias – whether conscious or unconscious – operated at every stage of the recruitment process, in the evaluation of applications and in interview procedures. Such bias continued into employment, where minoritized women characteristically found themselves blocked from promotion.

The intensified neoliberalization of the 2010s, especially the enactment of austerity policies, exacerbated the racial and ethnic disparities which already existed in the UK (Manfredi, 2016). In 2017, the United Nations launched an investigation into ethnic inequalities and racial discrimination in the UK, led by Professor E. Tendayi Achiume, its Special Rapporteur on racism, racial discrimination, xenophobia and related intolerance. The subsequent UN report showed extensive evidence of inequality and exclusion in areas such as employment and housing, as discussed in this chapter, as well as in health provision and police activity (Tendayi Achiume, 2018). The UN investigation noted the increasing virulence of Islamophobia, as well as some disturbing consequences arising from the Brexit referendum. According to Shankley and Rhodes, Tebdayi Achiume's report

> pointed to rising hate speech and violence in the wake of Brexit, the emboldening of far-right and extremist politics, and a widespread sense that such sentiments have gained ground within the political mainstream. The result of this, Achiume concluded, is 'the growth in the acceptability of explicit racial, ethnic and religious intolerance'. (Shankley and Rhodes, 2020: 267)

The greater casualization of employment and commodification of labour, covered in Chapters 3 and 4, has aggravated racial and ethnic disparities. Much platform work undertaken in the 'gig' economy involves migrants working for low pay in highly precarious and frequently unsafe conditions. Like much traditional work in the service sector, platform work is profoundly racialized (van Doorn, 2017). In a study of migrant women workers in the

Spanish care sector, Rodríguez-Modroño et al (2022) point to how race and gender intersect when it comes to the casualizing and commodifying effects of platform work – exacerbating disadvantage. For one thing, platforms 'rely on the longstanding historical and institutional factors which produce a cheap labour force, very often constituted by migrant women workers'.

Platforms feed on the fact that such workers are often excluded from alternative, more formalized sources of employment and are thus more vulnerable to exploitation and subjugation. As a consequence, 'domestic and care work, already devalued in itself, is re-segregated by race, social class and the country-of-origin in digital platforms' (Rodríguez-Modroño et al, 2022: 631–2).

Yet it is important to recognize that platform work does not operate just as a 'site of degradation'. For minoritized ethnic workers, who, because of employers' prejudices and discriminatory behaviours, would otherwise encounter considerable obstacles in securing conventional employment, it can be an 'opportunity' (van Doorn et al, 2023: 1101). Platform work provides them not just with a valuable income but also offers them scope to exercise some control over their working lives that might otherwise be absent.

Under conditions of intensified neoliberalization, increasing employer-controlled flexibility has driven greater casualization of employment – see Chapter 4. The resulting precarity is generally both highly gendered, with women workers employed in sectors such as retail being particularly prone to experiencing insecurity (Wood, 2020), and racialized. Migrant workers, especially those whose status is undocumented, often experience particular disadvantage and exploitative treatment in a system of employment relations which privileges employers' flexibility (FLEX, 2017). Efforts to prioritize action against so-called 'modern slavery' and other forms of hyper-exploitation at work are largely performative: they convey a moral concern with improving the conditions of particularly disadvantaged workers while legitimizing the operation of highly exploitative employment models that render such workers even more vulnerable (Kenway, 2021).

Governments in countries such as the UK, which have enacted increasingly harsh immigration rules in response to concerns stoked by the rise of nationalist and xenophobic right populist political parties about the supposedly adverse consequences of immigration (see Chapter 7), have exacerbated exploitation and racial disadvantage. Historically, the UK already had a poor record of welcoming immigrants, refugees and asylum seekers, with governments often keen to impose more restrictive conditions in response to racial prejudice whipped up by the popular press (Solomos, 2003).

Matters took a harsher turn during the 2010s, as Conservative and Conservative-led governments propagated a so-called 'hostile environment' approach to immigration policy, aimed at discouraging undocumented migrants, refugees and asylum seekers from settling in the UK (Goodfellow, 2019) – see, for example, the measures taken to criminalize so-called 'illegal working' under legislation such as the Immigration Act 2016. The 'hostile environment' policy was based on a tacit admission that it is legally difficult to prevent people from entering the country. Instead, the aim was to ensure that, once they had arrived, their lives were made as unpleasant as possible – prompting them to leave and deterring others from journeying in the first place (Fekete, 2020; Griffiths and Yeo, 2021).

As well as stoking racial prejudice and giving succour to the far right, the 'hostile environment' policy exacerbated migrant workers' vulnerability, thus amplifying disadvantage. Undocumented migrants are disinclined to report abuses by employers for fear of being subject to immigration enforcement action and possible deportation if they do so. Restrictive immigration rules in general exacerbate exploitation, commodification and precarity (Anderson, 2010) – even for migrant workers who are documented. In the UK, for example, there are widespread reports of the difficulties experienced by migrant agricultural workers, hired on seasonal work visas, whose lack of permanent residency leaves them particularly open to abuse (McKinney et al, 2022). While migrant workers have long experienced vulnerability, harsher immigration rules for so-called 'low-skilled' labour make it harder to tackle severe forms of labour exploitation such as modern slavery offences, exacerbating vulnerability and precarity and fuelling racial disadvantage (Hodkinson et al, 2021; Kenway, 2021). This is in the context of a highly neoliberalized employment relations regime which privileges employers' flexibility, offers workers weak and limited rights and protections and lacks effective mechanisms for enforcing labour standards (not just in the UK – see Milkman [2020] for the experience of the US).

Young people and precarity: futures in jeopardy

Older workers are often justifiably irate about their experience of age prejudice (Hunt, 2005; Bradley, 2016). Under neoliberal conditions, with organizations increasingly looking for short-term profitability, workers in their 50s and 60s may be seen as a liability: young people may be preferred by managers for their better levels of qualification, their IT skills and a perception that they will be better able to adapt to change. But the impact of neoliberalization on work and employment has been particularly challenging for young people, especially those from working-class and non-privileged backgrounds. They have borne the brunt of the precarity arising from greater labour market flexibilization and the diminished opportunities available for good jobs, limiting their ability to secure decent housing as a consequence. US President Joe Biden has remarked on the particular difficulties experienced by young people in our crisis-ridden age:

> 'This generation has really been screwed. These were really the most open, the least prejudiced, the brightest, the best-educated generation in American history. And what's happening? They end up with 9/11, they end up with a war, they end up with the Great Recession and then they end up with this [the COVID pandemic]. This generation needs help in the middle of this crisis.' (quoted in Osnos, 2020: 18)

Any such help does not seem to have materialized. As Osnos (2020) points out, following the financial crash young people entered the labour market in the worst recession since the 1980s. As we have emphasized in previous chapters, the jobs on offer are increasingly precarious, and young people are more vulnerable to unemployment than other age groups. A lack of good jobs and a dearth of affordable housing mean that in both the UK and US a greater number of young adults are living at home with their parents (Osnos, 2020; Booth and Goodier, 2023b).

For some, an intergenerational divide has arisen. For example, in 2010 David Willetts, a former Conservative education minister in the UK, published a book entitled *The Pinch: How the Baby Boomers Took Their Children's Future – and Why They Should Give It Back* (Willetts, 2010). The 'boomer' generation, roughly comprising people born between 1945 and 1964, benefitted from relatively benign economic circumstances, secure jobs, often with good occupational pensions attached and greater opportunities for home ownership – especially if they were employed in the kind of stable, white-collar roles which expanded rapidly during the second half of the 20th century. For those in the following generation, often termed 'millennials', comprising people who typically entered the labour market during the 2000s and 2010s, the situation was rather different. This generation of young workers was the first in modern history to be less financially well-off, on average, than that of their parents. The squeeze on young people's earnings preceded, but was exacerbated by, the 2007–8 global financial crisis and its consequences (Elliott, 2016). According to Torsten Bell, then Director of the UK's Resolution Foundation, which published a report on the topic of intergenerational pay inequality in 2016, it

> risks becoming a new inequality for our times, and nowhere is that clearer than on pay ... Far from earning more, millennials have earnt £8,000 less during their 20s than the generation before them. The financial crisis has played a role in holding millennials back, but the problem goes deeper than that. Even on optimistic scenarios they look likely to see much lower generational pay progress than we have become used to, and there is even a risk that they earn less over their lifetimes than older generations, putting generational pay progress into reverse. (Resolution Foundation, 2016)

However, academic research using data from the US shows that millennials are not uniformly less well-off than their parents' generation; rather social class plays a notable part in producing variations in financial rewards and thus influencing inequality. While millennials fortunate to be in prestige jobs are wealthier on average than their 'boomer' predecessors, such high-status and well-remunerated positions have become scarcer, with young workers often pushed into lower-status roles which attract lower rewards than was previously the case (Gruijters et al, 2023).

The influence of social class on the experience of young workers has been emphasized by Adkins et al (2020):

> Increasingly, the only way to buy property in major Western cities is with parental assistance. The division between people who do and do not have access to parental wealth is becoming particularly evident as a fault-line in the 'millennial' generation, who are the first since the post-war boom to really experience the impossibility of building up wealth and securing access to a middle-class lifestyle on the basis of wage-labour alone ... Intergenerational transfers have become a key mechanism in the new logic of class. (Adkins et al, 2020: 14)

Capital passed on within families is crucial to success in the neoliberal era (Piketty, 2014). Young women and men from working-class families lack access to the kind of economic and cultural capital amassed by their more privileged counterparts, meaning that their acquired educational capital – in terms of qualifications – is often insufficient for accessing and progressing in professional and managerial careers. Young working-class people without tertiary education are particularly badly disadvantaged. They are more likely to be unemployed, to experience long spells of unemployment and to be forced into low-paid, insecure jobs (Bradley et al, 2022). In March 2023, Statista reported that 11.3 per cent of people aged 16–24 in the UK were unemployed. This age group persistently has the highest unemployment rates, peaking in 2011 at 25 per cent as the impacts of recession and austerity hit home (Statista, 2023a). Youth unemployment has also been high across Europe: 28 per cent in Spain, 24 per cent in Greece and 22 per cent in Italy and Romania in 2023 (Statista, 2023b).

Bradley et al (2022) provide an overview of the kinds of occupations available to working-class youth. For young women, the traditional 'three Cs' – cooking, cleaning and childcare – remain major options. The ageing of the population means an expansion of care work, both in residential institutions and in people's own homes. These jobs, however, are tiring and typically low paid. Retail and hospitality may offer better conditions, and hairdressing and beauty qualifications are attractive to many young women. Options for young men, however, are more constrained:

> The decline of factory work and especially of heavy industry (coal, steel, shipbuilding) meant jobs became limited: there is unskilled work in the construction industry and other labouring work, bar work, while some may find a job as a kind of informal apprentice to a self-employed craftsman. They may reluctantly enter female specialities, such as retail and care. The decline of the traditional apprenticeship schemes, which offered a major route of labour market entry for boys in the past, has closed doors for young hopefuls. (Bradley et al, 2022: 31)

COVID-19 amplified the precarity experienced by young workers, not least by – temporarily at least – restricting their labour market opportunities. The kinds of jobs they often undertake – for example, in shops, restaurants, bars and hotels – were in sectors where businesses were forced to shut because of the pandemic. There is evidence from the UK that young workers were disproportionately adversely affected by the impact of measures aimed at preventing the spread of the coronavirus. Young workers were more likely than older workers to have been furloughed or to have lost their main job. Given that they are near the beginning of their working lives, the impact on young workers of exiting employment, even if only temporarily, can be particularly harmful. This is because they are more prone to unemployment and having their pay prospects damaged as a consequence (Gustafsson, 2020: 3).

The initial negative impact of COVID-19 on young workers' pay was also notable. Disregarding full-time students, over a third of 18–24 year olds experienced a reduction in their pay when the pandemic struck, compared to under a quarter of 35–49 year olds; older workers, those aged from 55 to 65, were also particularly prone to reductions in their pay (Gustafsson, 2020). COVID-19 was not the prime cause of the labour market precarity experienced by young workers. Neoliberalization, and the emphasis on flexibilization in employment which it propagated, meant that insecurity was already an ingrained feature of young people's working lives (Rydzik and Bal, 2023). However, one notable consequence of the pandemic was to exacerbate this insecurity (Christie and Swingewood, 2022). All this has to be seen in the context of the climate crisis and the uncertain consequences it portends for work and employment. It is young people today who are going to have to cope with a world apparently 'heading down the highway to climate hell' in the words of the Secretary-General of the United Nations, António Guterres (Harvey and Carrington, 2022).

Conclusion

Throughout this chapter, we have emphasized how the crisis of equalities is manifest in various dimensions of inequality and disadvantage relating to gender, ethnicity and age, which have been amplified under neoliberalization. Underlying them all, though, is the reality of class difference. Those with wealth, earned and unearned, can buy themselves out of the situation that disadvantage would otherwise generate. The chapter has also highlighted the interconnectedness of various crises. The crisis of equalities intersects with other crises, such as the crisis of housing – a crisis which is particularly acute for young people from working-class backgrounds. The experience of COVID-19 not only reflected and illuminated disadvantage in work but also reinforced it. Consider, for example, the implications of the pandemic for gender inequality and young workers' precarity.

All this symbolizes the crisis-ridden nature of the contemporary era in general. The antagonisms fuelled as a consequence demonstrate how the crisis of equalities is an integral component of the broader crisis of work which we are concerned with in this book. Sexual harassment – a phenomenon which is still widespread in employment settings – has prompted many women to mobilize and contest organizational structures and hierarchies dominated by men, challenging male power in the process. Racial and ethnic disparities, adversely affecting young working-class men of colour in particular, have produced contention, particularly in the aftermath of the 2020 murder of the African-American George Floyd Jr by a White police officer in the US, which triggered the Black Lives Matter movement, marked by waves of protest in the US and with repercussions in other countries, including the UK (see Chapter 8).

The escalating climate crisis, given the instabilities which it produces, exacerbates inequality and disadvantage, with new antagonisms arising as a result. Facing worse employment prospects than those in previous generations, and amid a profound crisis of housing, it is perhaps no surprise that many young people are becoming radicalized, prompting them to participate in and support climate activist groups (see Chapter 8) – a manifestation, it has been suggested, of an embryonic 'millennial socialism' (Adkins et al, 2020: 7). One particularly profound consequence of the developing climate emergency concerns the impact on migration and refugee movements. Many European countries already see themselves as experiencing a refugee crisis: in 2015, when this crisis flared up, more than 1.25 million refugees reached the borders of the EU; in one month alone, October 2015, over 221,000 arrived on the southern shores of the Mediterranean Sea (Greussing and Baumgaarden, 2017). Climate change is aggravating such a trend. Much of the world, particularly parts of South Asia and North Africa, are increasingly uninhabitable because of the effects of extreme heat – including the greater prevalence of famines, motivating the greater movement of people across borders. Playing on people's fears and anxieties about immigration has emboldened far-right political movements both in the US and Europe (see Chapter 7), whose nationalist and xenophobic politics have contributed to resurgent racial prejudice. Given the extent to which the contemporary age is marked and marred by conflict, war, climate and environmental disasters, displaced populations and, partly as a consequence, greater political polarization and hatred, it is unsurprising that inequalities are growing.

6

Trade Unions in Crisis

Introduction

In exploring the crisis of contemporary work, it is essential to examine the experiences and activities of the trade unions. There is a widespread understanding that unions, as collective organizations of workers, play a crucial part in ensuring that workers are well treated and have their interests represented effectively at work. Trade unions use their bargaining power to leverage pressure on employers to treat workers fairly, pay them appropriately and provide them with decent working conditions. During 2022–23, the popularity of Mick Lynch, the General Secretary of the Rail, Maritime and Transport (RMT) union in the UK, was based on his success in articulating the interests of the RMT's members in the media, especially their demands for higher pay and to maintain properly staffed train services and stations, amid a series of strikes on the railways.

Many of the profound problems workers currently experience – extensive insecurity and precarity (see Chapter 3), for example, and commodification pressures (see Chapter 4) – would not have become so acute if the trade unions had been stronger in recent years. Powerful trade unions capable of organizing and mobilizing workers to ensure their rights and protections are defended, and to advance them where necessary, clearly matter (Livingston, 2021). In the hospitality sector, for example, an industry marked by low pay and poor conditions, trade unions have helped workers benefit from higher pay (Papadopolous and Ioannou, 2023).

In general, though, since the 1980s trade unions have themselves been in crisis. This chapter begins by explaining how the crisis of trade unionism, one that is particularly manifest in reduced union membership, was a product of neoliberalization before examining how the unions have sought to respond to the crisis by looking to revitalize themselves. After 2020, the experience of the COVID-19 pandemic provided unions with opportunities to build back stronger. Moreover, one key way the trade unions have sought to demonstrate their relevance is by engaging with environmental issues and responding to the climate crisis. Unions are playing a key role in facilitating a 'just transition' to a net-zero world by ensuring that workers' interests are represented in the process of change, even though this has generated some notable tensions and challenges. Nevertheless, as a consequence, they are better able to demonstrate the important and effective contribution they make to advancing workers' interests, not least by fomenting activism and challenging employers and governments.

Neoliberal capitalism and the crisis of trade unionism

As collective organizations of workers, trade unions exercised a notable influence over work and employment matters during the 20th century, particularly because of the emphasis placed on supporting, representing and mobilizing working people. In bargaining collectively over pay and conditions with employers, and securing more than workers could otherwise have gained by acting on an individual basis, unions have an economic role within capitalism. Importantly, though, trade union methods can, to varying degrees, depending on the setting, be underpinned by a belief in the desirability of advancing the interests of working people as a class in opposition to capitalism. Moreover, in some countries, particularly in parts of Western Europe, unions have long had an interest in promoting greater social integration, improving the way that capitalism functions by ensuring that workers' interests are accommodated by being involved in designing and operating welfare mechanisms and through their close associations with left-of-centre, social democratic political parties (Hyman, 2001; Vandaele, 2019).

However, since the 1980s, trade unions have largely been on the defensive. Under neoliberal capitalist conditions, unions are viewed as obstacles to employers' efforts to secure greater flexibility for the purpose of improving their competitiveness. As a consequence, the trade unions' power and legitimacy has diminished markedly (Gumbrell-McCormick and Hyman, 2013; Baccaro and Howell, 2017; Holgate, 2021a).

One way of illuminating the crisis of trade unions is to focus on the trend of declining union membership. Across all Organization of Economic Co-operation and Development (OECD) countries, the proportion of employees who are union members – known as 'union density' – fell from 36.5 per cent in 1980 to 15.8 per cent in 2019; with little more than one in seven employees in the rich countries of the Global North being trade union members (OECD, no date). Unions have found it particularly difficult to attract young members into trade union membership (Vandaele, 2019). Generally, this is not because such workers are resistant to unionization; rather, unions themselves, and their structures and processes, have often been insufficiently receptive of young workers and their interests. Yet trade unions are making renewed efforts to accommodate young workers by facilitating their participation and leadership development, for example, for the purpose of strengthening labour movements around the world (Hodder and Kretsos, 2015; Simms et al, 2018; Tapia and Turner, 2018).

Changes in union density demonstrate how trade union power has diminished since the 1980s: lower membership means that unions have fewer 'associational' resources necessary to influence employers and governments from a position of strength (Gumbrell-McCormick and Hyman, 2013). Yet some comparative variation is evident. Trade union density has fallen in most of the Global North; however, the decline is most apparent in 'liberal' market economies – Australia, New Zealand, the UK and the US – countries where neoliberalization has been most acute (Ibsen and Tapia, 2017). Moreover, some care needs to be taken in using trade union density as a measure of union power. What union membership means, and the form it takes, can vary between countries (Sullivan, 2010; Metten, 2021). The high trade union density in Italy, for example, in part reflects the tendency for retired workers to retain their union membership.

Unions can benefit from being able to access other – structural – sources of power, including control over key parts of the economy – think about the disruptive effects of industrial disputes in transport, for example. They can use institutional power resources to influence electoral politics and government policy, particularly through their connections with social democratic political parties. Unions can also take advantage of organizational power resources, based on their ability to mobilize workers and engage in labour conflict (Sullivan, 2010; Gumbrell-McCormick and Hyman, 2013). Union density in France is very low, but that does not necessarily equate to weak trade unionism, since unions there generally enjoy strong organizing capabilities for the purpose of collectively mobilizing workers in general, irrespective of whether or not they are union members, and challenging the interests of capital.

While it is important not to assume that trade union power has declined just because of falling union membership levels, the diminished position of the unions, under neoliberal capitalism, is evident in other key respects. There is considerable evidence for the reduced role of collective bargaining as a method of determining workers' pay and conditions in the countries of the Global North (Waddington et al, 2019). There may well be little change in the proportion of workers who are covered by collective bargaining; however, its capacity to influence pay and conditions has been much reduced in more neoliberalized settings characterized by the exercise of greater employer flexibility (Baccaro and Howell, 2017; Hyman, 2018). Even in Germany, an archetypal 'coordinated' market economy, where institutionalized union involvement has traditionally been widely accepted, collective bargaining has been in decline as firms, under pressure to become more competitive, look to secure greater managerial flexibility (Addison et al, 2017). The marked decline in the level of recorded strike activity between the 1980s and 2010s suggests that unions enjoy far less 'organizational' power than was once the case (Frangi et al, 2018; Waddington et al, 2019). There is also clear evidence from Europe of the diminished political influence of unions and the more limited extent to which they can make use of 'institutional' power resources (Gumbrell-McCormick and Hyman, 2013; Lehndorff et al, 2018; Prosser, 2019).

What has caused the reduction in trade union power? One key factor in the countries of the Global North concerns long-term changes in the composition of employment. Unions were traditionally concentrated in highly industrialized sectors of the economy, which, since the 1980s, have experienced major declines in employment (Clark, 2018). At the same time, unions have struggled to attract members and organize in new and developing sectors of the economy, particularly in private services – IT, finance and hospitality for example. The ability of unions to do so has been hampered by the reduced bargaining power of labour under conditions of neoliberal, global capitalism (Gumbrell-McCormick and Hyman, 2013). By privileging employers' flexibility, neoliberalization has marginalized the role of trade unions, particularly in more globalized settings (Kelly, 2015; Baccaro and Howell, 2017). Industrial work that used to be carried out in highly unionized plants in the Global North is now typically undertaken in factories in the Global South, sites where independent trade unions are either absent or weak (Bartley, 2018; Frenkel, 2018).

A key problem for unions is that, as 'primarily national organizations' (Gumbrell-McCormick and Hyman, 2013: 158), they have struggled to respond to globalization effectively. Studies of highly integrated multinational firms, such as the steel-making company ArcelorMittal, demonstrate how they look to benefit from globalization by using the interconnectedness it gives them to push through efficiencies and weaken union bargaining power. Fears about the prospect of losing investment, and thus jobs, to plants in other countries encourage workers to moderate their expectations and demands (Aranea et al, 2021).

Suppressing trade unionism is an integral feature of globalization as a neoliberal project. This is epitomized by the activities of IKEA, the well-known furniture retailer. Despite the firm's espoused willingness to work with trade unions, in some parts of the world it has engaged in some notable anti-union campaigns – including veiled threats about the adverse consequences for jobs – designed to prevent workers from having union representation (IndustriAll, 2016; UNI Global Union, 2018). In the US, employers' opposition to trade unions is a longstanding feature of work and employment relations (Logan, 2006). Extensive and well-resourced campaigns against unions demonstrate just how crucial remaining union-free is to companies such as Amazon because of the perceived challenge to managerial control and flexibility posed by unionization (Logan, 2021). Importantly, anti-union efforts in the US have, at times, such as during the presidency of Donald Trump, been aided by governments which perceive unions as an enemy to be vanquished (Greenhouse, 2020). In the UK, employers benefit from a regulatory environment which imposes considerable legal restrictions on how trade unions operate and their capacity to engage in industrial action (Ewing and Hendy, 2010; Baccaro and Howell, 2017).

Even in European countries where trade unions have traditionally enjoyed a considerable amount of political influence through their involvement in, and connections with, state institutions and political actors, the decline of social democratic parties has contributed to the marginalization of the unions (Lehndorff et al, 2018; Prosser, 2019; Colfer and Prosser, 2022). In Germany, a country generally considered to offer a more supportive climate for trade unionism, discount retailers such as Lidl have pursued aggressive anti-union efforts (Geppert and Pastuh, 2017). One particularly striking consequence of the 2007–8 global financial crisis, and how European countries responded to it, was the greater exclusion of union influence over economic and social policy making. Governments sought to focus on promoting competitiveness by reducing employment rights and protections and weakening collective bargaining arrangements in order to enhance employers' flexibility and encourage wage moderation (Johnstone et al, 2019; Waddington et al, 2019; Rathgeb and Tassinari, 2022). The immediate aftermath of the 2007–8 global financial crisis saw an intensification of neoliberalization (López-Andreu, 2019), which had damaging consequences for the trade unions (Hyman, 2018), not only by undermining collective bargaining and reducing union influence over policy making but also weakening cooperation between union movements in different countries (Prosser, 2019).

The trends and developments covered in this chapter so far suggest that trade unions are in crisis, a crisis which has to a large extent been caused by neoliberalization and was amplified by the intensified neoliberalism characteristic of the period following the global financial crisis. However, it is important to note that not all unions have experienced decline – some have been able to take advantage of specific sources of power, including identity resources, to mobilize effectively and grow their memberships (Smale, 2020). Notable variations can exist between unions in different countries with regard to access to power resources, qualifying the assumption of a general decline in trade unionism (Schmidt et al, 2019; Vandaele, 2019). Moreover, unions have been increasingly active in responding to the crisis in which they have found themselves and in demonstrating their critical role in the contemporary world of work.

Trade union revitalization – responding to crisis

The crisis of the trade unions is important not just because of the debilitated position of the unions in and of itself but also because of how it has contributed to the broader crisis of work. Weak trade unions are both a consequence and a cause of the diminished bargaining power of labour under neoliberalism. Their difficulties have contributed to the problems in the labour market, work and employment, including the proliferation of precarious jobs and stagnant real wages (Blanchflower, 2019; Greenhouse, 2020).

It is important, then, to examine the efforts trade unions have been making to overcome their difficulties and improve their capacity to represent, bargain on behalf of and mobilize working people effectively for the purpose of challenging neoliberalization and its adverse consequences. That said, trade union initiatives have often had a rather defensive character in that they have largely been concerned with managing decline. One common response to such decline involves mergers between unions, predicated on the belief that a process of consolidation would make them more efficient and thus better able to provide services to members and improve membership retention as a result (Holgate, 2021a). Sometimes unions have also tried to reinforce their existing relationships in organizations by cultivating a cooperative, partnership-based approach, one predicated on the belief that a trade union presence is best secured by engaging positively with employers and promoting 'mutual gains' (Johnstone, 2015). Yet a concern with managing decline is an inadequate response to the crisis of trade unionism. It does little to expand unions' representational and mobilizing capacities and thus renders them unable to respond to the contemporary issues and problems people experience at work. An alternative approach, one concerned with how unions can revitalize themselves, potentially offers a much more effective response to the crisis of trade unionism (Ibsen and Tapia, 2017).

During the 2000s and 2010s, union revitalization efforts, manifest in attempts to expand their representational, organizational and mobilization capacities, were evident in a number of areas. One prominent aspect concerns a renewed appreciation of the value of collective bargaining in securing improvements to workers' pay and conditions (Moore et al, 2019). For collective bargaining to operate, trade unions need to be recognized by employers. Some unions have been successful in gaining recognition in firms that had previously upheld a non-union approach to managing employment relations. Despite having once espoused a very hostile approach to trade unions, operational difficulties caused by staff shortages and vigorous union campaigning activity have prompted Ryanair to recognize unions in some European countries. It also has a union recognition agreement covering directly employed UK-based cabin crew (Topham, 2018). The global online retail giant Amazon, a notoriously anti-union company, has been the target of unionization efforts among warehouse workers, both in the US and Europe. Although Amazon operates an array of 'union-busting' techniques to keep trade unions out of its sites in the US, often with some success (Logan, 2021), attempts by workers and labour activists to unionize the company and secure better pay and improved working conditions have escalated (Alimahomed-Wilson and Reese, 2021).

Efforts to unionize corporations such as Amazon point to the important way in which effective union revitalization is contingent on the mobilization of workers, often for the purpose of challenging employers. There is evidence that a confrontational approach – engaging in strike action, for example – is associated with membership growth (Hodder et al, 2017). The UK 'fast-food rights' campaign, initiated in 2014 by the Bakers, Food and Allied Workers Union, and influenced by the 'Fight for $15' movement to organize service sector workers in the US, points to the contribution an activist-based approach can make to union revitalization. The campaign involved a series of strikes for increased pay and better conditions by workers in McDonald's, a famously anti-union employer, as well as associated actions by workers in TGI Fridays, Wetherspoons and Uber Eats. Although the workers were not able to gain union recognition from McDonald's, the 'fast-food rights' campaign was a success to the extent that it 'allowed workers to reflect on and articulate perceived injustices' and 'raised expectations regarding working conditions'. Where workers' activists are present, 'store management more carefully adhere to rules and procedures and show more respect to workers' (Royle and Rueckert, 2022: 423).

The case of the 'fast-food rights' campaign and the involvement of young workers employed in the service sector highlights the important extent to which trade union revitalization is contingent upon a broadening of the union agenda to encompass groups whose interests have hitherto been largely neglected. The greater engagement of young workers is critical to trade union renewal (Tapia and Turner, 2018). Unions have made vigorous efforts to represent the interests of a more diverse workforce and broaden their constituencies, particularly by prioritizing equality issues (Kirton, 2018). One prominent way they have done this involves attempts to influence employers' approaches, including by emphasizing the importance of equality issues and ensuring that organizational policies and practices are implemented appropriately (Seifert and Wang, 2018). Unions can use the collective bargaining agenda to promote equality issues, such as commitments to reducing the gender pay gap and promoting effective work–life balance arrangements. One of the ways they have been able to do this is by changing their internal representative structures: unions have taken steps to ensure that the interests of previously underrepresented groups of workers – women workers, Black workers, disabled workers, LGBTQ+ workers and young workers – are better recognized in decision-making structures (Kirton and Greene, 2022).

Yet despite the formal commitments unions have expressed on equality issues, and the actions that have accompanied them, there are a number of reasons why the effectiveness of the equality bargaining agenda has been impaired, limiting the contribution it can make to promoting trade union revitalization. One difficulty concerns the unfavourable political and economic climate. Since 2010, the UK government has been unsupportive of equality interventions in general, and union-led activities in particular. Employers are less receptive to equality bargaining as a consequence (Kirton, 2018). There are also internal factors that inhibit unions' efforts to promote gender equality. They include a tendency for such issues to be marginalized in environments where trade union representatives are generally male and sometimes uninterested in, and even resistant to, engaging with equality concerns (Kirton, 2021).

The greater emphasis placed on equality issues illustrates the important ways unions have attempted to revitalize themselves by responding to external circumstances – specifically greater workforce diversity – and changing the way they operate. Union revitalization can also involve a shift in orientation, with a greater onus placed on organizing workers in new and growing sectors of the economy. Providing workers with services – representation, bargaining – is an essential function of trade unions. However, there is now an increased recognition of the important contribution that 'organizing unionism' can make to promoting union revitalization (Simms et al, 2013; Simms, 2015; Holgate, 2021a). The 'organizing unionism' model originated in the US but was subsequently taken up by some UK unions and is apparent in many other European countries too (Ibsen and Tapia, 2017). The model puts an emphasis on building trade union organization among workers in non-union parts of the economy – such as young workers and migrant workers – who, while often experiencing employment disadvantage and vulnerability, have often been neglected by trade unions. 'Organizing unionism' is characterized by the deployment of dedicated, professional organizers and the use of innovative techniques designed to engage workers, including mobilization around specific grievances (Simms et al, 2013; McAlevey, 2020) – see, for example, the successful organizing of low-paid, migrant cleaning workers in the US as a result of the Justice for Janitors campaign (Erickson et al, 2002).

The use of the 'organizing unionism' model has enabled some trade unions to attract new members, expand their reach and enhance their organizational capabilities in a way that contributes to union revitalization. However, some caution is needed. It is important not to exaggerate the impact of 'organizing unionism': there is little evidence that it has done much to address the decline in unionization in settings – the US and UK in particular – where employer hostility to trade unions is widespread (Kelly, 2015). By no means have all unions embraced, in part, let alone in full, the 'organizing unionism' model. One major difficulty is that such an approach, if it is to be effective, requires a process of empowerment, with workers and grassroots union activists themselves setting their own priorities and objectives for building unionization and formulating the means of achieving them (McAlevey, 2016; McAlevey, 2020).

Questions of power, though, have largely been ignored by union leaders when developing worker organizing campaigns. The 'organizing unionism' model has not been accompanied by the kinds of changes in culture and strategic union leadership necessary for rebuilding trade union power. Instead of being used as a means of devolving power to trade union members, who are thus empowered to engage in activism and build union power in workplaces, 'organizing unionism' tends to be used as a bureaucratic tool for managing them and rendering them supine (Holgate, 2021a).

One prominent benefit of the unions' focus on organizing is that it is associated with efforts to expand trade unionism among workers in precarious forms of employment who were previously considered difficult to unionize. Trade unions have increasingly sought to organize, represent and campaign on behalf of such workers, demonstrating how unionization can moderate and challenge precarity (Keune and Pedaci, 2020; Carver and Doellgast, 2021; O'Brady, 2021). Workers in the platform economy can be sceptical about the benefits of, or even the need for, union representation, on the basis that identifying as independent contractors, and to some extent viewing themselves as entrepreneurs, renders collective organization inappropriate or even undesirable (Wood et al, 2018). Yet there is some good evidence that platform workers, such as the food couriers studied by Tassinari and Maccarrone (2020), hold solidaristic values, making them open to collective methods for advancing their interests as workers, even if they differ from conventional forms of trade union action.

This directs our attention towards how trade unionism is evolving in ways that reflect changing work patterns and a more diverse workforce in order to be more responsive to workers and their interests. The process of union revitalization, then, involves greater diversity and fluidity of organizational forms. In the UK, a new breed of grassroots trade union has emerged, the most prominent being the Independent Workers' Union of Great Britain (IWGB), which is concerned with organizing, representing and mobilizing workers – often migrant workers – in low-paid and precarious forms of employment with online labour platforms or as contract cleaners, using a combination of litigation and direct action, including protests (Cant, 2020). Just how novel or distinctive unions like the IWGB, which often aspire to develop collective bargaining relationships with employing organizations, actually are is open to question. While their activities have attracted considerable attention compared with traditional, mainstream trade unions, the membership of such 'independent' unions remains small.

As part of their revitalization efforts, some trade unions have sought to widen their membership constituencies by organizing migrant workers (Holgate, 2021a). In doing so, a key issue concerns the necessity of not just seeking to engage with such workers in their workplaces but also to build relationships and be active within the communities they inhabit (Alberti, 2016). The concept of 'community unionism' refers to the ways in which unions and other worker-based organizations support, represent and mobilize people in particular communities, based not just on the geographical places where they live and work but also their social networks and relationships, arising from shared interests and identities (McBride and Greenwood, 2009). In some cases, unions themselves, such as Unite in the UK, with its community membership scheme, have developed their own community-based arrangements (Holgate, 2021b). In the US, so-called 'alt-labour' organizations (Eidelson, 2013), such as immigrant worker centres (Fine, 2006), support and campaign on behalf of workers in particular communities unions. The concept of 'community unionism' also captures the activities of coalitions between unions and community organizations (Tattersall, 2010). A good example of such coalition working is the involvement of trade unions in broader, community-based living wage campaigns (Heery et al, 2018).

Attempts by trade unions to build 'coalitional power' with community organizations and broader social movements can help to promote union revitalization (Ibsen and Tapia, 2017; Geelan, 2022). Yet the durability of such coalitions is questionable (Holgate, 2015). Cultural differences can generate tensions. Whereas unions tend to operate in a rather bureaucratic way, the cultures of community organizations and social movements are, as 'adhocracies', generally more informal, fluid and relationship-based (Tapia, 2013). Nevertheless, the development of community unionism, as a notable manifestation of union revitalization efforts, symbolizes how trade unions have sought to respond to the crisis in which they have found themselves – a product of declining membership, weakened bargaining power, challenges from employers and hostile government policy – by demonstrating their valuable role in representing and advancing working people's interests and promoting good jobs and decent work.

Stronger, revitalized trade unions have a key part to play in tackling the problems in contemporary work and employment relations – a surfeit of low-paid and precarious jobs, excessive commodification pressures and limited worker voice in particular. To be sure, the unions have been marginalized under conditions of neoliberal capitalism and have often struggled to adapt to changes in work and employment and demonstrate their relevance. Nevertheless, their growing popularity (Frangi et al, 2017; Brenan, 2021) is predicated on a belief that trade unions matter. This was particularly evident during the COVID-19 pandemic. Moreover, union efforts to address the climate emergency point to the major contribution they can make to enabling a 'just transition'.

COVID-19 and the trade unions

The experience of unions during the COVID-19 pandemic, a major epidemiological crisis, demonstrates the contribution they make to supporting, protecting and advancing workers' interests and thus the imperative for a revitalized trade union movement. According to the International Labour Organization (ILO) (2021a: 19), trade unions 'worldwide did and continue to do outstanding work throughout the pandemic in supporting their members and the population at large', including by formulating and influencing policies designed to protect jobs and livelihoods and using their bargaining relationships with employers to mandate improvements in health and safety at work. Yet there were some prominent instances of employers and governments using the pandemic as an opportunity to promote a resurgent anti-union agenda. In some South East Asian countries, Cambodia and Indonesia for example, the response to COVID-19 was marked by a notable degree of union repression (Ford and Ward, 2021). However, the most egregious anti-union offensives took place in the US, where a series of employers took advantage of pandemic-related disruption in their efforts to roll-back organized labour (Sainato, 2020).

In general, though, the experience of the pandemic highlighted just how important trade unions are. For example, by virtue of their engagement in social dialogue – interactions with governments, state agencies and employers' bodies – unions contributed to strengthening employment protection measures in a period when many people's jobs and livelihoods were threatened by the measures introduced to combat the pandemic, such as temporary business closures (ILO, 2021a). According to Brandl (2023: 167), the 'outbreak of the COVID-19 pandemic in early 2020 led to an unprecedented increase in tripartite social dialogue in many industrialized countries in the world'. Action was evident in two notable areas. One was the design and operation of job retention and income retention schemes, particularly in Europe (Müller et al, 2022), as discussed in Chapter 4. In the UK, for example, the Trades Union Congress (TUC) played a major part in urging the government to adopt a job retention scheme – what became the Coronavirus Job Retention Scheme or 'furlough' – and influencing its content (Ewing and Hendy, 2020).

Second, more generally, unions were often successful in ensuring that protections covered workers in non-standard forms of employment, such as the self-employed (ILO, 2021a). Trade union participation in social dialogue during the pandemic mattered in two other respects: first, the contribution they made to influencing occupational health and safety policy; and, second, their ability to shape policy responses relating to changing working patterns, particularly working-from-home arrangements (ILO, 2021b, 2022a).

While both the quantity and quality of social dialogue involving unions in general clearly increased as a result of COVID-19, there was some notable variation between countries. In Greece, for example, the extent of social dialogue was limited and its quality weak, much like before the pandemic (Eurofound, 2021; ILO, 2022a). Moreover, beyond Europe the role of social dialogue was less evident. In Australia, efforts to enhance cooperation and dialogue between unions, the government and employers when COVID-19 struck quickly dissipated (Gavin, 2022).

Trade unions also played a key role during the pandemic by regulating work and employment relationships in workplaces – engaging with managers to protect workers and advance their interests. This was particularly apparent when it came to health and safety matters, with unions and union representatives playing an important part in ensuring that proper risk assessments were undertaken for workers who were still required to attend their normal workplaces and that sufficient personal protective equipment (PPE) was provided (ILO, 2021b, 2022a). There is some good evidence from the food industry in the UK, where workers had to go in to work as usual because they were deemed 'essential', of the role that effective union workplace representation plays in reducing risks to such workers and protecting their health and safety (Cai et al, 2022). In the US, a stronger trade union presence reduced a worker's likelihood of dying from COVID-19. Unions, then, 'do indeed save lives' (Soares and Berg 2023: 16). A key contribution of the TUC in the UK has been to assert the importance of 'long COVID' – the enduring and often debilitating effects of infection – as an occupational disease which affects many people (TUC, 2023b).

Throughout the pandemic the importance of the unions could also be seen in the resurgence of labour activism which was evident. The early period of the pandemic in the spring of 2020 saw a series of strikes, walk-outs and protests by 'essential' workers in several parts of the US economy, including Amazon warehouses, who were demanding higher pay and better health and safety protection as the number of COVID-19 cases soared (Selyukh, 2020). Collective action by workers, organized by trade unions, over the issue of inadequate PPE and because of other health and safety concerns was also evident in the UK, such as in food processing plants for example (ITV News, 2020). The UK government agency responsible for handling driving licences – the Driver and Vehicle Licensing Agency, based in Swansea, Wales – was affected by a series of strikes because of workers' concerns that inadequate health and safety protections had been responsible for the large number of COVID-19 cases that had broken out on the site (Lewis, 2021).

Around the world, frontline workers, those responsible for delivering essential services – in food production, distribution and retailing, healthcare and social care for example – were motivated to take action and engage in conflict as a consequence of the pandemic either because of a lack of adequate health and safety protections, insufficient pay, increased workloads or a combination of all three. According to the ILO (2022a: 150): 'Disruptions and labour protests threatened the continuity of services in many parts of the world. Dissatisfaction with wages, insufficient PPE and work intensity were frequent triggers of work stoppages and other forms of labour unrest among frontline workers throughout 2020 and 2021.'

Research on 90 countries by Trapmann et al (2022) identified 3,873 examples of labour protests by healthcare workers and 466 examples of labour protests by retail workers between March 2020 and June 2021. Their key demands included higher pay but also concerned issues relating to the supply of PPE, working hours, labour shortages and workloads. According to Trapmann et al (2022: 5): '[K]ey workers have raised their concerns about their working conditions through different forms of protest, including demonstrations, petitions, "sick outs", public campaigning, or lobbying alongside conventional forms of strike action'. All this demonstrates how on 'a global scale, the experience of the pandemic seems to have shone a rather more positive light on trade unions than has hitherto been the case' (ILO, 2021b: xi).

In the context of the pandemic, there is a clear sense that the unions have looked to build back stronger, something which involves mobilizing to challenge employers and governments and engaging in activism. Perhaps the most obvious manifestation of trade union revitalization since 2020 is the resurgent labour activism and the conflict it produced. In a study of ride-hailing workers, Maffie (2022: 215) demonstrates how the COVID-19 pandemic 'created a global shock to the employer–employee relationship, where the power imbalance between labour and management became clear as employers placed their interests ahead of workers', with the result that workers became more interested in collective organization and representation.

Trade unions as environmental and climate actors

A powerful trade union movement is essential if the climate crisis is to be tackled effectively. While the role of trade unions as environmental and climate actors has often been neglected, there is now a clear understanding of just how important the unions are to addressing the climate emergency (Snell and Fairbrother, 2011; Hampton, 2018; Stevis et al, 2018; Räthzel et al, 2021). As Räthzel and Uzzell (2013: 5) argue, 'union movements across the world have been moving fast to incorporate a concern for nature by taking on climate change as an issue of trade union policies'.

There are some good reasons why trade union engagement with the climate crisis is essential. For one thing, there is a growing appreciation of just how important changes in production relations are when it comes to effective environmental and climate action measures, something that unions, as organizations of workers, can influence (Räthzel and Uzzell, 2011). Trade union involvement can ensure that workers are not only represented in efforts to enable a 'just transition' but that they also play an active part in contributing to such a process, rendering it more effective as a result. The role of unions in contributing to the 'greening' of organizations and workplaces has become more widely understood (Farnhill, 2018). Moreover, unions themselves have an interest in promoting environmental and climate action, particularly by ensuring that 'green' jobs are genuinely 'good', unionized jobs.

Yet the role of trade unions in addressing the climate emergency is by no means straightforward, not least because of the tensions that can arise between the imperative to promote green policy action on the one hand and demands to protect workers' jobs, particularly in 'dirty' industries such as coal mining, on the other (Baldry and Hyman, 2022). Unions may find themselves torn between pressure from members to preserve jobs, especially given the realities of the cost-of-living crisis and the crisis of work, and their commitment to sustainability policies, such as the Green New Deal.

Trade union involvement in environmental issues is not new. The development of 'labour environmentalism' in the US in the 1970s and 1980s signalled the efforts of some unions to engage in environmental matters (Stevis, 2011; Stevis and Felli, 2015; Stevis et al, 2018). Moreover, as Felli (2014: 373) observes, union concerns with workers' health, safety and well-being can 'spill over into broader demands for environmental alliances with community-based movements'. One prominent manifestation of just such a movement is the BlueGreen Alliance (BGA) in the US. Established in 2006 and regarded as 'probably one of the more sustained alliances between unions and environmentalists around the world' (Stevis, 2018), the BGA operates as a coalition of environmental organizations and trade unions, including the United Steelworkers. It seeks to reconcile economic growth with environmental improvements and action to tackle climate change through the promotion of 'good' – well-paid and unionized – 'green' jobs in areas such as clean energy production and transportation (Baldry and Hyman, 2022).

The increased engagement of international trade union organizations such as the International Trade Union Confederation (ITUC) and the European Trade Union Confederation (ETUC) with environmental and climate policy matters has been a further notable development (Snell and Fairbrother, 2010; Felli, 2014; ILO, 2018b). Within Europe, union bodies have made progress in incorporating green issues into processes of social dialogue with governments and employers' associations (Vitols et al, 2011; Felli, 2014; ETUC, 2018). In the UK, the TUC has been active in leading labour movement efforts to engage with environmental and climate matters (Hampton, 2018; TUC, 2019).

Trade union action not only involves engaging with policy makers but also encompasses efforts to shape employers' activities directly, particularly through so-called 'green bargaining' initiatives – see, for example, how union workplace representatives engage in activities designed to influence policy and practice within organizations (Farnhill, 2018). One prominent example from the UK is the TUC's 'Green Workplaces' project, which encompassed various joint union–management initiatives designed to stimulate environmental and climate action (Vitols et al, 2011; Hampton, 2018). There is clear evidence that union representatives' ideas and interventions have enabled organizations to significantly improve their environmental performance (Hampton, 2015). For example, the AB InBev brewery in South Wales saw a substantial reduction in water and electricity usage due to its participation in a Green Workplaces initiative, with the involvement and leadership of its workers central to the project's effectiveness (Goods, 2017).

The degree of such 'climate mobilization' symbolizes the important extent to which environmental and climate issues have become incorporated within the trade union bargaining agenda (Hampton, 2018). However, the overall impact of this kind of union activity is rather small. There is not much evidence that UK trade unions in general are particularly active when it comes to green issues (Holgate, 2021a). Moreover, unions are present in just a minority of private sector firms in the UK, limiting the extent of their potential contribution (Hyman and Baldry, 2022). Even where trade unions are present, employers can be wary of their involvement in environmental and climate activities given the perceived threat union activity poses to managerial control. As a consequence, managers often limit union representatives to making relatively modest, albeit not unimportant, contributions, on the basis that unions can act as a resource, helping to produce ideas and securing the support of employees for green initiatives. Given that such a modest 'technocratic' and 'apolitical' approach to engaging with environmental matters is consistent with a partnership orientation, whereby unions cooperate with, and are subordinate to, employers, there is little prospect of it contributing much to trade union revitalization overall. (Farnhill, 2018).

Trade unions, climate crisis and the 'just transition'

Trade unions are clearly important environmental and climate actors, even if their contribution to influencing organizational policy and practice can be rather modest. Potentially, though, as proponents of and active participants in a 'just transition' to a net-zero world, there is a notable opportunity for unions to affect how the climate emergency is tackled, with beneficial consequences for working people. In Chapter 4, we highlight the difficulties in relying on corporate efforts to manage employment relations for the purpose of enabling a 'just transition' and emphasized the importance of involving workers and unions (Klein, 2019). Indeed, the 'just transition' concept itself developed out of the US labour environmentalism movement and the growing engagement of unions with environmental issues (Felli, 2014; Stevis and Felli, 2015; Galgóczi, 2020).

In relation to climate change, the 'just transition' policy was advocated by international trade union organizations at the 1997 Conference of the Parties (CoP) meeting in Kyoto, Japan, referenced in the 2010 CoP agreement and finally accepted, in what Galgóczi (2020) calls a 'major success' for the unions, in the 2015 Paris CoP agreement (Stevis and Felli, 2015; Markey and McIvor, 2019). Campaigning activity by trade unions, particularly the advocacy of the ITUC, has ensured that workers' interests are prominent in global action to address the climate emergency and that unions should have a part to play in managing the shift to a low-carbon economy.

With this in mind, the 'just transition' approach comprises two integral elements. One is the necessity of developing 'green' jobs which are genuinely 'good' jobs, in the sense of work which is not just environmentally sustainable but also offers a living wage, employment security, opportunities for skills enhancement and union representation (Stevis, 2013; TUC, 2019). For the ILO, social sustainability, in the sense of decent work, and environmental sustainability are inseparable. In its 'guidelines' on a 'just transition', the ILO emphasizes that the key elements of its Decent Work Agenda, '[s]ocial dialogue, social protection, rights at work and employment – are indispensable building blocks of sustainable development and must be at the centre of policies for strong, sustainable and inclusive growth and development' (ILO, 2015: 3). The ILO also maintains that '[a] just transition for all towards an environmentally sustainable economy … needs to be well managed and contribute to the goals of decent work for all, social inclusion and the eradication of poverty' (ILO, 2015: 3).

In Chapter 4, we show that when employers' interests predominate many supposedly 'green' jobs are actually unhealthy, unsafe and exploitative. The second key element of the 'just transition', then, concerns the importance of involving workers and unions directly in designing and developing measures to promote greater sustainability and address the climate emergency (ILO, 2015; TUC, 2019; Markova, 2021; Hyman and Baldry, 2022). If 'green' jobs really are to be 'good' jobs, as they should be, then they need to be unionized jobs. Union representation can do more than simply ensure that workers' interests are represented and their voices heard in the process of decarbonization. It potentially allows workers to be 'protagonists' in, rather than 'victims' of, change (Saltmarsh, 2021: 100). According to the TUC:

> The workers and communities across the UK most affected by the move towards low-carbon industries must have a central voice in how

this is implemented. The best and most obvious way to achieve this is by working with trade unions. Trade unions were founded in the heat of the last industrial revolution to represent workers, and remain the best way to ensure that workers [sic] interests are protected throughout any period of industrial change. (TUC, 2019: 7)

An effective 'just transition', then, depends upon the involvement of trade unions as organizations that advocate for workers and represent their interests. Importantly, though, union interventions need to be sensitive to, and driven by, the priorities and aspirations of workers in local communities themselves. It is they who best understand the issues and challenges for jobs arising from the push to decarbonize, and what responses would be effective, depending upon the setting (Snell and Fairbrother, 2011).

From a trade union perspective, the key benefit of the 'just transition' concept is that it offers a means of reconciling two potentially competing imperatives – the desirability of addressing the climate emergency, on the one hand, and pressure to protect workers' jobs, especially those based in 'dirty', environmentally damaging sectors, on the other. There is not necessarily a trade-off between unions' environmental and job protection objectives in the sense that they are not irreconcilable, but they can lead to tensions and create antagonisms (Snell and Fairbrother, 2011; Goods, 2017). Thomas and Doerflinger (2020: 384) describe these tensions as the 'jobs-versus-environment dilemma'.

For many unions, the problem is particularly acute because they represent workers in environmentally 'dirty' industries where effective action to mitigate environmental pollution and reduce carbon emissions would result in plant closures and substantial job losses. In Poland, for example, unions have opposed the rationalization of the coal mining industry because of the job losses it would cause (Galgóczi, 2020; Thomas and Doerflinger, 2020). Union leaderships can be reluctant to emphasize environmental and climate advocacy and campaigning because of a concern that it would be opposed by their members. This is despite evidence that trade union members are generally more supportive of climate action than non-members (Ringqvist, 2022).

Given that traditional jobs in 'dirty', carbon-intensive industries are generally far more likely to be unionized than those in new, 'green' sectors, it is easy to understand trade unions' concerns (Vitols et al, 2011; Thomas and Doerflinger, 2020). Since the power base of unions is often located within older, more polluting sectors, it is difficult for them to support decarbonization because of the threat this poses to their members' jobs (Snell and Fairbrother, 2011). This has been a particularly notable difficulty in the Global South, where workers, and their unions, often oppose efforts to mitigate climate change in settings where economic growth, and thus jobs and livelihoods, are dependent upon carbon-intensive industries. In the countries of the Global South the concept of the 'just transition' is viewed with suspicion. It is perceived as an attempt by the richer Global North, which is less reliant upon economic growth powered by fossil fuels, to prejudice attempts by countries in the Global South to improve their prosperity by growing their economies and increasing their competitiveness (Stevis et al, 2018).

The experience of South Africa is instructive. Leading unions there were prominent supporters of the need for a 'just transition'. However since the 2000s, the perceived threat that decarbonization poses to jobs in the dominant mining sector, in a country with very high levels of unemployment and poverty, prompted a shift in emphasis towards a defensive orientation which privileges protecting existing jobs (Cock, 2021). For Sikwebu and Aroun (2021: 61), it was the failure of the 'energy transition to deliver on the promises of jobs, training and economic empowerment' that made workers 'sceptical or … turned them against the proposed shift to a low-carbon economy'.

In settings where trade unions are already in crisis because of declining membership, it is entirely rational for them to react defensively to the perceived threat posed to their existing constituencies by the economic and industrial challenges of decarbonization (Baldry and Hyman, 2022). Unions also have a concern that pressing firms to reduce their carbon footprint will increase their costs, making them less economically competitive and giving non-unionized competitors, which offer lower pay and inferior conditions, an unfair advantage. In the US, for example, the United Auto Workers (UAW) union worries that the greater costs associated with producing 'greener' vehicles threatens the competitive position of the major manufacturers with which it has collective bargaining agreements – General Motors, Ford and Stellantis (formerly Chrysler) – to the benefit of non-unionized foreign producers (Stevis, 2018). In this context, the 2023 efforts by the UAW to secure substantial improvements to its members' pay through industrial action were all the more notable.

Workers in new, so-called 'green' jobs generally lack union representation. Chapter 4 highlights the oppressive working conditions in Tesla, a firm which has pioneered the development of sustainable vehicles. The company has also opposed union representation for its workers, exhibiting a pronounced anti-union approach (Minchin, 2021). Given the hostility towards trade unions in 'green' sectors of the economy, it is easy to understand their concern with defending jobs in existing areas of membership strength, even if these are in industrial sectors with high carbon footprints. Unions are also duty-bound to represent their members' interests. In general, US energy workers in old, high-carbon sectors enjoy relatively well-paid and secure jobs and good conditions because of the bargaining efforts of their trade unions over many years. New, 'green' jobs in the renewable energy sector, though, are largely non-unionized – indeed employers often keenly pursue union avoidance strategies – and fail to offer workers comparable benefits (Vachon, 2021). This demonstrates why workers, and the unions that represent them, can be ambivalent about action to improve environmental sustainability and tackle the climate crisis.

When it comes to environmental and climate policy, notable divisions exist between and even within trade unions (Stevis, 2013; 2018; Baldry and Hyman, 2022). Unions' responses to the climate crisis vary according to the sector in which they operate (Räthzel and Uzzell, 2011). In the UK, it is trade unions that represent workers in parts of the economy which generate low-carbon emissions – public sector and education unions for example – which have been at the forefront of calling for action to mitigate climate change, including calls to curb airport expansion. Unions which represent aviation workers, though, support increases in airport capacity (Hampton, 2015; Markey and McIvor, 2019).

Within the US labour movement, there is a clear division between public sector and service sector unions, who emphasize the adverse effects climate change is having on their members and their communities, and energy unions, operating in industries with high carbon footprints, who worry about the adverse impact of efforts to tackle the climate crisis on their members' jobs and livelihoods (Vachon, 2021). Internal divisions exist within unions themselves. While union leaderships can be prominent advocates of the necessity of a 'just transition', it is local trade union representatives, operating in specific workplaces and communities, who must deal with the consequences (Galgóczi, 2020).

Conclusion

During the early 2020s, the COVID-19 crisis demonstrated the importance of unions and the valuable contribution that they make to supporting, protecting and advancing workers' interests, particularly when they are prepared to engage in contention and thus challenge employers and governments. Clearly, as this chapter demonstrates, trade unions matter, particularly when they are powerful. However, the unions have been in something of a crisis themselves, a function of falling membership levels and declining bargaining power in neoliberal settings which privilege employers' flexibility. The weakness of the unions has contributed to the broader crisis of work that is the focus of this book. Stronger unions would enhance workers' bargaining power and give them greater voice in, and influence over, their jobs. Through their efforts to advance decent working conditions, and by challenging commodification pressures, powerful trade unions can do much to challenge neoliberalization and the crisis of work it has induced. They can also help to facilitate a genuinely 'just' transition to a decarbonized economy by ensuring that workers not only have their interests represented but are also active participants in the process of economic and industrial change which is required if the climate emergency is to be tackled properly. This both demands and, in turn, would help to enable, a renewed trade union movement, one marked by resurgent grassroots activism and which, in mobilizing for greater economic, social and climate justice, is prepared to engage in contention. By 'building back stronger', union revitalization of this kind, based on enhancing workers' collective bargaining power, would do much to resolve the crisis of work. In the aftermath of the pandemic, the mounting 'cost-of-living crisis' further demonstrates just how important trade unions are when it comes to action to defend workers' interests, given the increasing number of strikes and episodes of labour conflict which have been evident – see Chapter 8.

7

Crises at Work: Broader Dimensions

Introduction

In other chapters, we explain why we believe that various crises which are *at* work – the adverse consequences of neoliberalization, the challenges posed by environmental degradation and the climate emergency and the implications of the COVID-19 pandemic – have contributed to a crisis *of* work. In this chapter, we place this crisis of work in broader perspective, centred on its economic and political dimensions. As we explain, the crisis of work we are concerned with in this book intersects with various other crises, in particular those arising from a dysfunctional economy and labour market and the unstable, turbulent and volatile nature of contemporary politics. The important point about these various crises is that they are not just consequences of the troublesome nature of paid employment but also contribute to it, fuelling the antagonism that lies at the heart of the contemporary crisis of work.

The first substantive topic we focus on in this chapter concerns the economic dimension of the crisis of work, drawing particularly on evidence from the UK. We highlight the dysfunctional nature of the economy and the labour market, pointing to the connections between economic stagnation, labour shortages, weak earnings growth and the 'cost-of-living crisis' that escalated during the early 2020s. The crisis of work is thus tied up with the vicissitudes of a neoliberal, overly financialized economic model which is inimical to sustainable growth.

We then move on to consider the crisis-ridden nature of contemporary politics, including the crisis of democracy, and its intersections with the troublesome nature of work. Generally, governments have played a notable part in advancing neoliberalization, particularly in relation to work and employment relations. But workers' expectations of greater protection, particularly in the context of COVID-19, have challenged the legitimacy of a neoliberal model that favours deregulated labour markets, employers' flexibility and weak trade unions. The consequence is a more volatile and turbulent political environment, one where support for traditional left-of-centre social democracy has waned. Moreover, 'populist' far-right politics has increasingly thrived in settings where, because of neoliberalization, working people feel more insecure and threatened.

Economic stagnation, the labour market and the crisis of work

The period of stagnant and uneven growth since the 2007–8 global financial crisis is perhaps the most prominent manifestation of the troublesome economic landscape. Figure 7.1 shows the annual percentage growth in UK gross domestic product (GDP) for the period between 2003 and 2022. The figure illustrates the notable fall in GDP that occurred in 2008–9 – marking the 'Great Recession' that followed the global financial crisis. During the 2010s, the UK experienced a very weak economic recovery by historical standards. The collapse in GDP in 2020 was a consequence of the restrictive economic measures enacted to tackle COVID-19, after which growth rebounded – briefly – in 2021–22.

However, the economic recovery from the pandemic soon dissipated. Although on the face of it the UK's headline growth rate of 4.3 per cent in 2022 seemed healthy, this was mainly a consequence of the continued bounce back from the economic difficulties arising from COVID-19 and was concentrated in the early part of that year. In the context of escalating inflation, the associated cost-of-living crisis, labour shortages and a wave of labour conflict (see Chapter 8), UK GDP growth deteriorated markedly during the course of 2022, while 2023 effectively saw no economic growth at all, as, according to initial estimates, the country entered a technical

Figure 7.1: UK annual GDP growth (%), 2003–22

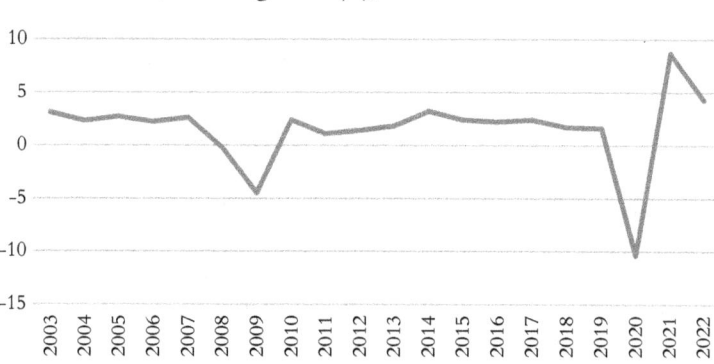

Source: Office for National Statistics

'recession' – as measured by at least two successive quarters of economic contraction (OBR, 2023; Elliott, 2024b). While the UK's economic performance in the early 2020s may not have been quite as poor as first thought, it was inferior to most other advanced economies (Harari, 2023). High inflation, and the rises in interest rates enacted to combat it, contributed to ongoing economic stagnation during 2023 (Inman, 2023b). Overall, the period between 2019 and 2023 amounted to 'five years of lost economic growth' (NIESR, 2023), exacerbating the longer-term economic stagnation in the UK. In the 15 years following the 2007–8 global financial crash, annual UK GDP growth averaged just 1.2 per cent, less than half that (2.8 per cent) during the 15-year period that preceded it (Resolution Foundation, 2024). The country is a lot poorer than it would have been if the pre-crash growth trend had been maintained.

The period of low growth and economic stagnation since the global financial crisis is not the only problem. Any economic growth that has occurred has been uneven, disproportionally benefitting relatively wealthy owners of assets, particularly property, in affluent parts of the UK, such as rural and suburban areas of South East England. One consequence of this has been increasing income inequality and a rise in relative deprivation (Resolution Foundation, 2022). There are pronounced regional differences in GDP growth across the UK.

Why has the UK's economic record been so poor, and what have been the consequences for work and employment? Globally, the propagation of neoliberal policies would seem to be a major cause of low and uneven growth since the 1980s. But the problems in the UK were amplified by the presence of a highly financialized economic model, based on the ownership and exploitation of assets and the expansion of private and public debt (Calafati et al, 2023). Its consequences, notably increased turbulence and instability, were particularly evident in the period following the global financial crisis as Conservative-led governments sought to uphold the privileges of rentiers (Lavery, 2019; Christophers, 2020). The focus on asset price inflation, including property, meant there was limited investment in both capital and people.

During the first half of the 2010s, the UK government's emphasis on austerity contributed to economic stagnation. It believed that rapid action was necessary to reduce government expenditure in order to reduce the budget deficit that had arisen because of the global financial crisis and subsequent economic recession. The UK was not alone in pursuing such an approach. It was widely propagated elsewhere in Europe because of structural problems in the Eurozone. For the UK Conservatives, though, austerity measures were less of a necessity and more of an ideological choice, based on a belief that deficit reduction was essential for securing the increased confidence of global financial markets and reducing the size of the state. However, in sucking demand out of the economy, austerity dampened economic growth (Tooze, 2018; Wren-Lewis, 2018). One of the principal consequences was a greater degree of political turbulence, as the 2016 vote to leave the EU and its aftermath illustrated. Even before the dramatic adverse impact of COVID-19 in 2020, economic growth in the UK had been weakened by the uncertainties arising from Brexit, including reduced prospects for investment.

A cursory look at the labour market data during the 2010s might give the impression that the UK economy was thriving in the period between the global financial crisis and the advent of the COVID-19 pandemic. In 2019, the official rate of unemployment fell to its lowest level – under 4 per cent – since the mid-1970s, and the number of people in employment rose to over 32 million, the highest on record. While the initial impact of COVID-19 was to cause a rise in the official rate of unemployment – to 5.2 per cent of the workforce at the end of 2020 – it subsequently fell again, to 3.7 per cent in the summer of 2022, the lowest rate for some 50 years (Strauss and Parker, 2022).

However, the headline level of 'unemployment' omits millions of people who are not actively seeking work, because of ill-health, for example, or because they have caring responsibilities – when they are aware of employers' reluctance to accommodate their needs. We also need to be aware of the phenomenon of 'underemployment', the incidence of which grew during the 2010s (Bell and Blanchflower, 2021). This encompasses involuntary part-time workers (people who would prefer a full-time position) and those who prefer part-time and other flexible arrangements, including zero-hours contracts (see Chapter 3), but who would like to increase their hours – and thus their pay.

Moreover, much of the employment growth during the 2010s involved a surfeit of 'bad' jobs (Blanchflower, 2019), marked by low pay and insecurity – a consequence of a labour market in which employers' flexibility, for the purpose of managing labour as efficiently as possible, is privileged – see Chapters 3 and 4. This points to the important ways in which economic stagnation intersects with the troublesome nature of work. Because they are often low paid and not all that productive in conventional economic terms, the proliferation of 'flexible' jobs during the 2010s helped to impede growth (Calafati et al, 2023). At the same time, the dysfunctional nature of the UK's financialized market economy, one that puts an onus on short-term cost savings to satisfy the interests of rentiers and financial institutions, necessitates using forms of employment which seek to treat labour as a commodity.

This highlights the important extent to which economic dysfunction is not simply a product of low growth. Importantly, it reflects a lack of *sustainable* growth, marked by efforts to share the proceeds of economic development more widely and equitably in a way that values workers, enriches the environment and would help to mitigate the climate emergency. Instead, economic activity in general, and managing workers in particular, are undertaken for the purpose of deriving immediate financial benefits for the owners of capital. This has invidious consequences for employment, of course, as is evident throughout this book; but it also contributes to the economic stagnation and dysfunction that has been evident since the 2000s.

An unhealthy and uncaring economy?

The intersection between economic dysfunction and the troublesome nature of contemporary work is evident in respect of health and social care. As already mentioned in this chapter, many people are excluded from employment because of health conditions or caring responsibilities that make them unattractive to employers. In Chapter 4, we draw attention to the unhealthy nature of much contemporary work, something that was particularly exposed during the COVID-19 pandemic. There is an important consequence of this in that it contributes to the broader crisis of ill-health in the UK, something which, in turn, has further troublesome implications for the economy and the labour market. By the end of 2023, record numbers of people in the UK, around 2.8 million, were classified as 'economically inactive' – that is, not in paid employment or actively seeking it – because of ill-health, an increase of 700,000 since the start of the pandemic (Elliott, 2024a).

Chronic pain and mental health conditions are the two most common causes of economic inactivity, with many affected by multiple conditions (Burn-Murdoch, 2022). COVID-19 has also clearly had an impact. Many people's health has been debilitated by conditions associated with the phenomenon of 'long COVID' (Marshall, 2023). For others with longer-term health conditions, the experience of being furloughed or of working from home during the pandemic led to them becoming more disconnected from paid work and leaving the labour market (Stewart, 2022). Long-term health conditions have a particularly marked impact among older workers, with 1.6 million of those aged 50 or over unable to work due to ill-health (Hill and Partington, 2023).

The growth in inactivity has aggravated the UK's economic difficulties by fuelling labour shortages, impairing productivity, contributing to inflation and exacerbating the 'cost-of-living crisis' – see later on in this chapter (Elliott, 2023). While inactivity has clearly been driven by the rise in long-term, and more complex, health problems, the unhealthy nature of much contemporary work, and the lack of interest among employers in implementing measures to promote workers' well-being and making the necessary adjustments to accommodate people with health conditions, have played a notable part too.

We also need to recognize the influence on the economy and labour market of a profound social policy problem, one which has become particularly acute since COVID-19, namely the delays and difficulties people encounter when trying to get health conditions treated. Excessive pressures on an insufficiently funded health service mean that people have to wait longer for treatment. A squeeze on funding has made it difficult for health employers to recruit and retain staff. High levels of sickness absence within the National Health Service (NHS) itself, a function of an overworked and often exhausted workforce, especially since the pandemic, have exacerbated resourcing difficulties. NHS waiting lists ballooned during the pandemic and its aftermath: in October 2023, the waiting list for treatment in England and Wales rose to nearly 7.8 million – a record number. Delays in treatment for health conditions not only impair people's capacity to be economically active and engage in, and benefit from, paid work opportunities but also limit their ability to live individually and socially fulfilling lives.

The unhealthy nature of work, society, the economy and the environment is interconnected and mutually reinforcing. Too much contemporary work has profoundly adverse consequences for health and well-being, putting greater pressure on the health service, which is less able to cope as a result, exacerbating delays to treatment. In turn, this impairs people's ability to lead full and active lives and make valued contributions to society, while also fuelling economic inactivity, labour shortages and economic underperformance in general. Employers often grouse about economic inactivity and staff shortages and the difficulties these cause them. But they would do well to reflect on their own responsibility for the crisis of ill-health. Under conditions of intensified neoliberalization, work has been organized largely on their terms, predicated on the desirability of securing efficiency savings in an environment where employment has become more precarious, labour more commodified, workers lack effective protections and trade unions are weak.

One of the biggest challenges facing contemporary societies, and one which is too often neglected by policy makers, involves ensuring that people who need support from others – children, people with disabilities and older people – receive the care they need to lead dignified lives. Ageing populations, especially in the UK and other Global North countries, are generating increased demand for care provision as health conditions common among older people, such as dementia, become more prevalent. Because 'care' in general involves personal and social relationships, it is not reducible to 'care work' (Dowling, 2022).

Nevertheless, care labour, whether paid (by workers) or unpaid (by family members or friends), is becoming ever more important both socially and economically. The provision of high-quality social care is critical to enabling people who need help and support from others to lead dignified and fulfilling lives. In addition to being socially and ethically necessary, a well-resourced and sustainable system of social care offers some important economic benefits. Working-age adults, whose care needs are supported effectively, are better able to participate in the labour market, giving them greater financial independence and thus improving the supply of labour.

Yet there are some profound difficulties with the system of care in general, and the organization and remuneration of care work in particular, that hamper its contribution to sustainable economic growth. Funding constraints, low pay and staffing shortages are a function of the highly marketized and financialized nature of social care (Dowling, 2022) – see Chapter 3. In terms of its intersection with the crisis of work, there is a further dimension of social care provision that should not be overlooked. This concerns the role of unpaid carers. As we explain in Chapter 1, this book is primarily focused on paid work, concerning jobs which are done by workers in return for wages or salaries. Yet undertaking unpaid caring activities also influences how people – mainly women – engage with the labour market.

The inadequacies of the social care system mean that a greater amount of responsibility for providing care falls to family members, especially women, adding to the obstacles that hamper their participation in the labour market and their advancement at work and thus reinforcing gender segregation and disadvantage (Busby and James, 2016). According to a survey of more than 4,000 women conducted in 2023 for the British Chambers of Commerce, two thirds of those with childcare responsibilities thought that their progression at work had been negatively affected because of the demands imposed by caring (Partington, 2023).

Women in particular are exposed to greater precarity because of the imperative to find jobs that offer the flexibility necessary to enable them to combine paid work with unpaid caring activities, jobs that are often low paid and insecure (Rubery et al, 2016). Not only is childcare provision in the UK very expensive; it is also in increasingly short supply, largely because nursery providers cannot recruit and retain sufficient numbers of staff and have sometimes even been forced to close (Marsh, 2023). A consequence of the resultant care gap is that working parents, especially women, are required to take time away from their jobs or reduce their hours of work in order to provide childcare. As well as the implications for gender disadvantage, this exacerbates labour shortages and constrains economic growth. It also contributes to the living standards difficulties already affecting many families, helping to fuel the 'cost-of-living crisis' – see later on in this chapter.

Excessive ill-health, an over-stretched health service and the inadequacies of the system of social care have made an important contribution to the dysfunctions in the UK economy and labour market. They hamper people's capacity to engage in paid employment, aggravating labour shortages – thus impeding economic growth and fuelling inflationary pressures. Moreover, the unhealthy and uncaring nature of the economy intersects with the troublesome nature of contemporary work in some important ways. In the UK's highly financialized market economy, a preference for short-term flexibility and low-paid employment over long-term investment in staff not only exacerbates economic and labour market inequalities but also contributes to the persistence of an economic growth model which fails to make the most of people's capabilities, lacks sustainability and, ultimately, compromises long-term prosperity.

The crisis of squeezed earnings

Relative economic stagnation in general, and the dearth of 'good' jobs in particular – those which are reasonably well paid, secure and offer scope for advancement – have made a major contribution to the crisis of stagnant earnings and compressed living standards. In the ten years following the global financial crisis, there was an unprecedented squeeze on wages – what Clarke and Gregg (2018: 11) describe as a 'decade of lost earnings growth'. When taking inflation into account, by 2023, following 'a decade and a half of pay stagnation', real wages had barely recovered to their 2007 level, leaving the average worker £11,000 worse off each year (Rawlinson, 2023). Historically, this was an unparalleled situation. For each decade between 1970 and 2007, wages rose by an average of 33 per cent; but during the 2010s there was no overall growth at all (Resolution Foundation, 2022).

What explains the failure of wages to grow in the period after the global financial crisis? In the public sector, austerity-driven funding cuts meant that earnings growth was constricted for government employees, teachers and health workers, among others. This caused severe difficulties in recruiting and retaining staff in key public services, resulting in labour shortages and constraining economic growth – for the reasons specified earlier in this chapter. More generally, weak and uneven economic growth played a notable part in suppressing wage levels. In a largely stagnant economy, employers can ill-afford to give workers pay rises. Compared to other large, advanced economies such as Germany, France and the US, the UK has had a poor productivity record since the global financial crisis. This reflects a lack of investment in capital (machinery and equipment) and people (training and skills development) (Resolution Foundation, 2022).

Given that rises in earnings are best funded by firms becoming more productive – increasing the output derived from each worker's input, in other words – the squeeze on wages was undoubtedly a consequence of meagre economic growth and low productivity. However, the experience of the

UK suggests the presence of a more complex set of connections between the labour market, productivity and wages. For one thing, poor productivity is not necessarily just a cause of squeezed earnings growth but can also be a consequence of it. Changes in the labour market, particularly the growth of a more flexible and disposable workforce, are associated with low-paying jobs – or at least jobs which offer limited prospects of much improvement in wages – that are not, in conventional terms, necessarily very productive. In this sense, low wages (or, rather, a surfeit of low-paid work) have contributed to the UK's productivity problem. The lack of real earnings growth reflects the climate of intensified neoliberalization, one where employers' flexibility is privileged, with labour disempowered and lacking in bargaining power. Calafati et al (2023) question the emphasis placed on raising productivity as a means of enabling economic growth, given the extent of the shift in the UK to a labour market based on low-wage, service sector jobs, which are difficult to make more productive. One important consequence of this shift has been the long-term fall in the share of economic output that goes to labour (in the form of wages) rather than capital (especially profits) from 57.3 per cent in 1979 to 48.7 per cent in 2019 (Calafati et al, 2023). Given this context, Calafati et al (2023: 64) contend that the 'dream of a high wage, high productivity economy is unrealisable and misconceived at the same time, as its non-realisation feeds into a sense of disappointment and cynicism that increasingly trouble our politics'.

The lack of real earnings growth in the aftermath of the global financial crisis has had some major adverse consequences, not least for household incomes, contributing to a profound 'living standards crisis' (Arnold et al, 2021). People on low and middle incomes in the UK have been particularly badly affected, leaving them substantially poorer than their equivalents in countries such as France and Germany and aggravating inequality. 'Having surged during the 1980s, and remained consistently high ever since, income inequality in the UK was higher than any other large European country in 2018' (Resolution Foundation, 2022: 9). A key driver of inequality is that while income growth during the 2010s was meagre, household wealth, driven by returns from the ownership of assets such as poverty, soared (Resolution Foundation, 2022). Taken together, weak economic growth, stagnant wages and increasing inequality are a 'toxic combination' (Resolution Foundation, 2022: 48), with ruinous effects for many working people and their families. One consequence is the 'crisis' of housing in the UK (Dorling, 2015; Tunstall, 2023) – see Chapter 5.

A particularly disturbing consequence of the crisis of squeezed earnings and diminishing living standards has been growing poverty in general, and in-work poverty in particular (Clark, 2023). Before the global financial crisis of 2007–8, poverty in the UK was generally a function of worklessness. However, while paid work generally acts as a buffer against poverty, it has become less effective at doing so. In 2022, some two thirds (68 per cent) 'of working-age adults in poverty lived in a household where at least one adult is in work' – a record high (JRF, 2022: 31). Over 4 million individuals in work in the UK are in poverty (Alston, 2019). Precarious work, and the irregular earnings and economic insecurity that often goes with it, is a key source of in-work poverty given the struggle workers often have in getting sufficient hours of work (JRF, 2022). It can also exacerbate the ill-effects of low pay, even among workers who hold multiple jobs yet often still have to rely on food banks for support (McBride and Smith, 2022). The economic insecurity experienced by workers in the platform economy means that it is often a considerable struggle for them to secure a sufficient living, and then only by taking exhaustingly long shifts (Clark, 2023).

Low wages and problems of securing sufficient hours of work mean that many workers have become reliant on in-work welfare benefits for support. Yet austerity-related cuts to public expenditure and a more punitive approach to people claiming, or trying to claim, welfare benefits have exacerbated the problem of in-work poverty (McBride and Smith, 2022). Low-paid workers in receipt of benefits can face severe penalties if they are not deemed to be sufficiently active in securing more working hours for themselves, jeopardizing their income and thus their livelihood (Wright and Dwyer, 2022). The related issues of low pay, squeezed earnings, diminished living standards and in-work poverty are the products of an overly financialized market economy under conditions of intensified neoliberalization. At the same time, though, their prevalence contributes to ongoing economic dysfunction, compromising efforts to promote sustainable development and address the growth-sapping problems of low investment, weak productivity and persistent inequality.

The 'cost-of-living crisis', 2021–23

The so-called 'cost-of-living crisis', which emerged in 2021 before escalating in 2022–23, aggravated the problems of low and stagnant earnings growth, squeezed living standards and in-work poverty. This specific crisis was a function of rapid increases in the price of food, energy and consumer goods. Rising prices during this period were a global phenomenon, caused by surging demand after pandemic-related economic restrictions were lifted, disruption to global supply chains and, from February 2022 onwards, the effects of the Russian war against Ukraine (Brewer et al, 2023). Yet the difficulties were particularly acute in the UK, with supply-side constraints, including labour shortages, and the disruptive consequences of Brexit making a large contribution to increasing prices. In October 2022, the annual level of inflation (the rate at which prices rise) reached 11.1 per cent, the highest in 40 years, while the price of food was 19 per cent higher in

March 2023 than it had been a year earlier (Harari et al, 2023). Although nominal ('take-home') wages grew rapidly during 2022 – at a faster rate than in over 30 years – they nonetheless lagged substantially behind inflation. As we have already seen, the decade of stagnant earnings during the 2010s meant that average real wages (taking inflation into account) had barely recovered to their pre-2007–8 global financial crisis level by 2022. Because of the surge in prices, though, real wages plummeted during 2022 – falling by 3.4 per cent – the largest decline on record, resulting in a pronounced – and escalating – cost-of-living crisis in the UK (Brewer et al, 2023; TUC, 2023a). Figure 7.2 shows that while real earnings grew substantially during much of 2021, as the economy opened up when the COVID-19 restrictions were eased, there was a marked decline in 2022 and early 2023 as cost-of-living pressures escalated.

The increasing cost of food and energy hit those on low incomes particularly badly, because such items account for a larger share of their expenditure. While cutting back on spending was a relatively common response to the escalating cost-of-living crisis, millions of UK households struggled to cope with rapidly rising prices. The least well-off households are expected to be 17 per cent poorer by the end of 2024 than they were in 2019 (NIESR, 2023). The financial consequences of this include increased levels of household debt, with more people falling behind on bills.

There were some profound social problems as a result. The cost-of-living crisis was associated with worsening of levels of mental and physical health and well-being. Over a quarter of people (27 per cent) reported not being able to heat their homes properly (Brewer et al, 2023). Perhaps the most disturbing aspect of the cost-of-living crisis was the increase in food poverty

Figure 7.2: Quarterly change (%) in UK real average weekly earnings, 2020–23

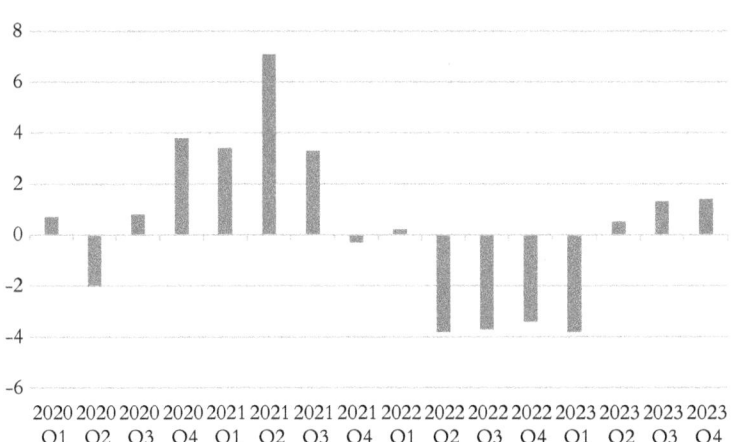

Source: Office for National Statistics

it generated, with a pronounced rise in the proportion of people going hungry (Brewer et al, 2023).

The level of inflation diminished during 2023, falling to 4 per cent by the end of that year, particularly because food and energy prices were not rising as quickly compared to the previous year. As a consequence, there was a resumption of – some modest – real earnings growth (see Figure 7.2). Nevertheless, average real earnings are not anticipated to return to their 2021 level until at least 2027 (Brewer et al, 2023). There are likely to be some notable long-term consequences of the lack of wage growth, not least the looming crisis of pensions as workers who are currently in their 30s and 40s near retirement. In previous generations, many people – particularly men – were able to rely on relatively generous occupational pension schemes which were calculated on the basis of their final salary (Major, 2023). Although workers in the UK now generally benefit from being automatically enrolled into workplace pension schemes, these are almost universally operated on a 'defined contribution' basis, which offer much more meagre payments in retirement (Otte, 2024).

Between 2021 and 2023, cost-of-living difficulties dominated the economic agenda in a specific context of rapidly rising prices. Yet we should not overlook the underlying, structural and long-term economic conditions which have contributed to stagnant real earnings and squeezed living standards. The magnitude of the cost-of-living crisis that emerged as the economy opened up following the COVID-19 pandemic may have been striking, but it was the symptom of a deeper malaise. For Calafati et al (2022), the cost-of-living crisis should be viewed as an 'episodic' event and situated in the context of the broader and longer-term 'crisis of household liveability' which has developed since the 2000s. Driven by intensified neoliberalization, it comprises a squeeze on earnings and living standards, but it also incorporates the much diminished quality of essential public services and the poor condition of social infrastructure – witness the impoverished state of social care for example – set against a context of austerity (Calafati et al, 2023).

The historically unprecedented squeeze on earnings after the global financial crisis reflected the nature of the UK's highly financialized economy, with the benefits of any growth disproportionately accruing to rentiers – owners of assets – rather than workers (Christophers, 2020). Viewed from this perspective, improving wage growth is not just a matter of greater investment to ensure that workers are more productive; it also involves addressing a model of neoliberal capitalist growth that depends upon the greater commodification of labour.

By privileging workers' interests and raising their bargaining power, the presence of stronger trade unions could help to deliver sustainable economic growth, with the benefits, including increased productivity levels and wages, being more equitably shared. Unfortunately, as we explain in Chapter 6, the bargaining power of organized labour has diminished markedly (Holgate, 2021a), particularly in highly liberalized market economies such as the US and UK. Before the early 2020s, when there was a resurgence of labour conflict (see Chapter 8), there was little pressure on employers to pay higher wages, especially in circumstances where workers were anxious about their job security (Blanchflower, 2019). The greater onus on employers to generate short-term financial value, based on efficiency savings, not only makes union avoidance more attractive but also encourages the use of precarious employment models and commodified labour arrangements in order to control costs (Grady and Simms, 2019; Gouzoulis, 2023).

Financialization also contributes to the diminished bargaining power of organized labour in another important respect. A feature of financialized economies, like that of the UK, is workers' greater reliance on private sources of credit. This has helped to maintain living standards in a period of low – or even no – wage growth. Yet increased dependency on such credit and the concomitant growth of personal and household indebtedness reduces the propensity of workers to engage in strike activity, because the consequences of losing their jobs are potentially more damaging (Gouzoulis, 2023). This is a notable illustration of how financialization disciplines workers, thus moderating their wage demands. Simply put, workers lack the collective muscle to ensure that a greater share of the returns from what economic growth does arise goes to them rather than being appropriated by capital. In other words, the squeeze on earnings reflects the way the labour market and the system of employment relations are organized, contributing to the problem of poor productivity and, in turn, reinforcing wage stagnation.

While global shocks – the effects of COVID-19 and the war in Ukraine – clearly played an important part in contributing to rising prices during 2022–23, the experience of the UK demonstrates that the cost-of-living crisis was also a function of the power of capital to extract greater profit at the expense of labour. Inflation is not purely a quantitative measure of how much prices are rising but a manifestation of the struggle between capital and labour over how the income from any economic growth should be allocated. Orthodox economic theory holds that rising inflation is largely the fault of workers and unions. In looking to maintain living standards by demanding pay rises that match or even exceed inflation, they cause employers to raise their prices and increase demand in the economy relative to supply, contributing to a 'wage–price spiral'. Yet it is generous pay rises going to the well-off, people who are already at the top of the earnings hierarchy, such as City of London bankers and traders, which have primarily been responsible for escalating inflation. Those on low and middle incomes, meanwhile, have seen their wage growth suppressed as prices rise faster than increases in take-home pay (Helm and Inman, 2023).

There is a growing appreciation of the flaws of such a 'wage-push' explanation of rising inflation, particularly in the period since the COVID-19 pandemic. Instead, greater attention has been devoted to the inflationary consequences of increased corporate profitability, caused by firms increasing their profits while squeezing wages (Weber, 2021; Weber and Wasner, 2023). Even institutions such as the International Monetary Fund and the Organisation for Economic Co-operation and Development (OECD), otherwise staunch advocates of economic orthodoxy and certainly no allies of labour, have recognized that recent inflationary pressures around the world are largely a consequence of increased corporate profits (Inman, 2023a; OECD, 2023).

Since the COVID-19 pandemic, corporate profitability in the UK has soared. Energy companies have benefitted from the increased cost of fuel supplies. A lack of effective competition in some key parts of the economy – the telecommunications sector for example – has given firms space to hike prices substantially leading to allegations of collusion. According to Lapavitsas et al (2023: 47), there has been a 'relentless rise in profits that takes advantage of rising prices, boosting profit margins, and keeping prices high'. Rising inflation was thus a function of efforts by capital to wrest more income from labour, in an environment where the bargaining power of the latter had been considerably weakened between the 1980s and 2010s.

Consistent with economic orthodoxy, the efforts of UK economic policy makers to tackle inflation have been dominated by two imperatives. One is the pressure exerted on workers and unions to exercise wage restraint, supposedly to avoid further stoking inflation. In the public sector, for example, the UK government has offered workers such as nurses, doctors and teachers lower-than-inflation pay rises – provoking considerable labour conflict as a consequence (see Chapter 8). The second imperative involves the tactic of increasing the price of money through a series of rises in interest rates, the purpose of which is to reduce demand in the economy and thus moderate inflationary pressures. But the effect of this was to increase – substantially – the cost of mortgage payments for homeowners, with tenants of rental properties also indirectly affected through higher rents paid to landlords. Attempting to tackle inflation through 'monetary austerity' (Haldane, 2023) by suppressing wages and raising interest rates further exacerbated the squeeze on people's living standards and aggravated the already escalating cost-of-living crisis. A more equitable and sustainable way of reducing inflation would involve increasing taxes on wealth or on corporate profits, perhaps accompanied by strategic price controls (Weber, 2021). In the UK, though, policy makers deliberately opted for approaches designed to make working people poorer rather than targeting the wealthy or corporations.

In a period of low growth, rising inflation and cost-of-living pressures have made the potential for distributional conflict between capital and labour more acute, aggravating economic turbulence and instability (Lapavitsas et al, 2023). One notable consequence concerns the diminished legitimacy of an economic model that disproportionately privileges the interests of large corporations and rentiers while keeping working people subordinated. The experience of the COVID-19 pandemic was influential in this respect insofar as it was responsible for amplifying expectations that work should be fairer and better in a context of greater re-regulatory pressures – see Chapter 1.

All of this has to be viewed in the context of the escalating climate emergency. The highly financialized economic model that prevails in the UK, one dominated by an emphasis on realizing value from the ownership of assets and the commodification of labour, is hardly conducive to the delivery of long-term, sustainable growth. Clearly, an effective 'just transition' to a low-carbon economy demands measures that promote sustainable and more equitably shared growth (Klein, 2019). This is particularly important since climate change and environmental degradation mean that supply chain disruptions and the scarcity of goods caused by such disruptions will become more likely, helping to fuel inflation and further squeezing living standards (Kerr, 2023). All this will likely exacerbate the potential for distributional conflict – between capital and labour – over how the proceeds of any economic growth are allocated. Moreover, from a 'foundational economy' perspective, it is not so much economic growth that is important but rather the capacity to promote sustainable economic development – marked by a concern with securing greater equity and social justice, building strong and effective public services for all and providing a robust social fabric, one which enables people to feel supported and protected and more capable of contributing to the economy and generating prosperity (Calafati et al, 2023).

Political turbulence I – the crises of democracy and social democracy

In covering the broader aspects of the crisis of work in this chapter, we have been concerned with the economic and labour market dimensions, including the causes and implications of the long-term squeeze on earnings and the 'cost-of-living crisis' that erupted during the early 2020s. Now, though, our attention shifts to the political dimensions of the crisis of work. As is evident at various points elsewhere in this book, the contemporary crisis of work is strongly infused with politics.

At the same time, the troublesome nature of work has made a major contribution to the increasingly unstable and turbulent political environment in the liberal democracies of the Global North, such as the UK. In acknowledging, first of all, how politics has influenced the crisis of work, it is important to appreciate the important extent to which governments played a notable role in the effort to advance neoliberalization, particularly by enacting measures designed to propagate flexibilization and weaken the influence of organized labour (Baccaro and Howell, 2017).

The purpose of mentioning this here is to emphasize just how important politics is to the contemporary crisis of work, given the basis of this crisis in the antagonism that arises from a neoliberal emphasis on privileging employers' flexibility. However, while some have emphasized the reinvigoration of neoliberal globalization in the 2020s (Slobodian, 2023), the legacy of the 2007–8 global financial crisis, the consequences of the COVID-19 pandemic and the imperative to address the climate emergency mean that circumstances have become less propitious for neoliberalism. One important consequence has been the marked degree of greater political volatility and turbulence (Hopkin, 2020). This points to the connections between intensified neoliberalization, work and the politics of crisis.

It is important, then, to consider the implications for politics of the troublesome nature of contemporary work and characterize the key features of the more turbulent and unstable political system it has engendered. There is a growing understanding that economic dysfunction, particularly a lack of sustainable economic growth and a failure to distribute the proceeds of any growth that does occur, has hollowed out liberal democratic politics (Wolf, 2023). The idea that democracy is in crisis is not a new one (Ercan and Gagnon, 2014). It was employed throughout the 20th century with regard to both fascism and the perceived threat to the West posed by the communist systems of the Soviet Union and China (Runciman, 2014).

These tendencies have been more marked since the onset of financialized neoliberalism in the 1980s under the influence of Milton Friedman, a strongly pro-capitalist, anti-democratic economic thinker (Klein, 2008; Walby, 2017; Slobodian, 2023). As a political ideology, neoliberalism takes a very narrow view of what democracy involves, one that disregards public participation (Della Porta, 2013). Neoliberalization, and the challenge to democracy it portends, has 'partly been a result of the decline in power of the social democratic project' (Walby, 2017: 128).

Although it deepened during the 2010s, the crisis of social democratic politics is a long-term phenomenon (Keating and McCrone, 2013). Social democratic political parties traditionally enjoyed close links with organized labour, particularly in Europe (Upchurch and Taylor, 2009). Indeed, at the beginning of the 20th century the UK Labour Party was largely established by trade unions as a means of achieving working-class political representation. From the 1980s, economic change saw the decline of traditional, male-dominated primary and manufacturing industries, which had been key areas of union membership and power (see Chapter 6) and sources of support for social democratic politics in a more globalized setting.

During the 1990s and early 2000s, social democratic and left-of-centre parties in the Global North looked to respond to globalization and the diminished significance of their traditional constituencies by engaging with neoliberalism and searching for a way of reconciling labour market flexibility with social protection (Keating and McCrone, 2013). In the UK, for example, this was manifest in Labour's 'third way' politics under the premiership of Tony Blair. Gerhard Schröder's Social Democrat-led administration in Germany enacted labour market and welfare reforms that aimed to increase employment participation while also encouraging more precarious and low-paid – 'flexible' – jobs (Brady and Biegert, 2017).

The 2007–8 global financial crisis, and the 'Great Recession' that ensued, provoked a political crisis for social democratic political parties as they struggled to find an effective response. They had become too enmeshed in neoliberalization and were either complicit in advocating neoliberal austerity themselves (for example, PASOK in Greece) or failed to articulate a convincing alternative (for example, Labour in the UK) (Ryner, 2010; Keating and McCrone, 2013; Bailey et al, 2014). Across Europe, support for left-of-centre, social democratic parties plummeted in the 2010s, including in Germany, Sweden, Italy and France. The fate of the Greek socialist party, PASOK, which had been one of the two major parties of government but now saw their electoral support virtually obliterated, prompted the coining of a new term that captured the hollowing out of social democracy in this period – 'Pasokification' (Cox, 2019).

Given the extent to which they had been complicit in neoliberalism before the global financial crisis, traditional social democratic political parties were unable to respond to, and indeed in some ways were themselves responsible for promoting, the intensified neoliberalization of the 2010s and the accompanying labour commodification and employment precarity that went with it (Bailey et al, 2014). In this way, then, the accommodation between social democracy and neoliberalism made an important contribution to the crisis of work. At the same time, though, social democratic parties were hollowed out and increasingly lacked the capacity to respond effectively to the troublesome nature of work – by promoting tougher employment protections for example – even if they had wanted to.

This provided an opportunity and a space for more left-wing political movements that explicitly rejected neoliberalism, not least because of its adverse effects on work and working people's lives. The rise of an 'anti-system' politics was evident during the 2010s (Hopkin, 2020). On the political left, this took the form of insurgent movements and mobilizations that rejected the accommodation reached between traditional social democratic parties and neoliberalism and instead made an explicit commitment to challenging the interests of corporations and advancing rights and protections for low-paid, underemployed and precarious workers – see, for example, the rise to prominence of explicitly left-wing political parties such as Podemos in Spain and Syriza in Greece – often framed as 'left populists' – and the widespread Gilets Jaunes 'populist' protests prompted by discontent with neoliberal capitalism that occurred in France during the latter part of the 2010s (Kioupkiolis and Katsambekis, 2017; Royall, 2020; Gerbaudo, 2023).

In countries where social democratic and left-of-centre parties are hegemonic because of how the electoral system operates, there was a marked leftward shift. In the UK, the Labour Party explicitly repudiated neoliberalism after the veteran left-winger Jeremy Corbyn became its leader in 2015, instead articulating a leftist, social democratic policy programme which initially attracted much popular support (O. Jones, 2021). Even in the US the political left was resurgent, evidenced by its growing base in the Democratic Party, the popularity of Bernie Sanders during his 2016 and 2020 presidential election campaigns and Sanders' influence on President Joe Biden's policy platform (Marantz, 2021; Pilkington, 2021). One of the most distinctive features of contemporary left-wing political mobilization is that the necessity of effective action to tackle the climate crisis, by means of a 'just transition' that privileges workers and their interests, is central to its critique – and rejection – of neoliberalism (Klein, 2019).

However, by the early 2020s the left revival seemed to have abated, particularly in Europe, with moderate social democracy showing signs of recovery in some places. Following elections held in 2021, the German Social Democrats returned to power at the head of a government that includes the Greens, although its record in office subsequently proved to be lacklustre and underwhelming. Biden's Democratic administration in the US adopted an explicitly interventionist economic programme designed to address the climate emergency, boosting green growth and creating good jobs for working people through its 2022 Inflation Reduction Act while also offering a generally more supportive environment for trade unions (Lowenstein, 2022; Scheiber, 2022). The socialist government in Spain made progress in tackling precarious employment and its ill-effects (O'Connor, 2023). Under the leadership of Keir Starmer, who took over from Corbyn in 2020, the Labour Party seems likely to return to power in the UK at the July 2024 general election. While it maintains an ostensible commitment to improving workers' rights and protections and envisions a 'green energy revolution' to invest in combatting the climate emergency (Labour Party, 2022; Helm, 2023), there are widespread concerns that Starmer's Labour has backtracked on popular left-wing policies (Allegreti, 2023a).

The left mobilization of the 2010s pushed established centre-left parties leftwards, contributing to a modest revival in social democratic fortunes, albeit not everywhere, as the French Socialist Party and Italian Democratic Party remain in a particularly parlous state. This mobilization was predicated on a repudiation of neoliberalism and posited an alternative vision of the economy, labour market and work based on a sensitivity to workers' interests and the necessity of developing a more sustainable model of work. The key question, though, concerns how far centrist and social democratic governments can moderate the crisis of work through re-regulatory interventions in settings where instability arising from neoliberalization, the consequences of the COVID-19 pandemic and the effects of the climate emergency is manifest and exacerbating antagonisms. Witness the considerable turbulence in France in 2023, for example, arising from efforts by President Emmanuel Macron's administration to enact neoliberal reforms in a range of areas, but especially a rise in the pension age, and the opposition they attracted from workers and trade unions (Wieviorka, 2023).

Political turbulence II – resurgent right populism

Staying with France, the popularity of the far-right Rassemblement National party (formerly Front National party, and led by Marine Le Pen until 2022) is testament to the appeal of an alternative kind of 'anti-system' politics (Hopkin, 2020). Despite being defeated by Macron in the second round of the 2022 presidential election, Le Pen still secured over two fifths of the popular vote. Her electoral support came from combining an appeal to poor and working-class voters, who were experiencing greater economic insecurity and often struggling financially due to neoliberal globalization and its effects, with a far-right racist and anti-immigrant platform. The 'right populism' invoked by Le Pen in France has become a more prominent feature of global politics since the 2007–8 global financial crisis, posing a challenge to liberal democracy and producing greater political instability and turbulence – witness the aftermath of Biden's defeat of Trump in the US presidential election of 2020. Egged on by the defeated candidate himself, Trump's extremist right-wing supporters rioted and invaded the Capitol in Washington DC in an attempt to overturn the legitimate election result, which they falsely claimed had been rigged. The prospect of Trump successfully standing for the office of president again in 2024, despite being embroiled and indicted in various legal cases, not only illustrates the growing political polarization in the US but also points to the potential for even greater instability and turmoil in future (Callinicos, 2023).

In general, right populism is characterized by a championing of national culture and identity, hostility to economic and social liberalism and resentment against 'others', such as immigrants, who are perceived as outsiders (Albertazzi and McDonnell, 2015). Right populist politics can thus be viewed as a defensive reaction by socially conservative groups who perceive themselves to be threatened by change in settings where economic globalization and neoliberal austerity have aggravated disadvantage and contributed to greater distrust of established political parties (Brubaker, 2017; Norris and Inglehart, 2019).

There is often a highly individualist, libertarian dimension to right populism, characterized by a distrustful attitude towards established science and an antipathy to state intervention, even when it is necessary to advance collective welfare. For example, during the COVID-19 pandemic right populists stoked opposition to public health protection measures such as vaccination and the wearing of face masks (Stecula and Pickup, 2021). Climate change scepticism is also an endemic feature of right populism, again based on doubts about the veracity of established science, and informed by a libertarian worldview which claims that actions by states and international bodies to tackle climate issues are unnecessary and driven by the illegitimate aim of restricting the individual liberty (Lockwood, 2018).

Around the world, authoritarian leaders – including Recep Tayyip Erdoğan in Turkey, Jair Bolsonaro in Brazil (until 2022), Narendra Modi in India and (since 2023) Javier Milei in Argentina – have invoked a right populist, nationalist agenda to win support. Their success exemplifies the broader challenge to liberal democracy since the 2007–8 global financial crisis, with attacks on 'free and fair elections, the rights of minorities, freedom of the press and the rule of law' becoming more commonplace around the world (Abramowi, 2018). Right populism has grown in popularity among the liberal democracies of the Global North. In 2022, the far-right Brothers of Italy party won power at the head of a coalition government, with its leader Giorgia Meloni becoming Italian prime minister. The experience of Italy demonstrates how extreme right-wing parties have achieved success by mobilizing antipathy towards supposedly cosmopolitan liberal elites and articulating a racist and xenophobic nativism which is manifest in hostility towards immigrants. Right populism is also marked by strong support for socially conservative values, often manifest in anti-LGBTQ+ sentiment, as in Poland and Hungary for example (Rankin and Walker, 2021).

While the cases of France and Italy, in particular, highlight the role played by the extreme far right in fomenting right populism, the experience of the UK points to the way in which right populist politics have been taken up by more established right-wing parties – specifically the Conservatives (Bale, 2023). During the 2010s, there was a 'resurgence' of right-wing authoritarian populism linked to the rise of the anti-EU United Kingdom Independence Party and its growing influence on the governing Conservative Party (Crewe, 2020). This found specific expression in the 2016 vote to leave the EU. In the UK, particularly England, the vote for Brexit in 2016 was predicated on a burgeoning nationalist political agenda and characterized by an aversion to economic and social liberalism, the greater salience of immigration as a political issue and rising anti-immigrant sentiment. At the same time, though, the prominence of right populism reflected demands for a more interventionist state, one that would protect (native) people from the adverse consequences of intensified neoliberalization and neoliberal austerity (Eatwell and Goodwin, 2018; Fetzer, 2019; Norris and Inglehart, 2019; Hopkin, 2020).

Right populism in the UK, particularly anti-immigration sentiment, has exacerbated the troublesome nature of contemporary work in two key respects. First, right populist politics is associated with greater exploitation of migrant workers – see Chapter 5. Second, by permitting the UK to withdraw from the EU freedom of movement regime, Brexit aggravated supply difficulties and labour shortages in sectors such as food, road haulage and social care (Portes and Springford, 2023), stifling economic growth and, indirectly, contributing to squeezed living standards. Brexit was fuelled by claims there were too many EU workers in the UK, particularly from Central and Eastern Europe, who were taking jobs that should have been done by indigenous British workers and driving down wages and labour standards. There is no evidence that EU migration did have any adverse impact on pay and jobs (MAC, 2018). That said, in certain parts of the economy – food processing, agriculture, social care – unscrupulous employers do treat migrant labour as a commodity, helping to erode labour standards (Fudge, 2018). Hand car washes overwhelmingly use migrant workers in low-paid, casual and precarious employment, often with poor health and safety standards (House of Commons Environmental Audit Committee, 2018).

As a form of politics, right populism is marked by paradox. It manifests as a reaction against the state – run by supposedly out-of-touch, socially and economically liberal 'elites' – yet portends a more interventionist role for states by controlling immigration, for example, as long as it serves the supposedly popular will of the 'people'. Right populism is – supposedly – a reaction against economic liberalism in general and has become more salient because of the harmful consequences of neoliberalization. Yet right populist politics operates to facilitate neoliberalization in some important ways. In the UK, for example, the Conservatives viewed Brexit as a vehicle for reducing (EU-derived) employment rights and protections. Finally, right populism often has a highly libertarian character. Yet it is also a vehicle for promoting socially conservative values, which seek to deny many people's right to express themselves and live as individuals, especially if they are Muslim or identify as LGBTQ+ for example. The most well-known protagonists of right populism are highly authoritarian leaders. Their authoritarianism is often associated with efforts to suppress trade unions. Trump, US president between 2016 and 2020, sought electoral support largely as a right populist. But his administration was extremely hostile towards organized labour (Greenhouse, 2021). Right populists and neoliberals tend to find common cause when it comes to exercising hostility towards trade unions, as the experience of Argentina under Milei's presidency bears out (Phillips and Iglesia, 2024).

All this demonstrates how greater state intervention is not necessarily devoted to supporting workers and advancing their interests but can be dedicated to weakening their rights and protections, especially under the influence of right populist authoritarians. This is particularly evident from the experience of the UK, where Conservative governments between 2019 and 2024 led by, first, Boris Johnson and then Liz Truss (very briefly) and Rishi Sunak, attempted to meld a more strikingly authoritarian and anti-democratic agenda with market liberal ideology and hostility towards trade unions. One particularly prominent manifestation of this approach involved the enactment of new legislation in 2023 designed to enforce minimum service levels during strikes involving certain groups of workers, including railway and ambulance staff – a major attack on such workers' capacity to engage in strike action. For Katsaroumpas (2023: 555), such a coercive, authoritarian intervention can be seen as part of a broader attempt to sustain neoliberalism amid challenges to its legitimacy in the aftermath of the 2007–8 global financial crisis.

The authoritarianism characteristic of right populist politics is evident in other important respects. Islamophobia is a key feature of the shift towards a more authoritarian neoliberal agenda (Callinicos, 2023), as is the UK government's obsessive focus on being seen to be tough on reducing migration into the UK – to the extent of proposing to send asylum seekers to Rwanda or housing them in offshore sea vessels, a manifestation of what Slobodian (2023) terms 'seasteading'.

At the same time, though, migration in general has been rising for economic reasons – because of greater demand for workers in the economy amid shortages of labour in the context of a UK immigration regime that is more accommodating of non-EU migrants, especially those aspiring to fill reasonably well-paid, skilled roles (Portes, 2022).

A key aim of the right populism advanced by the Conservatives in the UK following the Brexit referendum was to sustain neoliberalism in increasingly unpropitious circumstances. By promoting a right populist agenda based on appealing to 'identity conservatives' (Sobolewska and Ford, 2020) and – opportunistically – fashioning a more interventionist role for the state, particularly through the short-lived emphasis placed on addressing geographic inequalities by so-called 'levelling-up' (Jennings et al, 2021), the Conservatives sought to articulate a distinctive response to the diminished legitimacy of market liberalism in an attempt to attract electoral support and thus maintain power. Yet this fusion of right populist politics and neoliberal economics was an inherently unstable phenomenon, one that contributed to the greater political turbulence in the UK. It failed to respond to, let alone satisfy, the interests of workers looking for greater support and protection, specifically as a consequence of intensified neoliberalization, especially in the context of a profound living standards crisis. There was nothing to suggest any marked departure from a neoliberal belief in the desirability of a lightly regulated system of employment relations in which business flexibility is privileged, workers enjoy limited rights and protections and trade unions are suppressed.

Ultimately, then, efforts by the UK's Conservatives to use a right populist agenda for the purpose of reconciling neoliberalism in work and employment relations policy with aspirations for greater state intervention, amplified by the experience of the pandemic, proved ineffective. This was largely because of the markedly diminished legitimacy of neoliberalism itself – a consequence of hollowed out public services, an impoverished social fabric and the increasingly widespread belief that the economy and society are fundamentally broken (Califati et al, 2023).

Conclusion

The purpose of this chapter has been to place the crisis of work in broader perspective, centred on its economic and political dimensions. From the material covered in the chapter it is clear that the troublesome nature of work intersects with other crises in some important ways. The chapter commenced by covering the economic and labour market aspects of the crisis of work. At one level, issues such as low growth, supply-side constraints and labour shortages, weak productivity, the unhealthy and uncaring nature of the economy, stagnant wages, cost-of-living difficulties and squeezed living standards are further empirical manifestations of this crisis. They are a function of the degradation of work and employment – consequences of the greater disposability and commodification of labour in settings where employers' flexibility is privileged and organized labour is weak. As such, they reflect processes of neoliberalization and financialization at an 'actual' level while ultimately arising from the exploitative nature of capitalism at an underlying 'real' level. At the same time, though, the economic and labour market trends and developments we have focused on in the chapter have helped to fuel the antagonism that lies at the heart of the contemporary crisis of work. As Chapter 9 shows, addressing the crisis of work demands a more sustainable model of economic development, one that is sensitive to, and supports, decarbonization but also spreads the proceeds of growth more equitably – rejecting the neoliberal attachment to financialization and commodification.

The large extent to which politics has driven the crisis of work by promoting and enabling neoliberalization is also evident from the material covered in this chapter. But it is important to recognize just how far the consequent degradation of work, manifest in greater commodification, precarity and insecurity, has contributed to a more volatile and turbulent political environment, especially given increasing expectations of state intervention – expectations which the experience of COVID-19 and the necessity of responding to the escalating climate emergency have amplified. While traditional social democracy has struggled to respond effectively, right populists, who promote an authoritarian and socially conservative political agenda, have increasingly been able to thrive. While right populism conveys a strongly anti-elitist sentiment and expresses a concern with protecting the interests of indigenous working people, it is by no means incompatible with neoliberalism, as is evident from its hostility to organized labour. Indeed, contemporary right populism is concerned with upholding neoliberalism in circumstances where it increasingly lacks legitimacy. As we explore in Chapters 8 and 9, robust political action is crucial for addressing the crisis of work; to do so, it needs to explicitly reject neoliberal dogma and offer a new way of making work and employment relations better for working people themselves, centred on the principles of equity, inclusivity and sustainability.

8

Crises at Work: Implications and Responses

Introduction

The purpose of this chapter is to examine some of the key implications of, and responses to, the crisis *of* work; a crisis which has been profoundly affected by crises which are *at* work, namely the experience of the COVID-19 pandemic and the effects of the escalating climate emergency. We start by exploring the implications for neoliberal capitalism itself. Marx famously argued that capitalism in general was continually being undermined by its own contradictions, such as states of overproduction and underconsumption or the continual search for profits leading to overexploitation of workers and thence to labour unrest and contention. Intensified neoliberalism, particularly in the aftermath of the 2007–8 global financial crisis, has fuelled antagonism, not least because of greater employment precarity (see Chapter 3), the way in which labour is increasingly treated as a commodity (see Chapter 4), prevailing inequalities (see Chapter 5), the weakness of the trade unions (see Chapter 6) and escalating cost-of-living difficulties (see Chapter 7). As a consequence, neoliberal capitalism itself seems to have become immersed in crisis, arising from a backlash against free market and deregulatory policies, a backlash exacerbated by the experience of the COVID-19 pandemic and a growing recognition that pro-market policies which favour big corporations are inimical to addressing the climate crisis.

As this chapter shows, neoliberalism has responded by taking a more authoritarian guise, accommodating the rising influence of right populist politics (see Chapter 7). How far this can sustain neoliberal capitalism is open to question, however, given the extent to which neoliberalism has become subject to challenge. Resistance to work, manifest in the anti-work movement, is one illustration of this, especially given the influence of the COVID-19 pandemic in changing workers' attitudes. Moreover, integral to the crisis of neoliberalism are the collective efforts of workers, activists and campaigners to challenge it. Simon Springer's vehement and controversial diatribe, *Fuck Neoliberalism* (2021), demonstrates that moments of crisis almost inevitably fuel protest and opposition. While individuals may be powerless in the face of the ravages of neoliberalism, crises such as those described in this book tend to provoke collective responses. As Springer (2021) notes, the financial crash of 2007–8 promoted the Occupy movement of encampments in sites of power, which is generally taken to have started in New York before spreading around the globe, notably to Britain and Spain. Similarly, neoliberal austerity also generated a significant degree of contention (Bailey et al, 2018). In this chapter, we focus in particular on responses by organized labour, particularly the surge of strike activity in the aftermath of the pandemic, and what such contention means for understanding labour activism and its capacity to challenge neoliberal capitalism. We also examine the burgeoning climate activism movement and the repertoires of contention which it uses, typically forms of non-violent direct action. Its efforts to promote climate justice imply a 'transformative' approach to achieving a decarbonized economy based on rejecting neoliberalism and privileging a socially and economically just transition.

Neoliberalism in crisis?

By the first half of the 2020s, it appeared that neoliberal capitalism itself was in the midst of a major, perhaps even terminal, crisis of its own. As we have explained in previous chapters, the crisis *of* work is an expression of the antagonism arising from crises which are *at* work: intensified neoliberalization and its consequences, especially in the aftermath of the 2007–8 global financial crisis, aggravated by the the COVID-19 pandemic and the effects of the escalating climate emergency. In an important sense, then, the crisis of work is also a crisis of neoliberal capitalism, given its harmful impact – greater inequality, precarity and commodification – on workers. Are we, perhaps, witnessing, if not the demise of neoliberalism, then at least its shrinking influence, amid pressures for greater state intervention in, and re-regulation of, the economy, labour market and work?

Yet going back a few decades – to the 1980s and 1990s – neoliberalism seemed hegemonic, triumphant even. Economic competitiveness and prosperity were dependent upon the promotion of free markets, marked by a process of deregulating labour markets, privileging employers' flexibility and subordinating trade unions – with the latter's legitimate role envisaged as being restricted to supporting businesses in their efforts to become more competitive (Williams et al, 2013). But given its scope and magnitude, the 2007–8 global financial crisis seemed to signal a turning point. In particular, it pointed to the apparent failure of a neoliberal capitalist economic model, particularly unregulated global finance (Tooze, 2018). The short-term impact of the crisis itself was tackled by governmental and intergovernmental action to prop up financial institutions and guarantee their funds, helping to restore economic confidence. However, predictions of the passing of neoliberalism in the aftermath of the global financial crisis proved wide of the mark (Crouch, 2011; Mirowski, 2013). Neoliberalism not only emerged and struggled onwards, faltering zombie-like following its presumed demise (Peck et al, 2010; Quiggin, 2012), but actually ended up resurgent (Mirowski, 2013; Hendrikse, 2018).

In Europe, for example, the EU and national governments sought to tackle the sovereign debt crises that arose as a result of the global financial crisis by enacting reductions in public expenditure, weakening employment regulations and restricting the scope of trade unions to bargain collectively. Such an archetypal neoliberal policy prescription was viewed as essential for the purpose of upholding financial stability and gaining the confidence of international financial markets (Davies and Gane, 2021). In the UK, the Conservative–Liberal Democrat coalition government embarked on an explicitly neoliberal programme of austerity between 2010 and 2015, focused on diminishing the size of the state, reducing public expenditure and cutting welfare benefits for the espoused, and ultimately unsuccessful, purpose of eradicating the budget deficit that had swelled due to the global financial crisis and subsequent 'Great Recession' (Williams and Scott, 2016).

As we show in other chapters, the intensified neoliberalization of the 2010s was particularly evident in work and employment. Consider, for example, the rise to prominence of online platforms and the commodified and precarious nature of the work associated with them (Prassl, 2018). Platforms benefitted from being able to operate within highly permissive regulatory environments in which business flexibility is privileged and workers' rights and protections are disregarded. The development of artificial intelligence (AI) and algorithmic management systems at work (see Chapter 4) have facilitated greater exploitation of workers by exposing them to greater surveillance, reinforcing managerial control over their activities and intensifying their work in highly neoliberalized settings where upholding the prerogatives of employing organizations, especially their control over labour, is paramount.

Far from dissipating, then, during the 2010s neoliberal capitalism appeared resurgent as governments, intergovernmental bodies and international financial institutions strove to restore the finance-based growth model marked by the primacy accorded to market competition, business flexibility and lightly regulated labour markets that had preceded the 2007–8 global financial crisis. However, by the end of the decade, the harmful consequences of this period of intensified neoliberalization – greater precarity, labour commodification and burgeoning inequalities – had clearly done major damage to the legitimacy of neoliberal capitalism itself. Even before the onset of the COVID-19 pandemic in 2020, neoliberalism's failure to deliver sustainable economic growth, and the greater inequalities it had produced, meant that its possible demise was again attracting critical commentary (see for example Stiglitz, 2019).

The experience of the pandemic reinforced a sense that neoliberalism was on the wane given the need for government interventions to protect workers, their jobs and their incomes from the ill-effects of temporary business closures designed to prevent the coronavirus from spreading (Natali, 2022). Such measures amounted to a kind of 'crisis' or 'COVID Keynesianism', characterized by the role of an activist, interventionist state in protecting the economy and jobs and, subsequently, stimulating an economic and employment recovery (J. Wood et al, 2023). Another departure from neoliberal doctrine during the pandemic was the emphasis accorded to valuing and recognizing the contribution of key workers, including those in the public sector, and the importance of treating them with greater respect and fairness rather than as economic inputs whose cost should be minimized (de Beer and Keune, 2022). Government intervention to regulate household energy prices during the 2022–23 'cost-of-living crisis' (see Chapter 7) marked a further departure from the neoliberal belief that, in the interests of competitiveness and economic prosperity, market forces should be allowed to prevail.

The imperative for action to tackle the escalating climate emergency has further diminished the relevance and legitimacy of neoliberal capitalism. There is a widespread understanding that market-based solutions – such as economic incentives – are an ineffective means of progressing decarbonization and achieving a net-zero world (Klein, 2019; Buller, 2022b). Tackling the climate emergency effectively, then, requires that neoliberalism be abandoned (Ball, 2022). It demands, instead, a more activist role for states, appropriate interventions by governments, especially at a local level, and the involvement of workers and trade unions in facilitating the transition away from a reliance on fossil fuels and unsustainable – environmentally and socially – production methods (Klein, 2014; 2019).

Neoliberalism's demise had been anticipated in the immediate aftermath of the 2007–8 global financial crisis – erroneously as it turned out. Yet there are strong reasons for believing that, in the 2020s, neoliberal capitalism is itself in crisis, one which could end up being terminal (Gerbaudo, 2021). Could this time be different? The troublesome legacy of the global financial crisis, the experience of the COVID-19 pandemic and the imperative to address the climate emergency mean that continued support for neoliberalism is by no means guaranteed. In the UK, this is evident from the harmful effects of austerity, the lack of sustained economic growth, weak productivity, stagnant wages, rising inequality, the increased commodification of labour and greater precarity (Lavery, 2019; Davies et al, 2022; Stanley, 2022).

Although 'post-neoliberalism' is not a new idea (see Peck et al, 2010), there is renewed interest in the nature and prospects of an emergent 'post-neoliberal' regime. For Davies and Gane (2021: 4–5), the concept of 'post-neoliberalism' does not 'refer to something that comes exclusively after neoliberalism, but rather ... to a set of emergent rationalities, critiques, movements and reforms that take root in neoliberal societies and begin to weaken or transform key tenets of neoliberal reason and politics'. While neoliberalism itself first gained significant traction during the economic crises of the 1970s, marked by a large increase in the price of oil, high inflation, rising unemployment and extensive labour conflict, a nascent 'post-neoliberal consensus' can be detected in the 2020s. According to Davies (2023), 'few ... are demanding less government intervention and more markets. On the contrary, dramatic price movements are met with the demand that governments do something to protect national populations from the impact of international shocks' (Davies, 2023).

There have been increasing signs of a 'shift to a post-neoliberal future' in the US, marked by a greater focus on government intervention in the economy, regulation of business activity and support for labour unions (Foroohar, 2022). After entering office in early 2021, Biden's Democratic administration enacted an economic stimulus package worth $1.9 trillion, including, among other things, direct cash payments of $1,400 to low-paid workers and their families. Later the same year, it passed new legislation to invest $1 trillion in new infrastructure, including large-scale investment in public transport and clean energy (Green, 2022). The 2022 Inflation Reduction Act provided an additional $369 billion of investment in climate and clean energy measures (Lowenstein, 2022). For Green (2022: 326), the Biden administration's 'approach cleaves closely to the legacy of Keynesian demand-side intervention', one which 'sees government spending and taxation policies as critical to financing the green transition and realising ambitious goals of green job creation, renewable energy infrastructure and other public benefits'. The initial impact of the Biden administration's measures seems promising: investment in manufacturing has risen, the economy is performing better than anticipated, employment growth is robust and the level of unemployment has declined (Reich, 2023).

Partisan opposition in Congress stymied the Biden administration's proposal to increase the federal minimum wage to $15 per hour and establish an ambitious social spending plan that would have funded a massive expansion of childcare support and a system of paid family and sick leave. Congressional opposition also prevented the Biden administration from progressing legislation that would have made it easier for workers to organize in trade unions and bargain collectively. Nevertheless, the policy approach is striking, with greater political support for unions being a notable contrast with a neoliberal agenda concerned with hollowing out organized labour (Foroohar, 2022).

Neoliberalism resurgent?

The diminished legitimacy of neoliberal capitalism, arising from growing pressures for re-regulating the economy, labour market and work, which were aggravated by the experience of the COVID-19 pandemic, imply that a shift to a 'post-neoliberal' era may be underway (Gerbaudo, 2021). Yet as the continuing influence of markets, competition and flexibility over EU employment policy and the experience of the UK under the Conservatives show, the resilience of neoliberalism, and its adaptive capacity, cannot be disregarded. For some, the turn away from neoliberalism evident during the pandemic – manifest in 'crisis' or 'COVID Keynesianism' – was a short-lived, transient phenomenon and not a lasting break with neoliberal capitalism (Montgomerie, 2023; J. Wood et al, 2023).

Neoliberalism's durability, and its contemporary vitality, are the subjects of Quinn Slobodian's disturbing book, *Crack-Up Capitalism*. Slobodian (2023) describes how 'market radicals', among whose number he includes former Conservative UK prime ministers Margaret Thatcher and Boris Johnson, along with variously labelled groups of libertarians and 'anarcho-capitalists', have been inspired by the very successful capitalist free-market economies of Hong Kong and Singapore to set up distinct 'zones' around the globe free from normal state regulations, taxes and duties. Zones can take a variety of forms: enterprise zones under Thatcher, gated communities across the United States, tax havens in the Caribbean and export-processing zones, such as Dubai's Jebel Ali Free Zone. Liberalized zones, where normal governmental laws do not apply, supposedly offer a 'free market utopia' where capitalists can operate with little political interference, circumvent democratic scrutiny and avoid regulation – thus relieving themselves from obligations to uphold workers' rights and protections. They speak to anxieties that capitalism, in its contemporary neoliberal guise, is inconsistent with, and acts to undermine, established democratic politics centred on the role of nation-states (Wolf, 2023).

What makes Slobodian's (2023) account so compelling is that so much of what he covers has already been happening as part of the project of neoliberal globalization. During the 2000s and 2010s, the market radical agenda informed efforts by 'Eurosceptics' to pull the UK out of the EU, based on a vision of the future centred on the role of distinct 'zones' in London – the Docklands, Canary Wharf and the City of London – where global financial capitalism congregates. Under this 'Singapore scenario', the purpose of Brexit was to liberate UK capitalism from EU legislation and bureaucracy and thus emulate successful East Asian economies whose rapid growth was ascribed to the presence of low taxes, light-touch regulatory environments and weak trade unions (Woolfson, 2017). One obvious problem with this perspective is that the economic development of countries such as Singapore was contingent on the presence of a strong state – to direct investment, promote workforce development and secure cooperation from organized labour through corporatist industrial relations arrangements (Leggett, 2007).

As Slobodian (2023) recognizes, states and governments play a key role in advancing the 'free market utopia' envisaged by proponents of 'crack-up capitalism'. Indeed, central to neoliberalism's resilience is the extent to which it is capable of mutation (Hendrikse, 2018; Davies, 2021; Davies and Gane, 2021). Neoliberalism's mutability has been emphasized by those who highlight its capacity to evolve and exist in varied forms, particularly its adaptability to an era of greater political authoritarianism and state intervention (Peck and Theodore, 2019; Callison and Manfredi, 2020; Šumonja, 2021). To be sure, neoliberalism has always embodied a strong role for states (Davies, 2018; Slobodian, 2021). Their interventions are required to coerce, encourage and incentivize societal actors into tolerating, and even accepting, the seemingly inexorable advance of market relations, competition and deregulation – see Chapter 1. That said, though, the resilience of neoliberalism and its seeming ability to transcend the crisis of legitimacy it faces is based on a process of accommodation with the pressures for a stronger role for states and governments that have arisen as a consequence of the particularly crisis-ridden nature of contemporary capitalism.

One key manifestation of this was the rise to prominence of a more authoritarian kind of neoliberalism in the aftermath of the 2007–8 global financial crisis (Bruff, 2014; Peck and Theodore, 2019), something which has been reinforced by an accommodation with growing right populist politics (Davies, 2021) – see Chapter 7. Given the antipathy to economic and social liberalism it supposedly represents, right populism is often viewed – with some justification – as a reaction against, or even a rejection of, neoliberalism (Bang and Marsh, 2018; Norris and Inglehart, 2019). Rather than marginalizing neoliberalism, though, right populism seems to have facilitated its adaptation and recovery, through the development of what Hendrikse (2018) calls 'neo-illiberalism'. Right populist politics provided neoliberalism with a 'toxic protective coating', helping to 'shield the economic core of the neoliberal project' (Hendrikse, 2018: 170).

One of the most distinctive features of this more authoritarian mutation of neoliberalism involves the explicitly more coercive role played by states in efforts to subjugate working people and render them compliant and thus more amenable to capital through the use of highly punitive welfare and labour market policies (Davies, 2021). Influenced by the politics of right populism, the more authoritarian mutation of neoliberalism also serves the purpose of neutralizing potential challenges from organized labour and its allies (Šumonja, 2021). As we point out in Chapter 7, hostility towards trade unions is common to right populists and neoliberals. There is often a kind of bogus anti-elitism evident in right populist attacks on organized labour interests. In Turkey, for example, the authoritarian right populist Justice and Development Party government's 'neoliberal populism' combines wide-ranging and largely successful efforts to appeal to, and secure support from, working people, including through the promise of increased material rewards, with the widespread suppression of trade unions (Bozkurt, 2013; Özdemir, 2020).

Government responses to COVID-19 reinforced the authoritarian neoliberalism that had arisen during the 2010s (Šumonja, 2021). As we have seen, some claim that interventions to protect workers, their jobs and their incomes during the pandemic accelerated an already existent 'turn away from neoliberalism' (Meadway, 2021). Others, though, are more cautious about proclaiming the demise of neoliberal capitalism based on the belief that neoliberalism depends on strong states – to exercise coercion over workers and organized labour. Duncan (2022) contends that the UK government's haphazard and often chaotic response to COVID-19 reflected an underlying neoliberal belief that imposing restrictions on economic activity and using state resources to support workers were undesirable. At the same time, the pandemic provided the government with 'new avenues to expand and deepen neoliberalization' (Duncan, 2022: 509), not least by providing a justification for renewed austerity in its aftermath.

While short-term 'crisis-Keynesian' policies were necessary to cope with the immediate impact of COVID-19, a set of 'crisis narratives' – over the necessity of reverting to fiscal conservatism to reduce government debt through low taxation and restrictions on public expenditure – were deployed to justify the resumption of 'normal' neoliberalism (J. Wood et al, 2023: 20). In the UK, this was also apparent from how far the Conservative government emphasized the desirability of operating a lightly regulated system of employment relations in which business flexibility is privileged and workers enjoy limited rights and protections – an approach which exacerbated the difficulties experienced by many workers during the COVID-19 pandemic (Bettington, 2021).

From all this, it is clear how the fusion of right populism and neoliberalism has not only helped to sustain neoliberal capitalism but has also given it a more authoritarian character. This would suggest that, far from being in crisis, under the influence of right populism, and in a more authoritarian guise, neoliberalism is resurgent. Suggestions that the experience of COVID-19 and the government interventions deployed to protect workers, jobs and incomes during the pandemic have accelerated progress towards a 'post-neoliberal' era seem rather fanciful. Yet re-regulatory pressures, exacerbated by the experience of the pandemic and the impact of the 2022–23 'cost-of-living crisis', continue to escalate, linked to workers' aspirations for protection, fairness and security.

The current epoch of authoritarian neoliberalism is a deeply unstable state of affairs and thus likely to lack durability. It is highly unlikely to do anything to counter the overarching sense that 'nothing works' in the UK, particularly public services (Calafati et al, 2023), and cannot respond effectively to the climate emergency, given its incompatibility with efforts to involve workers and unions in leading a democratic, just transition to a net-zero world. Paradoxically, by further diminishing its legitimacy, the resilience, resurgence even, of neoliberal capitalism has exacerbated the crisis of neoliberalism itself. Its failure to deliver good jobs, sustainable employment, decent work and effective workers' rights and protections has never been more apparent. Irrespective of whether or not the label 'post-neoliberalism' is justified, the contradictions produced by market fundamentalism are more acute than ever. As a consequence, neoliberalism increasingly lacks legitimacy and is subject to greater challenge.

'Alienation' and the growing 'anti-work' movement

People's experiences of work are now more often characterized by insecurity and temporariness, and this can lead to a declining belief that work is meaningful and can bring about meaningful change. While we do not concur with David Graeber's characterization of much contemporary employment roles as 'bullshit jobs' (see Chapter 1), we can identify an increase in work alienation, specifically as a result of the COVID-19 pandemic (Lagios et al, 2023), and in general as a consequence of ongoing neoliberalism (Sennett, 1998; Jaeggi, 2014). Alienation in work is corrosive, disconnecting the worker from the product of their work – highlighting the neoliberal ideological emphasis on individual autonomy, individual responsibility and individual pecuniary reward as the prime outcome of the employment contract. This is not irreversible, though, and there are examples of people seeking more meaning in their work through 'downshifting', often at the expense of higher incomes. Such choices are, of course, not available to many working people, particularly given the economic climate. But the point remains that alternatives are viable and resistance is possible.

The growing 'anti-work' movement constitutes one such alternative. It is clear that the economic crisis has been exacerbated by the pandemic and large changes have taken place across work, labour markets, the economy and society. The disruption brought about to patterns of work, the most notable of which was enforced working from home for millions of workers, had an unintended consequence. Many workers' attitudes towards work changed, and the 'anti-work' movement suddenly grew. Not coincidentally, the anti-work movement is most visible in its online presence through subreddits such as r/antiwork.

Workers who must work from home and online reappraised their work, their working conditions and their lives, and many drew the conclusion that work was not for them, or at least not in its present form. There are some parallels here to Graeber's respondents in *Bullshit Jobs* (2018), who identified deep dissatisfaction with meaningless and often low-paid jobs, but the anti-work movement, and it is a movement in that it actively advocates for an end to work in its current form and actively recruits to its cause, is a wider phenomenon. It is also different from the 'inertial characters' that psychoanalyst Josh Cohen identifies as emergent in contemporary society: the daydreamer, the slob, the slacker and the burnout (Cohen, 2020). The slacker, whose ethos can be seen as 'against work' (but not anti-work), is, perhaps, recognizable to many of us:

> Useless, shiftless, good-for-nothing – the contemptuous words and phrases we use to denigrate the slacker attest to the secret fear he induces in us. No sooner does his 'anarchic subjectivity' appear, whether in the form of Romantic reverie, Bohemian intoxication, hippy freak-out or punk nihilism, than it's attacked for its brazen parasitism, irresponsibility and delinquency. So invested is our manically productive culture in the image of us as active and purposeful beings that we seek to erase or destroy all evidence to the contrary – the slacker must put on a suit, get a job, lose his benefits and make himself useful. Harmlessly ineffective as he may be, we hate and fear him for showing us the useless dimension of our own selfhood, for voiding our own impulse not to go to work today, or tomorrow. (Cohen, 2020: 173–4)

The anti-work movement can be characterized as comprising a 'bunch of slackers' but the underlying analysis of meaningless, underpaid and undervalued work in capitalism is the root of the movement, not laziness or avoidance, and the message of the anti-work movement is a positive one: that work, and capitalism, must be reformed and improved.

The ur-text of the contemporary anti-work movement is Bob Black's (1986) *Abolition of Work*, an anarchist take on the world of work, with the, possibly ironic, clarion call at the end: 'Workers of the world ... *relax!*' Black's argument is that work under capitalism is forced labour, that industrialization has accelerated the pace of work and that work has caused untold misery and damage: 'Work is the source of nearly all the misery in the world. Almost any evil you'd care to name comes from working or from living in a world designed for work. In order to stop suffering, we have to stop working' (Black, 1986: 17). Black's argument isn't that we become slackers, that we just stop doing things: it is that we take control and turn our lives into a game, where work becomes play – a *ludic* phenomenon.

Contemporary anti-work activists (there are 2.8 million members of the r/antiwork subreddit) have a wider and more practical focus, offering online advice on how to stand up to bosses, how to unionize, how to oppose discrimination in workplaces; they use Reddit as a general forum for ideas, debates, complaints, rants and just lots of letting off steam – a typical post on the site is: 'Was told for months that I'd get a bonus on December 15th. 10 days before, my supervisor tells us we're not getting it after all. How the frack am I going to afford Christmas for my kid now?! This is just a vent. I'm so angry/irritated beyond words' (posted by Awkward-Pineapple424 on 6 December 2023 to the r/antiwork subreddit).

The future of the anti-work movement is unclear, but it has certainly grown since Kathi Weeks' *The Problem with Work: Feminism, Marxism, Antiwork Politics, and Postwork Imaginaries* was published in 2011. Weeks' radical feminist take on the problem of work and the need to move to a 'post-work' world, a world where work is not the centre of our lives (Weeks, 2011), chimes with the contemporary themes of much of the anti-work movement. However, we can also note that these themes – that we work too much, that technology can replace much work, that work is corrosive and exploitative – can be traced back a long way, not just through the Marxist genealogy but also to the work of Bertrand Russell in the 1930s.

The experience of the COVID-19 pandemic clearly affected attitudes to work and boosted anti-work ideas, manifest in the interest taken in the so-called 'great resignation' phenomenon as the pandemic receded in 2021–22. In the US, this period saw an exceptionally high number of workers voluntarily leaving their jobs, creating labour shortages as a result (Carillo-Tudela et al, 2022). While COVID-19 clearly did generate a greater degree of flux in the labour market, in retrospect the overall significance of the supposed 'great resignation', based on the belief that the experience of the pandemic had caused people to reappraise their priorities in life, is questionable. Where workers did quit their jobs, it was generally in order to secure positions with better pay and conditions, not to leave the labour market and reject paid work entirely (Carillo-Tudela et al, 2022; Fuller and Kerr, 2022).

The immediate aftermath of the pandemic also generated a flurry of concern about the phenomenon of so-called 'quiet quitting', something characterized by a supposedly greater tendency of workers, having re-evaluated their role and aspirations, to seek to stay in their jobs while minimizing their work effort, or only doing what is specifically required of them (Tapper, 2022). Yet the novelty of the 'quiet quitting' phenomenon is questionable (O'Connor, 2022a). There has long been a concern that people are insufficiently committed to their work and employing organizations – manifest in a supposed 'employee engagement deficit' (Rayton et al, 2012). Moreover, 'quiet quitting' is only a problem if you take a rather unsophisticated, managerialist view which assumes that workers both should, and want to, contribute more effort to their work organizations (Purcell, 2014; Harney et al, 2018). As decades of sociological studies have demonstrated, such assumptions are largely unwarranted. Yet while the prospect of the 'end' of work, or work as 'play', seems to be very distant, neoliberalism does face profound challenges arising from collective organization and mobilization and the contention they generate.

The surge of strike activity, 2022–24

One particularly prominent manifestation of contention during the first half of the 2020s was the post-pandemic upsurge of collective labour conflict, especially strikes organized by trade unions. As Chapter 6 explains, the experience of COVID-19 generated a considerable amount of contention. Subsequently, in 2022–23 trade unions in the UK responded to the 'cost-of-living crisis' (see Chapter 7) with widespread strike action, described by *Tribune* as the biggest fightback in decades by the 'organized working class' (Hansen, 2022; Ali, 2023). This surge of strike activity was all the more noteworthy given the pronounced decline in the prevalence of strikes between the 1980s and 2010s and the belief that they were 'withering away' around the world (Frangi et al, 2018). In the UK, any strike action that did occur during the 2000s and 2010s was concentrated in the public services and in strongly unionized parts of the private sector that were once in the public sector, such as the railways. Strikes were largely defensive in character, concerned with protecting pay, pensions and jobs (Lyddon, 2015). The climate of neoliberal austerity meant that the 2010s were a difficult period for trade unions and labour contention in Britain (Bailey, 2023).

Yet amid the crises arising from the experience of COVID-19 and escalating cost-of-living difficulties, the early 2020s saw a pronounced upsurge in labour conflict. As economies and businesses reopened following pandemic-related closures and restrictions, there were significant labour shortages in sectors such as hospitality and retailing. The increased bargaining power enjoyed by workers stimulated demands for better wages and conditions and, as a consequence, a flurry of labour activism (Partington, 2021). During 2022 and 2023, the 'cost-of-living crisis' (see Chapter 7), arising from global supply chain difficulties and energy price rises exacerbated by the Russian war against Ukraine, generated further contention. Workers engaged in collective strike action to demand wage rises that reflected increases in prices, fomenting renewed interest in the relevance of trade unionism as a result – see, for example, the experience of the Southampton-based Red Funnel ferry workers in the UK:

> Nobody on the Red Funnel picket line in Southampton can remember a previous strike; the company says that the last one was in 1966. Ian Woodley, the regional organiser for the Unite union, is surprised by the speed at which young workers have been radicalised: 'They've never been in a union before, let alone on strike.' (The Economist, 2022)

The period between 2022 and 2024 saw a mass wave of strikes take place in the UK, primarily over the issue of pay, involving postal workers, teachers, university staff, lorry drivers, refuse workers, lawyers, railway staff, train drivers, civil servants, airport workers, local BBC journalists, environment agency staff and charity and care workers. February 2023 saw the UK's biggest day of industrial action in more than a decade as teachers, university staff, train drivers, civil servants, bus drivers and security guards all went on strike (Sky News, 2023).

One particularly prominent example of actions resulting from the ongoing crisis of work has been the series of strikes occurring within the UK's National Health Service (NHS), which commenced in the summer of 2022. The Royal College of Nursing (RCN) union voted to strike for the first time in its history, and unions in the ambulance service called a national strike for the first time in some 40 years (Ali, 2023: 65). NHS employees ranging from porters, nurses – one in seven of whom are reported as regularly having to use food banks to supplement their pay (Ali, 2023: 66) – to junior doctors and consultants took part in strike action between 2022 and 2024. The 'cost-of-living crisis' was clearly a major source of contention. But the actions of workers in the NHS were also influenced by the experience of COVID-19 based on the belief that, in presiding over a substantial real terms decline in their pay and the continued decline in health provision, the government had failed to show that it valued the contribution they had made to getting the country through the pandemic.

The upsurge of strikes and labour conflict during this period was not just evident in the UK but around the world (Hodder and Mustchin, 2024). There was a marked increase of contention in the US, for example, involving workers in the hotel, health, education and automobile sectors. According to Greenhouse (2023b): 'Employee frustration and anger have fuelled the work stoppages. Many frontline workers are still fuming about how poorly they were treated during the pandemic, and many are upset that their pay increases have lagged far behind inflation.'

In the UK, the surge in labour contention is evident from the data on strike activity. In total, 2.472 million working days were not worked between June and December 2022 because of strikes. During the first six months of 2023, the figure was over 1.6 million. Between June 2022 and December

2023, over 5 million days were not worked because of strike activity, the most intensive period of labour conflict for over 30 years (Jones, 2024). The increased prevalence of strikes in the UK during 2022–23 was notable by historical standards (Cominetti et al, 2023). According to Hodder and Mustchin (2024: 240): '2022 saw the most striker days (2,518,000) since 1989 (4,128,000). In terms of the number of stoppages, July to August 2022 saw the most stoppages in a 6-month period since February to July 1984, and the months February to April 2023 each saw more than 600 stoppages in progress.'

During this period, strike activity was concentrated in sectors where unions are well organized – in transport, for example, particularly on the railways, and in public services, such as health and education (Hodder and Mustchin, 2024). Perhaps unsurprisingly, the immediate cause of strike action involved disputes over pay, as workers grappled with the consequences of inflation (Cominetti et al, 2023; Hodder and Mustchin, 2024), particularly in areas, such as public services, 'where pay has suffered the sharpest squeeze during a prolonged stagnation in wages' (Smith et al, 2023).

How effective was this upsurge of strike activity in improving workers' pay, and thus moderating the cost-of-living crisis for workers? There is some good evidence of how labour contention, in the form of disputes and (threatened or actual) strike action, can procure benefits for workers (Unite, 2023). In August 2022, for example, following a threat of strike action, the Unite trade union secured an overall pay rise of 13 per cent for some 16,000 British Airways staff working as cabin crew, engineers and staff, making up for pay cuts enforced when COVID-19 struck (Partington, 2022). In December of the following year, Oxfam staff won a significantly improved pay rise after taking strike action and closing the charity's shops – the first instance of such activity in the organization's history (ITV News, 2023). And in the US major strikes organized by the United Auto Workers union, involving workers in the major vehicle manufacturers General Motors, Ford and Stellantis, forced the firms to negotiate agreements, providing for substantial wage rises, to settle the disputes (Sainato, 2023a).

One important reason for the magnitude of the strikes involving public sector workers in the UK was the Conservative government's determination to resist union pay demands, claiming they would be unaffordable and – unsupported by any evidence – exacerbate inflation. As Chapter 7 explains, such an emphasis on wage restraint, as a means of combatting inflation, fails to appreciate that in the period following the pandemic rising prices were caused by other factors, including decisions by firms to take increased profits. Rather than addressing the causes of labour contention, the UK government responded to the surge of strike activity by enacting legislation which provides for further restrictions on strike activity, on top of the already existing body of laws that regulate industrial action by trade unions. The Strikes (Minimum Service Levels) Act 2023 gives the government new powers to promote the enforcement of minimum service levels in specific sectors, such as rail transport and health, during strikes, for the purpose of undermining the effectiveness of the strike action (McCulloch, 2023). The Conservatives had long considered legislating for such a purpose (Gall, 2022), with the wave of strikes that erupted over the 'cost-of-living crisis' giving them a pretext for action.

The Strikes (Minimum Service Levels) Act 2023 is a potentially highly repressive instrument, constituting 'yet another legislative episode in the never-ending "death by a thousand cuts" of UK trade unions' ability to take effective lawful industrial action' (Katsaroumpas, 2023: 514). As we observe in Chapter 7, it is a notable manifestation of the authoritarian turn which neoliberalism has taken in the period since the 2007–8 global financial crisis. Importantly, though, the introduction of a new, potentially more powerful tool for repressing strike activity reflects the weakness of neoliberalism in the context of growing challenges to its authority, credibility and appeal, and its diminishing legitimacy, rather than its strength. As Katsaroumpas (2023: 558) explains: 'Due to the government's inability or unwillingness to negotiate or secure consent, let alone to alter the neo-liberal model of regressive income and wealth distribution, the Government resorts to authoritarianism for defending neo-liberalism by moving the statutory goalposts.'

The highly coercive basis of the Strikes (Minimum Service Levels) Act 2023 is thus a function of efforts to uphold neoliberalism in an increasingly unpropitious environment, not least because of the extent to which it has been challenged. A remarkable feature of the post-pandemic strike wave was the high level of public support for striking workers. According to Hansen (2022): 'The unprecedented support for striking workers has been a remarkable feature of the year, with the likely explanation that a nation suffering the longest squeeze on real wages since Napoleonic times can empathise with the minority of workers with the tools to do something about it.' Public support and sympathy for the strikes, as reported by Hansen (2022), was all the more remarkable given the disruption they often caused. Nearly one in five people reported having their travel plans disrupted by rail strikes in December 2022 and early January 2023, although fewer than one in ten of those disrupted were unable to work, using alternative means such as buses and taxis to travel. The teachers' strike bit even deeper: over half of parents reported they would be affected if schools closed because of strikes, with 31 per cent saying they would have to work fewer hours – 28 per cent said they would be unable to work (ONS, 2023b).

However, not all industrial action during the period in question resulted in success. In UK higher education (HE), for example, the main academic trade union was able to secure a restoration of pension benefits for staff in one part of the sector following industrial action; however, a series of strikes and associated actions in 2023, including a marking and assessment boycott, failed to win an improved pay offer from employers (Adams, 2023). This points to the importance of trade union power – see Chapter 6 for a discussion. In HE, the unions have little structural power: industrial action is disruptive for students but has no noticeable effect on the economy. Low union density in HE means that any associational power is weak. And most staff in HE did not participate in the industrial action, translating into low organizational power. As the surge of post-pandemic strike activity demonstrates, contention by unions is an important means by which working people can collectively advance their interests. However, the process of mobilization is by no means easy or straightforward, particularly in settings where unions have little bargaining power. And in much of the UK's private sector economy, unions are barely present anyway.

Underlying sources of labour contention – a revitalized labour movement?

As we have explained, the 'cost-of-living crisis' was the major cause of the upsurge in strike activity between 2022 and 2024, as workers, organized by unions, looked to protect their incomes in the context of rapidly rising prices.

Irrespective of the immediate, substantive outcomes arising from the upsurge in strike activity and its impact on pay – important as these are – perhaps the most notable result of the resurgence in labour contention is to emphasize the importance of trade unions when it comes to protecting and advancing working people's interests. As inflation recedes, though, and the immediate catalyst for strike action diminishes, can we expect labour conflict to wane in significance? There are good grounds for believing that the increase in labour contention in the first half of the 2020s was more than just a transient, episodic phenomenon, and that it is instead a function of broader, underlying issues in a way that signals the prevailing discontent with neoliberal capitalism. Antagonism, then, is inevitable as neoliberalism comes under challenge and its legitimacy further diminishes, aggravating the broader crisis of work.

Strikes by US actors and screenwriters in 2023, called by the Writers Guild of America (WGA) and the actors' union, SAG-AFTRA (Screen Actors' Guild-American Federation of Television and Radio Artists), offered unusual but high-profile illustrations of this. The strikers were asking for more money, but there was also a political edge to their dispute, relating to the digitalization processes described in earlier chapters. The film and television actors were concerned about the use of AI: 'AI programs that can convincingly replicate lead actors, visually and verbally, and write their scripts as well' (Morrison, 2023). As professionals, they saw their jobs and livelihoods being threatened, especially given the entry into film and television production of streaming providers Google, Amazon and Apple alongside Netflix and Disney. Writers traditionally get repeat fees for TV show re-runs, but streaming services only pay them a fixed, one-off fee. While the film industry has always depended on rich backers, the streaming companies simply want to improve their returns out of revenue from consumer subscriptions, so cutting costs becomes paramount. Particularly at risk are the less well-paid and insecure entry-level actors and bit-part players (Beckett and Paul, 2023).

Leaders of the strike action made the political angle clear. Liz Alper of WGA declared that the strikers were acting for "all the workers across America who have been hurt and disenfranchised by Wall Street and big tech" (Morrison, 2023); and Zeke Alton of Sag-Aftra pointed out that celebrities supporting the strike have powerful voices, with actors such as Susan Sarandon, Lily Tomlin, George Clooney, Bryan Cranston and Cillian Murphy speaking up for the strike (Beckett and Paul, 2023).

Underlying sources of discontent, a function of intensified neoliberalism and its consequences, particularly stagnant wages, disempowered labour and an increasingly impoverished public realm (see Chapter 7; Calafati et al, 2023), allied with the experience of the pandemic, meant that the 'cost-of-living crisis acted as a release flashpoint of accumulated discontent. For workers facing another reduction in their living standards, the concrete demand for pay restoration reflected an overall regressive perception' of a 'drift from one "disaster" to the next, from emergency to emergency, from slump to slump, from crisis to crisis' (Katsaroumpas, 2023: 556).

Workers' claims for immediate pay rises need to be understood in the context of the general real-terms failure of real wages to recover in the years following the global financial crisis of 2007–8 – see Chapter 7. Viewed in this light, workers' demands were an expression of 'grievances against a chronic failure of neo-liberalism to deliver on its promises. This is visible in union strike demands, which tend to place calls for pay restoration in the broader post-2008 real pay reductions' (Katsaroumpas, 2023: 556). Strikes, and other manifestations of labour conflict, may well be sparked by immediate economic grievances, but they also reflect the difficulties and challenges experienced by working people in a climate of intensified neoliberalism (Bailey, 2023).

One particularly notable manifestation of this concerns the consequences of efforts to commodify labour (see Chapter 1), including the difficulties caused by the intensification of work (see Chapter 4). In 2023, the UK's Trades Union Congress (TUC) published a survey exposing the levels of work intensification and the stress it put on workers (Creagh, 2023). The report focused especially on the responses of teachers, one of the striking groups of workers. It is noticeable that public sector workers predominate in the list of strikers. This is partly because public sector pay, controlled by the government, lagged behind wages in the private sector, but also because the cuts to public services and the partial privatization, processes central to neoliberal economic policy, have extremely negative impacts on workplace relations. Characteristically, both resources and staffing have been cut, leading to work overload and stress. Thus, the TUC found that teachers were experiencing increasing workloads, and this was having a serious impact on teacher retention (Creagh, 2023). Although pay and rewards are important, they are not the only things that influence a teacher's decision to quit the profession (Bradley et al, 2016). The features of the work they value are the culture and relationships within the school and the teaching environment. These have been eroded and damaged by excessive workloads, which involve increasing bureaucracy and imposition of a stringent testing and monitoring culture (Creagh, 2023).

Collective efforts by workers in Starbucks and Amazon to mobilize and contest the power of the corporate behemoths that employ them are driven by a desire for better pay and conditions, but they are also underpinned by the urge to challenge the commodification to which their work has been subjected, primarily through attempts to organize unions. In the US, for example, the

> remarkable success of the Starbucks Workers United (SBWU) and Amazon Labor Union (ALU) organising campaigns has been well documented. They have shown that unions can take advantage of the opportunity created by the pandemic labor market; that even the wealthiest, most anti-union corporations are not invincible; that many young workers want bold leadership from unions and the opportunity to lead. (Logan, 2023: 87)

To be sure, both Amazon and Starbucks have fiercely resisted attempts to unionize their sites (Loomis, 2023; Sainato, 2023b). But, as the experience of Amazon in the UK demonstrates, discontent among workers over their pay and conditions has been growing, manifest in the increasing numbers of strikes affecting its facilities. Amid greater unionization, the company has had to intensify its anti-union efforts accordingly (Shenker, 2023).

Previous chapters in this book have highlighted the growth of the platform economy and its commodifying tendencies in a climate of intensified neoliberalism, with greater precarity being a notable consequence. Yet there is good evidence of how growing discontent among platform workers over the perceived poor treatment and unfairness they experience has informed the development of a sense of shared identity and increased solidarity, thus stoking contention in the form of strikes, labour protests and other forms of collective action (Della Porta et al, 2023; A. Wood et al, 2023). While grievances over pay are the main source of contention, the experience of the COVID-19 pandemic seems to have exacerbated platform workers' feelings of injustice, particularly over health and safety issues, contributing to the incidence of labour protests around the world (Bessa et al, 2022). There is some good evidence that contention by platform workers is a significant, international phenomenon, with pay being a particularly notable cause of labour conflict. This contention is a function of the increasing associational power resources accrued by such workers. Even in the absence of unions, platform workers can develop a greater sense of shared, collective identity and solidarity, informed by their experiences of community activity and political activism as appropriate (Cini, 2023; Stuart et al, 2023).

In the UK, instances of labour conflict have also been informed by discontent arising from the parlous and diminished state of many public services (Calafati et al, 2023), including health and education. As we mention in Chapter 7, pronounced recruitment and retention difficulties have arisen in such areas, causing labour shortages and further compromising service delivery, thus aggravating the crisis of public services. The surge of strike activity between 2022 and 2024 was, of course, primarily sparked by disputes over pay. But in many public services – health, education, transport, postal delivery – it also reflected discontent over inadequate staffing provision and service quality (Hodder and Mustchin, 2024). While a common demand from striking workers in the NHS was for pay rises that matched the increase in inflation, underlying (and largely political) sources of contention were also evident: the underfunding of the NHS; a gradual but persistent process of privatization; discontent arising from the highly stressful conditions caused by the COVID-19 pandemic, including the deaths or illness of many staff; and the backlog of patients needing treatment which had accumulated as a result – exacerbating already gruelling work pressures. As a doctor explained:

> 'Morale is at an all time low in the NHS ... We have seen growing waiting lists for elective care, problems retaining the medical workforce, and the worst waiting times for emergency care on record. I have seen many colleagues, both junior and senior, sobbing behind closed clinic room doors, as they try to tackle the ever increasing daily challenges.' (Darlow, 2023: 588)

The pandemic caused a major crisis for the NHS and its employees. The 2022 NHS staff survey revealed that 79 per cent of nurses felt that there were insufficient staff to carry out their jobs (Ali, 2023: 67). Importantly, the public has repeatedly supported their strikes, despite efforts by the government to drive a wedge between strikers and the public (Ali, 2023: 75).

In the UK, there have been many stories of ambulances queuing for hours and patients stuck on trolleys in corridors – patients may have to wait weeks to see a GP or even to get a phone consultation with one. It is no surprise that some doctors are leaving the NHS to go to Australia and New Zealand to attain better pay and conditions. Unions warned of this, as reported in a House of Commons briefing: they were concerned that people would leave the NHS and that recruiting new staff would be difficult. Unions also expressed concern over patient safety being compromised by inadequate staffing levels and staff burnout (Garratt, 2023). This is a major source of contention between the staff and the government over the future of 'our NHS', the great product of the post-war epoch and the Beveridge plan. It also exemplifies the crisis of deterioration of work: '[E]verybody should feel valued when they work' (Darlow, 2023: 588). This crisis is not confined to the UK, however. In Sweden, there is a major concern about 'job-hopping' among young nurses who are dissatisfied with their pay and conditions and who are leaving their positions in search of better prospects (Selberg and Mulinari, 2022). All this is a further manifestation of the problems affecting the provision of care under neoliberal capitalism (see Chapters 3 and 7), given the contradiction that exists between the paradigm of relations of production and reproduction and the realization of value (Fraser, 2016).

While there was a – justified – focus on the impact of cost-of-living issues, overall the magnitude of labour conflict during the early 2020s highlighted the extent to which, in the aftermath of the COVID-19 pandemic, the neoliberal model of work and employment relations, characterized by austerity, deregulation and disempowered labour, has been subject to challenge. What does all this mean for organized labour, though, and the prospects for a revitalized trade union movement? The manifest contention we have described did not appear to translate into any immediate notable increases in trade union membership in the UK and US, with the proportion of workers who are union members continuing to fall. Yet unions in these countries face major obstacles, especially hostility from employers, in their efforts to organize workers. The remarkable wave of labour conflict highlights the deep feeling of unrest that exists about the state of work and the conditions experienced by workers which has arisen as a consequence of the era of intensified neoliberalism and which can contribute to the revival of labour movements around the world.

Writing about the US, Cornfield (2023) identifies a 'new labour activism' associated with the surge of union organization and mobilization in the aftermath of the COVID-19 pandemic in the context of growing discontent among workers with their experiences of precarity and inequality and informed by an intersectional approach which holds that racial and gender politics are integral to understanding workers' struggles, the revitalization of the labour movement and, thus, the prospects of challenging neoliberal capitalism.

The rise of 'grassroots' unions in the UK, such as the Independent Workers of Great Britain, which organize and mobilize precarious workers, particularly migrant workers, illuminates this in practice. In developing 'communities of struggle' which are 'cohesive and effective', based on workers' own lived experiences and identities, building alliances with sympathetic organizations and campaigns and through the shrewd use of contentious tactics – online activism and direct action, for example – independent, grassroots unions have won tangible gains for workers who otherwise lack conventional bargaining power and whose interests had been neglected by established unions (Però, 2020: 901). While their significance has been questioned (see Chapter 6), according to Weghmann (2022: 145), self-styled 'independent' unions 'have reinvigorated worker-led militancy', posing a challenge to the bureaucratic and risk averse behaviour of traditional organizations and creating 'communities of resistance that amplify the struggles of low paid, migrant workers'.

In the US, there is a growing understanding of the racialized dimension of resistance by labour to corporations such as Amazon (Alimahomed-Wilson and Reese, 2021). Viewing labour conflict through an intersectional lens necessitates an appreciation of just how much contention is a function of structural racial and gender disadvantage in employment relations (Lee and Tapia, 2021, 2023). Protests against sexual harassment by workers in McDonald's in the US demonstrate the influence of the #MeToo movement on labour activism (Fortado, 2018). Taking an intersectional perspective means that we have to recognize how social identities other than those related to class, those arising from gender and 'race' in particular, influence labour contention. The experience of the US demonstrates how broader movements for social justice, such as the Black Lives Matter mobilization, can underpin workers' struggles against capitalism and demands for greater justice in an environment where, because of the inbuilt racism in the economy, discrimination against people of colour is rampant (Lee and Tapia, 2023).

Environmental and climate activism

A resurgent labour activism is clearly one response to the crisis of work, linked to the adverse effects of intensified neoliberalism, amplified by the COVID-19 pandemic and the impact of cost-of-living difficulties, and informed by demands for social justice among workers from marginalized and disadvantaged groups. Moreover, the climate crisis has also prompted a surge of activism. Consider the phenomenon of 'climate strikes', often led by young people, which have become a commonplace form of contention in protest against the failure of corporations, governments and international organizations to take meaningful action to address the escalating climate emergency (Buzogány and Scherhaufer, 2023; Richardson, 2023). The March 2022 wave of 'school strikes' were organized and coordinated by the Fridays for Future campaign, involving walk-outs from schools and colleges by young people around the world (Gayle, 2022).

To be sure, there is a long history of environmental and climate activism (Gunningham, 2019). Local struggles against extraction, what Klein (2014) describes as 'Blockadia', since road-blocking has been a key strategy, have succeeded in stopping or halting fossil fuel operations, for example. But the increasing severity of the climate crisis, and the prospect of reaching a tipping point, has galvanized the climate movement. July 2023 was the hottest month ever recorded on earth. As UN Secretary-General Guterres has pointed out: "For vast parts of North America, Asia, Africa and Europe it is a cruel summer. For the entire planet it is a disaster. And for scientists, it is unequivocal – humans are to blame" (Niranjan, 2023).

In this context, a global climate justice movement has developed, as the example of the 'climate strikes' demonstrates, one which is marked not just by protests but other, more disruptive forms of contention, such as the use of direct action and civil disobedience tactics (Buzogány and Scherhaufer, 2023: 366). Behind these lie grassroots social movements and activist campaigns, which have emerged for the purpose of challenging fossil fuel capitalism and taking meaningful, transformative action to tackle the climate crisis (Gunningham, 2019, 2020; Buzogány and Scherhaufer, 2023; Farrer et al, 2023). In the UK, for example, the Just Stop Oil (JSO) campaign has organized activities which involve protestors gluing themselves to roads, climbing motorway gantries, slow marching in city centres and throwing orange powder at sporting events. JSO is part of the action network A22, which is committed to facilitating non-violent civil disobedience and mobilizing mass support and connects groups in ten countries.

Another prominent social movement which has been involved in organizing direct action as a way of inciting meaningful action to tackle the climate emergency is Extinction Rebellion (XR), which originated in the UK in 2018. Within a year, around 130 local XR groups had been established in the UK, and the movement grew so quickly it spread to 45 other countries (Gunningham, 2019). For XR and other such movements, non-violent, direct action, designed to cause substantial 'economic disruption', was the principal means of raising the awareness of, and securing effective action from, policy makers – in governments, corporations, international organizations and non-governmental organizations. Until it seemingly disavowed direct action in 2023, XR had organized relatively small-scale but highly disruptive non-violent activities 'including street blockades, parliamentary occupations, disruptions of commuter traffic, or activists sticking themselves to protest sites' (Buzogány and Scherhaufer, 2023: 360). XR argued that the escalating climate emergency had left the planet 'on the brink and the only option left is civil disobedience, to disrupt the ordinary working of things, so that decision makers HAVE to take notice' (Gunningham, 2019: 198).

Although reviled as 'eco-terrorists' by the right-wing press and often provoking angry reactions from the public, groups such as JSO and XR hit the headlines in a way that less disruptive actions would fail to do. Hundreds of JSO activists have been arrested, some of them many times in an attempt to clog up a struggling justice system and cost the government money. The effectiveness of disruptive direct action can be seen from its positive impact on pushing climate change up the political agenda and its success in influencing efforts by governments and others to address the climate emergency (Gunningham, 2019, 2020; Buzogány and Scherhaufer, 2023).

An important dimension of the new climate activism discussed here, and indeed other activist mobilizations such as the anti-war movement, concerns the belief that effective action demands an economic transformation, one that repudiates neoliberal capitalism, given the extent to which it privileges corporate excess and negates sustainable development. The growth of the climate justice campaign has been influenced by the revulsion caused by the behaviour of profit-hungry corporations in traditional extractive industries. For gas and oil companies, 2023 was a year of massive profits: British Gas (which raised UK household bills massively that year) reported annual profits of £969 million, BP £2 billion and Shell £3.9 billion, a figure described as 'obscene' by Greenpeace activists who mounted a protest outside Shell HQ in London (Ambrose, 2023).

This points to the interconnectedness of climate activism and demands for economic and social justice (Klein, 2014). Tackling the climate crisis effectively necessitates a social and economic transformation, one which repudiates neoliberal capitalism, for the purpose of securing a genuinely 'just' transition. As Buzogány and Scherhaufer (2023: 363) explain, a 'defining feature in the narratives of the climate movement is the contestation of the existing political and economic system – which is perceived as unjust, undemocratic and capitalist'. The extent to which climate activism can find common cause with labour movements is moot. Given their often, albeit not universally, espoused advocacy of a 'just transition' towards a decarbonized economy (see Chapter 6), trade unions can be viewed as important allies of the climate movement and its constituent parts (Stevis et al, 2018). But there can be profound obstacles to collaboration, especially where unions represent workers in industries with high carbon footprints, given the threat to jobs posed by climate action. According to Gunningham (2019: 201), this is where 'the climate movement's increasing emphasis on a just transition to a low-carbon economy, and a clear articulation as to how displaced workers would be treated and new jobs in renewables created, will be crucial'.

Conclusion

One thing that is very clear from the material covered this chapter is the extent to which contention has been a response to the crisis *of* work, and thus an integral feature of the crises *at* work which we are concerned with in this book. The effects of intensified neoliberalism, the experience of the COVID-19 pandemic and the impact of the escalating climate emergency have exacerbated antagonism and thus fuelled challenges to neoliberal capitalism. The upsurge in strike activity we have described was not just a function of demands from workers for wage rises that would match inflation, in a pronounced 'cost-of-living crisis'; it also fulfilled what Katsaroumpas (2023: 556–7) calls a 'disclosure function'. Growing labour contention highlighted some profound problems facing society and the economy and demonstrated how these were a consequence of intensified neoliberalism and the austerity, deregulation and disempowered labour it had propagated. Much recent climate activism is informed by the belief that neoliberal capitalism has been responsible for the perilous position in which our planet is now in, and that it should be rejected as a result. Linked to this, then, is the strong sense that neoliberalism itself is in a state of crisis, as it has become subject to increasing challenge, with its legitimacy diminished accordingly. One key response to this is neoliberalism's increasingly authoritarian 'turn' – a function of its weakness, in a context where demands have escalated for greater state intervention to promote sustainable employment, protect workers' interests and tackle the climate emergency. The resilience of free market capitalism, especially under the auspices of increasingly authoritarian states, should not be underestimated (Slobodian, 2023). This is why it is so important to offer alternative scenarios, setting out how the crisis of work covered in this book can be addressed effectively, something we do in the final chapter of this book.

9

Beyond Crisis?

Introduction

The crisis *of* work with which we are concerned in this book is a product of some notable crises that are *at* work, namely the harmful consequences of intensified neoliberal capitalism, the effects of the COVID-19 pandemic and the impact of the escalating climate emergency. In this final chapter we consider the prospects for transcending the crisis, starting with an emphasis on how work can be made fairer, healthier and greener, particularly by means of a more empowered workforce, represented by stronger trade unions.

Fairer, healthier and greener work – empowered workers and unions

In a context of greater pressures for re-regulation, and amid escalating activism and contention, market fundamentalism may itself be in crisis (see Chapter 8), as people reject the profoundly exploitative model of work with which it is associated. They are increasingly rejecting prolonged wage stagnation and aspiring to improved employment rights and protections. Whether or not a shift in the balance of power away from capital and towards labour is occurring (O'Connor, 2022b), there is clearly a growing expectation that moderating employers' flexibility is desirable and that workers should be better valued. Indeed, the demands of a 'just transition' for the purpose of tackling the climate crisis makes transcending neoliberal capitalism and the – socially and environmentally – unsustainable model of work and employment which characterizes it all the more imperative.

In the field of work and employment relations, there are incipient signs of a greater concern with workers' interests. Consider, for example, the growing attention being devoted to the 'good work' agenda, based on the idea, first of all, of determining certain measures of job quality – for example, pay and rewards, job design, health, safety and well-being and voice – and then advancing ways of improving them (Dobbins, 2022b). The growth in the number of employers who have voluntarily chosen to pay workers a 'real' living wage demonstrates the potential effectiveness of interventions driven by a corporate commitment to operating ethically (Heery et al, 2023). The importance of such efforts, along with calls to address other troublesome aspects of contemporary work, through demands for a four-day week, for example, or for workers to have greater scope to 'disconnect' from their work outside of standard working hours, should not be disregarded. These things can make a positive difference to people's working lives. Yet their overall effect is ameliorative rather than transformative, not least because they operate on the terrain of employers themselves, with the justification for any changes often resting on the desirability of business case arguments – having a better motivated, engaged and highly performing workforce – which can be partial and limited in scope.

Efforts to address the contemporary crisis of work effectively cannot just be restricted to employers, or governments for that matter, but require the active involvement of workers themselves, collectively organized, represented and mobilized in trade unions. Empowering workers and unions, then, is critical for making work and employment better, not just for raising living standards but also for improving the quality of people's working lives, enhancing public services and developing a fairer, greener economic model (Calafati et al, 2023). How, then, can a stronger role for unions help to address the contemporary crisis of work and, indeed, take us beyond the crisis?

We can start at the level of the workplace, where important changes are needed to make it easier for unions to represent and support workers. As the experience of the COVID-19 pandemic showed, a union presence in the workplace can make an important contribution to protecting workers' health, safety and well-being (Cai et al, 2022) – see Chapter 6; unions can also bargain with employers over effective measures for 'greening' the workplace (Farnhill, 2018). Among other things, a trade union presence in the workplace could ensure that artificial intelligence (AI) and related technologies are used in a way that does not damage workers' interests, moderating the potential for surveillance and work intensification for example.

Yet employers are often strongly opposed to the presence of trade unions in the workplace. The existing legal mechanism operating in the UK that enables a trade union to claim recognition by an employer has manifold weaknesses (Bogg, 2012), as do the equivalent arrangements in the US. Accordingly, some interest has been shown in alternative ways of improving the workplace presence of unions in the face of often hostile employers, such as the 'union default' proposal, which would entail that, subject to certain conditions, workers are automatically enrolled into union membership unless they choose to opt out. This would inevitably boost the union's bargaining power, allowing it to represent workers from a greater position of strength (Gall and Harcourt, 2019). In the UK, the Labour Party emphasizes that the 'right of unions to operate effectively in the workplace, in each sector of the economy is vital for achieving fairness, dignity and democracy at work for all' (Labour Party, 2022: 10). If and when it returns to government, it has promised to introduce some measures to make it easier for unions to operate, including a pledge to 'simplify the process of union recognition and establish a reasonable right of entry to organize in workplaces' (Labour Party, 2022: 10). Yet there are doubts about how far Labour is committed to advancing workers' and trade union rights (Hansen, 2023), and the experience of the US shows just how determined some employers, such as Starbucks, can be when it comes to resisting unionization (Jamieson, 2023).

As well as at the level of the workplace, empowering unions so they have a more powerful presence in the labour market would do much to improve people's working lives (Calafati et al, 2023). There is clear evidence of the effectiveness of collective bargaining by unions as a means of improving workers' pay, conditions and living standards, often backed by (the threat of) industrial action (Moore et al, 2019; Unite, 2023). Yet the much diminished position of collective bargaining in the UK has been a major reason for the reduced share of income going to labour, as opposed to capital (see Chapter 7). The workers most in need of union representation and collective bargaining are least likely to have access to them: low-paid workers in precarious employment in sectors such as social care. Nevertheless, through collective bargaining at industry-sector level, unions can regulate labour markets, particularly by setting minimum pay rates and basic employment standards. As a consequence, there have been calls for measures to establish collective bargaining arrangements of some kind, at sector level, in order to address low pay, tackle exploitation and improve living standards in areas such as social care (Hunt, 2023). The UK Labour Party's plan to establish 'fair pay agreements' could see a revival of sector-level bargaining. Labour has proposed that these agreements would be negotiated by representatives of workers and employers and 'establish minimum terms and conditions, which would be binding on all employers and workers in the sector' (Labour Party, 2022). Should Labour be returned to government, it will be interesting to observe how, if at all, these proposals are enacted and what their impact will be.

Boosting the power of unions in the workplace and the labour market could not only improve workers' living standards as a result of collective bargaining but also reverse the precarity and commodification trends noted elsewhere in this book. In doing so, a stronger role for the unions would do much to foster a fairer, healthier, more caring and greener economy: a fairer economy by virtue of the potentially redistributive effects of extending and strengthening collective bargaining and the implications for moderating inequality; a healthier economy because of the pressure unions can exert on employers to ensure that the safety and well-being of workers is prioritized; a more caring economy due to the potentially increased value placed on care work as a consequence of collective bargaining; and a greener economy because of the efforts of unions to promote a 'just transition' to a net-zero world. At a global level, there is an appreciation of the important extent to which collective bargaining can give workers agency, increasing their power to influence patterns of employment relations in supply chains (Kumar, 2020).

Through collective bargaining and its benefits for workers, trade unions can advance a genuine 'levelling up' of the economy (Bryson, 2023), helping to redistribute both income and power, a marked contrast with the phoney approach to 'levelling up' propagated by the Conservatives. A stronger role for the unions is an important but far from the only feature of a transformed economic model that would help to overcome the crisis. This change must be seen alongside the operation of a progressive taxation agenda, focusing on extracting revenue from wealth and polluting industries for example rather than income from employment, which would also moderate inequality. The development of a more activist state role in promoting economic growth and innovation, in partnership with firms but also other stakeholders, such as unions, would also be highly desirable (Mazzucato, 2021). One outcome of such a process of economic democratization would be the marginalization of finance capitalism and rentier interests, helping to moderate employment precarity, labour commodification and work intensification. As we have discussed in other chapters, a 'just transition' to a net-zero economy requires a more sustainable economic model, one where workers and unions themselves are actively involved in the process of change, not treated as the casualties of a short-term, financial imperative to reduce costs (Klein, 2014, 2019; Saltmarsh, 2021).

Empowered workers and unions would have important benefits for society as well as the economy. One of the most serious social problems in the UK is the shortage of workers in key public services, such as health, education and social care; this has been fuelled by staff recruitment and retention difficulties as a consequence of low and stagnant pay. There is now massive under-capacity, imperilling the ability of providers to offer services and contributing to some of the economic difficulties we outline in Chapter 7. Stronger unions could play an important part in enhancing the delivery of public services by moderating staff shortages – a consequence of raising pay levels and improving working conditions – funded by a progressive tax agenda. As previously discussed in this chapter, by prescribing minimum rates of pay and working conditions, a system of sectoral collective bargaining would do much to alleviate some of the difficulties in social care, particularly the prevalence of low pay and hyperflexibility.

Stronger unions, then, can play an important part in promoting greater social justice, with implications for work and beyond. The example of the successful campaign against rail ticket office closures in 2023 highlights how a broader focus, one which engages with advocacy and community organizations – those representing people with disabilities for example – can help to renew the labour movement – see Chapter 6. Coalition working between trade unions and community-based organizations can help to improve the lives of workers in precarious forms of employment which unions find difficult to penetrate on their own (Preminger, 2018). The emergent 'grassroots' style of trade unionism we mention in Chapters 6 and 8 is particularly evident in hyperflexible forms of work, such as that which typifies the platform economy. Importantly, such unions are adept at mobilizing workers collectively in a way that puts pressure on platforms and challenges how they operate (Della Porta et al, 2023). Going beyond trade unions, growing attention is being paid to the role that social movement organizations play in supporting and advocating and campaigning on behalf of working people, sometimes in coalition with trade unions but often on their own account (Williams, 2024). The international Clean Clothes Campaign, for example, actively campaigns for improvements in labour standards in garment factories which are part of global supply chains (Balsiger, 2014).

The extent to which trade union action can make such contributions to improving the quality of people's working lives, with notable benefits for the economy and public services, depends on the presence of a favourable political climate. Since the 1980s, though, unions have faced considerable difficulties stemming from the predominance of a neoliberal ideology which emphasizes the importance of privileging employers' flexibility and suppressing trade unions as a supposed means of improving competitiveness and growth (see Chapters 1, 4 and 6). The damage this has caused, particularly in work and employment, has been a major theme of this book, not least the extent to which it has fuelled greater instability, turbulence and – ultimately – crisis. Clearly a transformed politics is necessary if the contemporary crisis of work is to be abated, one which is not only more supportive of trade unions and the extension and strengthening of trade unions but also advocates a fairer economy. This should be based on a progressive taxation system designed to further the redistribution of wealth, promote a 'just transition' and support public services while confronting the interests of rentiers.

In the UK, the Conservatives are clearly uninterested in any of this; but what about Labour, a party that was originally formed to give working people a voice in Parliament? As mentioned already in this chapter, the Labour Party has published proposals to make it easier for unions to operate and to extend and strengthen collective bargaining by means of new 'fair pay agreements' (Labour Party, 2022). Its 'New Deal for Working People' policy agenda also contains other proposed measures which would improve workers' rights and protections with the aim of moderating precarity and commodification. These include proposals to end bogus self-employment, to ban exploitative zero-hours contracts, to give all workers employment rights and protections from their first day in a job, to enact a new right for workers to 'switch off' from work and not be available outside of working hours and to prohibit the practice of 'firing and rehiring' workers (see Chapter 4) as a cost-saving measure (Labour Party, 2022). However, as already mentioned in this chapter, during 2023 the Labour leadership signalled a potential retreat from its commitment to improving workers' rights and protections and rebalancing power at work in order to demonstrate its supposed business credibility (Hansen, 2023). It also stated its aversion to introducing a wealth tax (Crerar, 2023). Labour's ambitious proposal to invest £28 billion a year in green industry and jobs has seemingly been ditched as the party leadership seeks to emphasize its unwillingness to depart from an orthodox economic model that fetishizes fiscal discipline and austerity (Mason and Allegretti, 2023; Stacey and Harvey, 2024).

Labour's seeming failure to grasp what's required to tackle the contemporary crisis of work effectively suggests that we cannot rely on party politics alone. Rather, it requires a broader democratic transformation, one that involves greater sharing of power with people themselves and their active involvement in politics. A reformed electoral system would help, replacing the 'first-past-the-post' method of electing MPs to the UK's House of Commons, which entrenches the two-party (Labour and Conservative) model in England, with a more proportional arrangement – so that people's votes matter more (Lawson, 2023). This could diversify the range of voices represented in Parliament and give working people a greater stake in the political system. More political decentralization is also desirable, devolving power to regions and communities and thereby energizing politics. The experience of Scottish and Welsh devolution provides an indication, albeit limited, of the possibilities that exist. In contrast to the Conservatives' approach at UK level, both the Scottish government, run by the Scottish National Party, and the Labour-led Welsh government have made efforts to develop a more explicitly re-regulatory employment relations agenda, characterized by an emphasis on promoting greater social partnership and fairer work (Scottish Government, 2019; Welsh Government, 2021).

Empowering workers and unions is an inherently political process, necessitating a supportive political climate. Importantly, though, it also requires a transfer of power to working people and their unions. Measures such as giving workers a 'right' to 'switch off' from work, for example, or changing the law to enhance their ability to work flexibly, including remotely where relevant, are beneficial in and of themselves. But their effectiveness will depend on the capacity of workers, organized collectively in trade unions, to enforce such measures in the workplace and ensure that employers respect them. A more favourable political climate would be helpful, but genuine, transformative change at work is a function of the effective collective organization and mobilization of workers and the power to challenge employers, and secure benefits for workers, that stems from this.

Of course, this requires that unions operate in ways that enable workers to organize, mobilize and empower themselves, acting 'through' rather than on 'behalf of' working people and building their capacity 'to increase collective control over the way that work (but not just work) is organized in society' (Holgate, 2021a: 204).

Moving on from the 'polycrisis'

Having established the importance of building a fairer, healthier and greener economy by empowering workers, and the integral contribution of a revitalized trade union movement in doing so, what are the prospects for transcending the crisis of work? As we explain in the Prologue of this book, there is a sense in which, taken together, the crises which we are concerned with constitute a 'polycrisis' of the kind highlighted by Tooze (2021), with profound and far-reaching consequences. What, then, can be done to move on from this 'polycrisis', given the extent to which the logic of resource extraction seems to predominate in a financialized, asset-based economy which privileges the wealthy and the powerful while exposing working people to greater casualization and commodification? Three broad scenarios can be identified (Figueres and Rivett-Carnac, 2020; Hickel, 2020): first, a 'business-as-usual' approach (Macy and Johnstone, 2020), marked by the continuation of neoliberalism, albeit with increasingly unstable and adverse consequences; second, the development of a more benign model of capitalism, characterized by a social democratic emphasis on balancing the interests of capital and labour; and third, a transformative paradigm, one which rejects and seeks to move beyond capitalism.

Neoliberal 'business-as-usual'

The highly pessimistic 'business-as-usual' scenario posits the continued predominance of a neoliberal agenda, one with scant concern for empowering workers and revitalizing labour movements and which, partly as a consequence, would fail to transcend the crisis of work. During the neoliberal era, capitalism has expanded into most spheres of social, cultural and political life – on a global scale. In its neoliberal form, capitalism is based on processes of human and environmental extractivism that are incredibly damaging – harming people and threatening the entire planet. A 'business-as-usual' scenario portends a 'protective' approach to the 'just transition' (Vachon, 2021), one which is narrowly concerned with establishing mechanisms designed to ensure that workers whose jobs are at risk from the process of decarbonization are shielded in some way from its effects, including through access to re-training and re-skilling opportunities. Such an approach is consistent with a market-based, neoliberal agenda (Hampton, 2015), one which holds that change is inevitable and that the job of unions is to smooth the process, facilitating it in a way that moderates the impact on workers. Such a 'protective' way of facilitating the 'just transition', one concerned with facilitating the adaption of workers to the challenges of decarbonization, would do little to strengthen the unions, and indeed may even undermine them.

Mark Fisher's book *Capitalist Realism* (2009) presents a pessimistic view of our present and future. Starting from the quotation, attributed to both Fredric Jameson and Slavoj Žižek, that 'it's easier to imagine the end of the world than the end of capitalism', Fisher (2009) shows how neoliberalism and capitalism have become entrenched and embedded in all aspects of social, political and, particularly, cultural life; capitalism has become the only reality we know, hence 'capitalist realism'. Our way of life, especially the privileging of consumerism, makes it exceedingly hard to think beyond this reality, as the strength of climate denial among ordinary citizens shows (Figueres and Rivett-Carnac, 2020).

Change is very uncomfortable when it threatens the 'taken-for-granted' facts of our lives. For example, people find it very difficult to accept the idea of a world without the ability to travel around persistently in planes and cars powered by fossil fuel. However, unless we accept the necessity for change and start to reconstruct our culture, a terrible future portends, as starkly outlined by Figueres and Rivett-Carnac (2020). Extreme weather will batter us with wildfires, floods, hurricanes and heatwaves. In many places, the air will be unbreathable. Parts of the globe will become uninhabitable, causing the numbers of refugees fleeing to the remaining, more temperate areas to soar, further fuelling right-wing and authoritarian populist politics (see Chapter 7). Crops will fail, and food will become scarcer and more expensive within the next two decades. As the hunger for profits consumes more and more resources (including the forests which are the lungs of our planet), poverty and inequality will continue to rise as more jobs and sources of livelihoods are displaced by AI and digitalization. The greater use of new forms of 'generative' AI, such as ChatGPT, which are highly resource intensive, is likely to have very damaging environmental consequences (Crawford, 2024). It is possible that violence and unrest will become even more commonplace, even within the liberal democracies of the Global North, than is currently the case. Clearly, despite aspiring to 'business-as-usual', a major consequence of the continued predominance of neoliberal capitalism is that its effects – on work, the environment, life in general – would be so profoundly disruptive as to negate such an aim. As we explain in Chapter 8, the turn towards authoritarianism is itself a manifestation of the contemporary crisis of neoliberalism and the greater instabilities it has engendered.

Reforming capitalism

A second broad scenario with regard to moving on from the 'polycrisis' concerns the revival of an alternative, social democratic capitalist model, one which seeks to be responsive to, and reflective of, the interests of working people in attempting to balance the interests of capital and labour and which seeks to promote a 'greener' form of capitalism. During the 20th century, social democracy was associated with Keynesian economic policies that privileged full employment, a strong role for the state in providing education and welfare provision and a favourable attitude towards trade unions as representatives of workers that had a legitimate role in bargaining over pay and conditions with employers. Traditional social democratic politics, though, was highly gendered in the sense of privileging the interests of male (industrial) workers. As we explain in Chapter 7, one consequence of the crisis of work has been the diminished significance of social democracy as a political force, especially in much of Europe – partly because social democratic political parties have struggled to adapt to social, economic and employment changes.

Nevertheless, the key advantage of a renewed social democratic political agenda concerns the extent to which it would recognize and incorporate workers' interests, and even empower them. As we have already seen in this chapter, a stronger role for trade unions is integral to the development of fairer, healthier and greener work. It can also facilitate a more 'proactive' 'just transition' (Vachon, 2021), of a kind sometimes labelled 'green Keynesianism' – something which is particularly favoured by the official trade union movement, such as the Trades Union Congress in the UK (Hampton, 2015; Stevis and Felli, 2015). Such an approach is valuable to the extent that it can guarantee the involvement of unions and thus ensure that workers' interests are represented in responses to the climate crisis. However, the problem with this way of articulating the 'just transition' is that it pays little attention to matters of social justice and leaves untouched existing economic and 'social relations of property and production that are at the heart of the growth imperative and the climate crisis' (Felli, 2014: 380).

A shift away from neoliberalism towards a more benign form of capitalism, consistent with a renewed social democracy for the 21st century, necessitates some profound economic and social changes. A key priority is to secure effective decarbonization by substituting fossil fuels with renewable – wind, solar, geothermal and hydro – sources of energy. Costa Rica already has 98 per cent renewable energy sources. To limit the use of private cars, a strong role for the state is needed to promote greater investment in public transport systems – trains, buses and trams. According to Figueres and Rivett-Carnac (2020), building a massive electric train network across the US would also provide large numbers of green jobs as well as reducing private car use.

Greater provision of affordable public transport would help to offset the cost-of-living crisis, as would the provision of mass affordable housing, especially when publicly owned. Klein (2014) advocates the renationalization of certain key public utilities – energy, water, transport. This return to public control of common goods could be paid for by increasing taxes on wealth, perhaps accompanied by a carbon pricing system for the use of existing oil, gas and coal stocks (Mann, 2021). Much of the $600 billion used by governments around the world to keep the price of fossil fuels artificially low would be better employed in reinvesting in the public sphere.

State-led, public investment would have widespread benefits. In order to offset the substantial flooding caused by the escalating climate emergency, new sea walls and flood defences could be built, once again providing more good, green jobs. In terms of agriculture, major changes are already being trialled: replanting forests, rewilding farmlands, supporting small farms to practise agroecology, shifting from meat production to crops for plant-based food, the setting up of food cooperatives and community gardens. To make such a programme of change effective, consumers would need to accept changes to their lifestyles. To cut the immense costs and wastage of transporting food around the globe, there would need to be a switch to purchasing local food products, as is already commonplace in Scandinavian countries. People will need to minimize waste – of food, of throwaway fashion, of endlessly upgraded technical devices – based on the principles of 'reduce, reuse, recycle'. Sustainability is essential. As Klein (2014: 91) puts it, 'if we want to live within ecological limits, we would need to return to a lifestyle similar to the one we had in the 1970s, before consumption levels went crazy in the 1980s'.

Yet some evince scepticism that the current crisis, especially the ecological dimension, can be addressed effectively within a capitalist system, irrespective of how far it has been reformed (Hickel, 2020; Buller, 2022a). For example, Hickel (2020) claims that actions amounting to a 'greening of capitalism' cannot be effective, given that processes of resource extraction, exploitation of labour, accumulation and profit maximization are so integral to the capitalist economic system. Efforts to ameliorate the adverse consequences of capitalism are inevitably inadequate. Claims by businesses to be tackling the ecological damage of their activities, such as those by airlines asserting that they are pioneering ways to reduce carbonization from planes, or the practice of 'offsetting' carbon release by planting a bit of forest, can be seen as propaganda – 'greenwashing' exercises (Wright and Nyberg, 2017) – designed to justify continuing with 'business-as-usual'.

Buller (2022a) is withering about 'the myth of green capitalism'. Using the concept of 'maladaptation', which was originated by the Intergovernmental Panel on Climate Change, Buller (2022a) contends that many actions undertaken by businesses which are aimed at mitigating the climate crisis are not only insufficient but may also make things worse in the long run. The switch to electric vehicles is a prominent example: such vehicles rely on extracting lithium for their batteries, creating extreme environmental damage as a result while making it apparently 'green' to continue driving constantly. It is not enough to switch to electric cars: people need to severely limit private car use. As Buller (2022a) puts it, 'affluent consumption is the primary driver of ecological crisis'. The fundamental problem with the notion of 'green capitalism' is that the state still privileges private interests and market actions over public provision when it comes to tackling the climate emergency.

Beyond capitalism?

For some, such as Buller and Lawrence (2022), a more radical, transformative approach is necessary, one which rejects and seeks to move beyond capitalism. From this perspective, it is the fundamental antagonisms produced by capitalism which are at the heart of the contemporary 'polycrisis', and it is only by renouncing the capitalist system entirely that the crisis of work can ever truly be resolved – as part of the process of achieving a better world. To invoke the words of Fisher (2009: 77), there must be 'a credible and coherent alternative to capitalism' – if we are to stop the juggernaut that is rolling over our societies, condemning working people around the globe to stress, misery and, in many cases, poverty while threatening the long-term existence of humanity along with so many of the species that inhabit the planet.

Thus a 'transformative' approach to the 'just transition' is imperative. Integral to the 'transformative' approach is the idea that the climate crisis can only be tackled effectively by challenging capitalist market relations and repurposing economic systems to prioritize social and environmental justice (Hampton, 2015; Stevis and Felli, 2015; Galgóczi, 2020). For Vachon (2021), a 'transformative' approach involves:

> A radical reorganization of society and envisions a post-capitalist world order. Where the protective frame makes minor demands on the state to participate in the economy and the proactive vision makes a stronger challenge on free market ideology by demanding some limited economic planning and a voice for labour in policy making, the transformative vision blows the entire free market ideology out of the water by calling for a radical reorganization of the political economy of the world to eliminate the distinction between the owners of capital and labour. (Vachon, 2021: 120)

A 'transformative' approach to the 'just transition', then, offers the prospect of a more effective response to the climate crisis by challenging the capitalist model responsible for the degradation of both work and the environment and envisioning a more socially and economically just world. Central to this is the role of an energized and renewed trade union movement, one characterized by grassroots mobilization and activism and alliances with broader social movements for the aim of achieving increased economic democracy, with workers and their unions enjoying greater control over how work is organized and undertaken. An effective 'just transition' needs a revitalized union movement, one characterized by greater grassroots activism, involvement in progressive alliances and a commitment to economic democracy (Gunderson, 2019; Klein, 2019; Saltmarsh, 2021). At the same time, trade union revitalization itself can be enabled through unions' engagement with, and involvement in, the push for a just, inclusive, equitable and democratic transition to a net-zero world – and to a better society.

Such a new society would operate in a way that challenged existing inequalities – for example by ensuring that everyone has access to free healthcare, education, sufficient healthy food and clean water. This would require a major shift in thinking, away from consumerism and towards a more community ethos. The need for a more caring and equal society is paramount, one which privileges economic and social justice over markets and competition (Hickel, 2020). It is a society where people have more time for leisure and family activities – arising from a shorter working week – with the provision of guaranteed jobs upholding security and stemming the tide of anxiety and mental ill-health.

There are two main problems with such a vision. One is that it is far too utopian. Yet Ruth Levitas (2013) argues that utopian visions have always been, and still are, crucial to our thinking about how existing societies can develop in fairer ways. Second, what about the practical difficulties that arise? Capitalist market relations are so embedded and taken for granted that it is difficult to conceive that things could be different. Nevertheless, there are actions that could be taken as a priority – the provision of affordable, free even, public transport on a mass scale, for example, and the progressive scaling down of destructive industries such as fossil fuel extraction, armaments and private jets (Hickel, 2020). None of this is feasible, though, without two fundamental political shifts. The first concerns the need to strengthen democracy and the public commons, challenging one of the major principles of neoliberalism, privatization of the economy. Second, related to this, political structures and institutions have to be recaptured for democracy, rejecting kleptocratic and plutocratic governments and breaking the systems which allow 'dark money' to influence policy and the funding of governments by corporate interests (Geoghegan, 2020), thus challenging the second great principle of neoliberalism: the domination of the market.

Conclusion

We have used this chapter to emphasize how empowering working people and strengthening trade unions are essential to tackling the crisis of work and to sketch out three alternative scenarios for transcending the broader 'polycrisis' – upholding ('business-as-usual') neoliberalism, reforming capitalism and rejecting capitalist relations. In thinking of a future beyond crisis, the reorganization and reform of work must be central. Clearly, neoliberal capitalism, in its current iteration, cannot deliver the change that is necessary, especially if (further) environmental and climate devastation are to be avoided. Continued neoliberalism, by exacerbating antagonisms and instabilities, would only prolong, and intensify, the crisis.

A post-capitalist future may be possible in the long term – consistent with aspirations for a fairer, more socially just and greener world of work. In the short and medium terms, though, there is much that could be done to reform capitalism in order to facilitate a just transition and thus help transcend the crisis of work. Ensuring the provision of more 'good' (green) jobs that are fairly distributed, rewarded and recognized is essential. Much can be done to improve workers' rights and protections – helping to address the preponderance of highly casualized and often very commodified jobs. A key task is to enhance the rights of trade unions to organize in workplaces and to take appropriate industrial action when workers want it. Beyond this, the relentless audit and managerial culture that surrounds many forms of work can be confronted and changed through collective workplace and political action. This points to the crucial role of contention. Labour conflict and environmental and climate activism are not just manifestations of the crisis of work but can also play an important part in helping to transcend this crisis (see Chapter 8). As the experience of the climate movement illustrates, contention is an effective way of stimulating progressive and purposeful change (Buzogány and Scherhaufer, 2023).

Collective mobilization and activism have the potential to undermine the legitimacy of neoliberal capitalism and even challenge it. Campaigning for a better world in general, and a better world of work in particular, is increasingly informed by the realization that much of the wealth hoarded in the Global North reflects the legacy of colonialism and its plunders. It is critical that the countries most exposed to the damaging effects of the escalating climate emergency – generally those that are relatively poorer – have a voice on the international stage to oppose global capital's push for further extraction and emission of carbon resources. The crisis *of* work, understood as a function of three crises which are *at* work – economy, pandemic and climate – can only be addressed effectively through collective action, at local, national and global level. This seems a daunting task, especially given the reluctance of elite interests (in politics, the media and business) to take the 'polycrisis' seriously and their lack of concern with effecting meaningful change (a preference for 'business-as-usual'). But the experience of COVID-19 showed that collective awareness, empathy and solidarity are palpable under certain circumstances, as manifest in the actions people took to hinder the spread of the coronavirus. Challenging the processes of extraction, exploitation and appropriation which are integral to neoliberal capitalism is a profound struggle. But it is an important struggle if the crisis of work is to be addressed effectively.

References

Abramowi, M. (2018) 'Democracy in crisis', Freedom House, Available from: https://freedomhouse.org/report/freedom-world/2018/democracy-crisis

Adams, R. (2023) 'University staff union backs away from UK-wide strikes as support wanes', *The Guardian*, 22 September, Available from: https://www.theguardian.com/education/2023/sep/22/university-staff-union-backs-away-from-uk-wide-strikes-as-support-wanes

Adams-Prassl, A., Boneva, T., Golin, M. and Rauh, C. (2020) 'Inequality in the impact of the coronavirus shock: evidence from real time surveys', *Journal of Public Economics*, 189: 1–33.

Adams-Prassl, J. (2019) 'What if your boss was an algorithm? The rise of artificial intelligence at work', *Comparative Labor Law and Policy Journal*, 41(1): 123–46.

Addison, J., Teixeira, P., Pahnke, A. and Bellmann, L. (2017) 'The demise of a model? The state of collective bargaining and worker representation in Germany', *Economic and Industrial Democracy*, 38(2): 193–234.

Adisa, T.A., Antonacopoulou, E., Beauregard, A., Dickmann, M. and Adekoya, O. (2022) 'Exploring the impact of COVID-19 on employees' boundary management and work–life balance', *British Journal of Management*, 33(4): 1694–709.

Adkins, L., Cooper, M. and Konings, M. (2020) *The Asset Economy: Property Ownership and the New Logic of Inequality*, Cambridge: Polity.

Advisory, Conciliation and Arbitration Service (ACAS) (2021) 'Dismissal and re-engagement (fire-and-rehire): a fact-finding exercise', London: ACAS.

Ahuja, A. (2020) 'COVID-19 is really a syndemic – and that shows us how to fight it', *Financial Times*, 9 October, Available from: https://www.ft.com/content/34a502b1-5665-42ff-8a8d-1298b71f1e7b

Ainsley, C. (2018) *The New Working Class*, Bristol: Policy Press.

Albertazzi, D. and McDonnell, D. (2015) *Populists in Power*, Abingdon: Routledge.

Alberti, G. (2016) 'Moving beyond the dichotomy of workplace and community unionism: the challenges of organising migrant workers in London's hotels', *Economic and Industrial Democracy*, 37(1): 73–94.

Ali, T. (2023) 'How a historic strike wave rocked the NHS', *Tribune*, 3 July, Available from: https://tribunemag.co.uk/2023/07/how-a-historic-strike-wave-rocked-the-nhs

Alimahomed-Wilson, J. and Reese, E. (2021) 'Surveilling Amazon's warehouse workers: racism, retaliation, and worker resistance amid the pandemic', *Work in the Global Economy*, 1(1–2): 55–73.

Allan, S., Faulconbridge, J. and Thomas, P. (2019) 'The fearful and anxious professional: partner experiences of working in the financialized professional services firm', *Work, Employment and Society*, 33(1): 112–30.

Allegretti, A. (2023a) 'Keir Starmer denies abandoning Labour leadership pledges', *The Guardian*, 23 February, Available from: https://www.theguardian.com/politics/2023/feb/23/keir-starmer-denies-abandoning-labour-leadership-pledges

Allegretti, A. (2023b) 'Workplace accidents increasingly ignored by UK safety regulator', *The Guardian*, 27 April, Available from: https://www.theguardian.com/global-development/2023/apr/27/workplace-accidents-increasingly-ignored-by-uk-safety-regulator-hse-health-and-safety-executive

Aloisi, A. and De Stefano, V. (2022a) *Your Boss Is an Algorithm: Artificial Intelligence, Platform Work and Labour*, Oxford: Hart Publishing.

Aloisi, A. and De Stefano, V. (2022b) 'Essential jobs, remote work and digital surveillance: addressing the COVID-19 pandemic panopticon', *International Labour Review*, 161(2): 289–314.

Alston, P. (2019) 'Visit to the United Kingdom of Great Britain and Northern Ireland: report of the Special Rapporteur on Extreme Poverty and Human Rights', New York: United Nations.

Altura, T., Lawrence, A. and Roman, R. (2021) 'The global diffusion of supply chain codes of conduct: market, nonmarket, and time-dependent effects', *Business and Society*, 60(4): 909–42.

Ambrose, J. (2023) 'Shell's "obscene" $5bn profits reignite outrage amid climate crisis', *The Guardian*, 27 July, Available from: https://www.theguardian.com/business/2023/jul/27/shell-profits-oil-gas-price-shareholders

Anand, K. (2022) '"I became a slave in order to put food on the table for my family": unheard voices of undocumented migrants on survival on the margin', Presentation to British Sociological Association seminar on the cost-of-living crisis, 1 December.

Anderson, B. (2010) 'Migration, immigration controls and the fashioning of precarious workers', *Work, Employment and Society*, 24(2): 300–17.

Antràs, P., Redding, S. and Rossi-Hansberg, E. (2023) 'Globalization and pandemics', *American Economic Review*, 113(4): 939–81.

Appelbaum, E. and Batt, R. (2014) *Private Equity at Work: When Wall Street Manages Main Street*, New York: Russell Sage Foundation.

References

Apple (2022) 'Apple supplier code of conduct', Available from: https://www.apple.com/supplier-responsibility/pdf/Apple-Supplier-Code-of-Conduct-and-Supplier-Responsibility-Standards.pdf

Aranea, M., González Belega, S. and Köhler, H.-D. (2021) 'The European Works Council as a management tool to divide and conquer: corporate whipsawing in the steel sector', *Economic and Industrial Democracy*, 41(3): 873–91.

Armstrong, M. (2020) 'Discover Society: COVID-19 Chronicles, Available from: https://archive.discoversociety.org/2020/04/18/the-hidden-impact-of-covid-19-on-single-motherhood/

Arnold, S., Harper, A. and Stirling, A. (2021) 'The UK's living standards crisis: the case for a living income', New Economics Foundation, Available from: https://neweconomics.org/uploads/files/Living-Income-Report_FINAL.pdf

Aronowitz, S. (1997) 'The last good job in America', *Social Text*, 51: 93–108.

Ashley, L. (2022) *Highly Discriminating: Why the City Isn't Fair and Diversity Doesn't Work*, Bristol: Bristol University Press.

Ashton, D. and Maguire, M. (1984) 'Dual labour market theory and the organisation of local labour markets', *International Journal of Social Economics*, 11(7): 106–12.

Aust, I., Muller-Camen, M. and Poutsma, E. (2018) 'Sustainable HRM: a comparative and international perspective', in C. Brewster, E. Farndale and W. Mayrhofer (eds) *Handbook of Research in Comparative Human Resource Management* (2nd edn), Cheltenham: Edward Elgar Publishing, pp 358–69.

Aust Ehnert, I., Matthews, B. and Muller-Camen, M. (2020) 'Common good HRM: a paradigm shift in sustainable HRM?', *Human Resource Management Review*, 30(3): 1–11.

Baccaro, L. and Howell, C. (2017) *Trajectories of Neoliberal Transformation: European Industrial Relations since the 1970s*, Cambridge: Cambridge University Press.

Bailey, D. (2023) 'Worker-led dissent in the age of austerity: comparing the conditions of success', *Work, Employment and Society*, Available from: https://doi.org/10.1177/09500170231169675

Bailey, D., de Waele, J.-M., Escalona, F. and Vieira, M. (eds) (2014) *European Social Democracy during the Global Economic Crisis: Renovation or Resignation?*, Manchester: Manchester University Press.

Bailey, D., Clua-Losada, M., Huke, N., Ribera-Almandozd, O. and Rogers, K. (2018) 'Challenging the age of austerity: disruptive agency after the global economic crisis', *Comparative European Politics*, 16(1): 9–31.

Bain, P., Taylor, P. and Baldry, C. (1999) 'Sick Building Syndrome and the industrial relations of occupational health', *International Review of Employment Studies*, 7(1): 125–48.

Baines, D. and Cunningham, I. (2015) 'Care work in the context of austerity', *Competition and Change*, 19(3): 183–93.

Baines, D. and Cunningham, I. (2020) 'Understanding austerity: its reach and presence in the changing context of work and employment', in D. Baines and I. Cunningham (eds) *Working in the Context of Austerity: Challenges and Struggles*, Bristol: Bristol University Press, pp 3–26.

Baldry, C. and Hyman, J. (2022) *Sustainable Work and the Environmental Crisis: The Link between Labour and Climate Change*, London: Routledge.

Bale, T. (2023) *The Conservative Party after Brexit: Turmoil and Transformation*, Cambridge: Polity.

Ball, J. (2022) 'Joseph E Stiglitz: "everything the neoliberals said was wrong"', *New Statesman*, 23 March, Available from: https://www.newstatesman.com/spotlight/sustainability/energy/2022/03/stiglitz-everything-the-neoliberals-said-was-wrong

Balsiger, P. (2014) *The Fight for Ethical Fashion: The Origins and Interactions of the Clean Clothes Movement*, Farnham: Ashgate.

Bang, H. and Marsh, D. (2018) 'Populism versus neo-liberalism: is there a way forward?', *Policy Studies*, 39(3): 251–9.

Barnes, T. (2018) *Making Cars in the New India: Industry, Precarity and Informality*, Cambridge: Cambridge University Press.

Barron, R. and Norris, G. (1976) 'Sexual divisions and the dual labour market', in S. Allen and D. Barker (eds) *Dependence and Exploitation in Work and Marriage*, London: Longmans, pp 47–69.

Bartley, T. (2018) *Rules without Rights: Land, Labour and Private Authority in the Global Economy*, Oxford: Oxford University Press.

Batt, R. (2018) 'The financial model of the firm, the "future of work", and employment relations', in A. Wilkinson, T. Dundon, J. Donaghey and A. Colvin (eds) *The Routledge Companion to Employment Relations*, Abingdon: Routledge, pp 465–79.

Bauman, Z. (1998) *Work, Consumerism and the New Poor*, Milton Keynes: Open University Press.

BBC News (2020a) 'Manchester University students "occupy" building in rent protest', 12 November, Available from: https://www.bbc.co.uk/news/uk-england-manchester-54921866

BBC News (2020b) 'Morrisons supermarket axes 3,000 managers in huge shake-up', 23 January, Available from: https://www.bbc.com/news/business-51223217

Beckett, L. and Paul, K. (2023) 'Bargaining for our very existence: why the battle over AI is being fought in Hollywood', *The Guardian*, 22 July, Available from: https://www.theguardian.com/technology/2023/jul/22/sag-aftra-wga-strike-artificial-intelligence

Belcher, O., Bigger, P., Neimark, B. and Kennelly, C. (2020) 'Hidden carbon costs of the "everywhere war": logistics, geopolitical ecology, and the carbon boot-print of the US military', *Transactions of the Institute of British Geographers*, 45(1): 65–80.

REFERENCES

Bell, A. (2021) *Our Biggest Experiment: An Epic History of the Climate Crisis*, Berkeley, CA: Counterpoint.

Bell, D. and Blanchflower, D. (2021) 'Underemployment in the United States and Europe', *ILR Review*, 74(1): 56–94.

Bessa, I., Joyce, S., Neumann, D., Stuart, M., Trappmann, V. and Umney, C. (2022) 'A global analysis of worker protest in digital labour platforms', Geneva: ILO, Available from: https://www.ilo.org/wcmsp5/groups/public/---dgreports/---inst/documents/publication/wcms_849215.pdf

Bettington, P. (2021) 'Work in 2021: a tale of two economies', London: CLASS.

Beynon, H. (2019) 'After the long boom: living with capitalism in the twenty-first century', *Historical Studies in Industrial Relations*, 40: 187–221.

Black, B. (1986) *The Abolition of Work and Other Essays*, Port Townsend: Loompanics Unlimited.

Blakeley, G. (2020) *The Corona Crash: How the Pandemic Will Change Capitalism*, London: Verso.

Blanchflower, D. (2019) *Not Working: Where Have All the Good Jobs Gone?*, Princeton: Princeton University Press.

Blauner, R. (1964) *Alienation and Freedom*, Chicago: University of Chicago Press.

Bloodworth, J. (2018) *Hired: Six Months Undercover in Low-Wage Britain*, London: Atlantic Books.

Blyth, M. (2015) *Austerity: The History of a Dangerous Idea*, New York: Oxford University Press.

Bogg, A. (2012) 'The death of statutory union recognition in the United Kingdom', *Journal of Industrial Relations*, 54(3): 409–25.

Booth, R. (2022a) 'England's affordable housing scheme falls 32,000 homes short of target', *The Guardian*, 7 December, Available from: https://www.theguardian.com/society/2022/dec/07/englands-affordable-housing-scheme-falls-32000-homes-short-of-target

Booth, R. (2022b) 'Half of care workers in England earn less than entry level supermarket roles', *The Guardian*, 24 August, Available from: https://www.theguardian.com/society/2022/aug/24/half-of-care-workers-in-england-earn-less-than-entry-level-supermarket-roles

Booth, R. (2023) 'Five million people in England and Wales are unpaid carers, census shows', *The Guardian*, 19 January, Available from: https://www.theguardian.com/society/2023/jan/19/5m-in-england-and-wales-provide-unpaid-care-census-shows

Booth, R. and Goodier, M. (2023a) 'Five care chains thought to make £150m a year for low-rated homes in England', *The Guardian*, 25 March, Available from: https://www.theguardian.com/society/2023/mar/25/five-care-chains-thought-to-make-150m-a-year-for-low-rated-homes-in-england

Booth, R. and Goodier, M. (2023b) 'Number of adults living with parents in England and Wales rises by 700,000 in a decade', *The Guardian*, 10 May, Available from: https://www.theguardian.com/society/2023/may/10/number-adults-living-parents-england-wales-up-700000-decade

Boseley, S. (2020) 'Germany confirms first human coronavirus transmission in Europe', *The Guardian*, 28 January, Available from: https://www.theguardian.com/science/2020/jan/28/germany-confirms-first-human-coronavirus-transmission-in-europe

Bozkurt, U. (2013) 'Neoliberalism with a human face: making sense of the Justice and Development Party's neoliberal populism in Turkey', *Science and Society*, 77(3): 372–96.

Bradley, H. (1999) *Gender and Power in the Workplace*, Basingstoke: Macmillan.

Bradley, H. (2016) *Fractured Identities* (2nd edn), Cambridge: Polity.

Bradley, H. (2018) *Gender* (2nd edn), Cambridge: Polity.

Bradley, H., Erickson, M., Stephenson, C. and Williams, S. (2000) *Myths at Work*, Cambridge: Polity.

Bradley, H., Waller, R. and Bentley, L. (2022) *Selling Our Youth: Stories of Class and Gender in a Precarious Labour Market*, Bingley: Emerald Publishing.

Brady, D. and Biegert, T. (2017) 'The rise of precarious employment in Germany', in A. Kalleberg and S. Vallas (eds) *Precarious Work* (Vol. 31, Bingley: Emerald Publishing, pp 245–71.

Brandl, B. (2023) 'The cooperation between business organizations, trade unions, and the state during the COVID-19 pandemic: a comparative analysis of the nature of the tripartite relationship', *Industrial Relations*, 62(2): 145–71.

Braverman, H. (1974) *Labour and Monopoly Capital: The Degradation of Work in the Twentieth Century*, New York: Monthly Review Press.

Brenan, M. (2021) 'Approval of labor unions at highest point since 1965', *Gallup News*, Available from: https://news.gallup.com/poll/354455/approval-labor-unions-highest-point-1965.aspx

Brewer. M., Fry, E. and Try, L. (2023) 'The living standards outlook 2023', London: Resolution Foundation, Available from: https://www.resolutionfoundation.org/publications/the-living-standards-outlook-2023

Brown, W. and Wright, C. (2018) 'Policies for decent labour standards in Britain', *The Political Quarterly*, 89(3): 482–9.

Brubaker, R. (2017) 'Why populism?', *Theory and Society*, 46(5): 357–85.

Bruff, I. (2014) 'The rise of authoritarian neoliberalism', *Rethinking Marxism*, 26(1): 113–29.

Bryson, A. (2023) 'Collective bargaining in the UK: the key to "levelling up"', *Unions 21 blog post*, 21 August, Available from: https://unions21.org/ideas/collective-bargaining-in-the-uk-the-key-to-levelling-up

Budd, J. (2011) *The Thought of Work*, Ithaca, NY: Cornell University Press.

Buller, A. (2022a) 'Green capitalism is a myth', *Tribune*, 3 August, Available from: https://tribunemag.co.uk/2022/08/green-capitalism-climate-crisis-finance-market-solutions

Buller, A. (2022b) *The Value of a Whale: On the Illusions of Green Capitalism*, Manchester: Manchester University Press.

Buller, A. and Lawrence, M. (2022) *Owning the Future: Power and Property in an Age of Crisis*, London: Verso.

Bunting, M. (2021) *Labours of Love: The Crisis of Care*, London: Granta Books.

Burki, N. (2020) 'The indirect impact of COVID-19 on women', *Lancet*, 20(8): 904–5.

Burn-Murdoch, J. (2022) 'Half a million missing workers show modern Britain's failings', *Financial Times*, 6 October, Available from: https://www.ft.com/content/b197e9e0-dd53-4d77-a84f-a94824100ed5

Busby, N. and James, G. (2016) 'Regulating work and care relationships in a time of austerity: a legal perspective', in S. Lewis, D. Anderson, C. Lyonette, N. Payne and S. Wood (eds) *Work–Life Balance in Times of Recession, Austerity and Beyond*, Abingdon: Routledge, pp 78–92.

Butterick, M. and Charlwood, A. (2021) 'HRM and the COVID-19 pandemic: how can we stop making a bad situation worse?', *Human Resource Management Journal*, 31(4): 847–56.

Buzogány, A. and Scherhaufer, P. (2023) 'The new climate movement: organization, strategy and consequences', in H. Jörgens, C. Knill and Y. Steinebach (eds) *Routledge Handbook of Environmental Policy*, Abingdon: Routledge, pp 358–80.

Cai, M., Moore, S., Ball, C., Flynn, M. and Mulkearn, K. (2022) 'The role of union health and safety representatives during the COVID-19 pandemic: a case study of the UK food processing, distribution, and retail sectors', *Industrial Relations Journal*, 53(4): 390–407.

Calafati, L., Froud, J., Haslam, C., Johal, S. and Williams, K. (2022) 'The crisis of everyday liveability, policy and politics', *The Political Quarterly*, 93(4): 640–8.

Calafati, L., Froud, J., Haslam, C., Johal, S. and Williams, K. (2023) *When Nothing Works*, Manchester: Manchester University Press.

Callinicos, A. (2023) *The New Age of Catastrophe*, Cambridge: Polity.

Callison, W. and Manfredi, Z. (eds) (2020) *Mutant Neoliberalism: Market Rule and Political Rupture*, New York: Fordham University Press.

Calvert, J. and Arbuthnott, G. (2021) *Failures of State: The Inside Story of Britain's Battle with Coronavirus*, London: HarperCollins.

Cant, C. (2020) *Riding for Deliveroo: Resistance in the New Economy*, Cambridge: Polity.

Care Workers Union (CWU) (2022) website, Available from: https://careworkersunion.org

Carillo-Tudela, C., Clymo, A. and Zentler-Munro, D. (2022) 'The truth about the "great resignation" – who changed jobs, where they went and why', *The Conversation*, 28 March, Available from: https://theconversation.com/the-truth-about-the-great-resignation-who-changed-jobs-where-they-went-and-why-180159

Carver, L. and Doellgast, V. (2021) 'Dualism or solidarity? Conditions for union success in regulating precarious work', *European Journal of Industrial Relations*, 27(4): 367–85.

Carver, N. (2019) '"So far from justice": on the frontline of the hostile environment', Bristol: Migration Mobilities website, Available from: https://migration.blogs.bristol.ac.uk/2019/12/05

Cavazotte, F., Heloisa Lemos, A. and Villadsen, K. (2014) 'Corporate smart phones: professionals' conscious engagement in escalating work connectivity', *New Technology, Work and Employment*, 29(1): 72–87.

Centre for Labour and Social Studies (CLASS) (2022) 'The UK race class narrative report', Available from: https://www.academia.edu/108845747/The_UK_Race_Class_Narrative_Report_Building_solidarity_across_race_and_class_to_win_progressive_change_and_inoculate_against_the_powerful_few_that_seek_to_divide_us?uc-sb-sw=38122863

Chagnon, C., Durante, F., Gills, B., Hagolani-Albov, S., Hokkanen, S., Kangasluoma, S. et al (2022) 'From extractivism to global extractivism: the evolution of an organizing concept', *The Journal of Peasant Studies*, 49(4): 760–92.

Chan, J., Selden, M. and Ngai, P. (2020) *Dying for an iPhone: Apple, Foxconn and the Lives of China's Workers*, London: Pluto Press.

Charlwood, A. and Guenole, N. (2022) 'Can HR adapt to the paradoxes of artificial intelligence?', *Human Resource Management Journal*, 32(4): 729–42.

Chartered Institute for Personnel and Development (CIPD) (2022) 'The four-day week: employer perspectives', Available from: https://www.cipd.co.uk/knowledge/fundamentals/relations/flexible-working/four-day-week#gref

Christie, F. and Swingewood, A. (2022) 'The impact of COVID-19 on young workers in England: young people navigating insecure work in Greater Manchester during the COVID-19 pandemic', Project report, Manchester Metropolitan University.

Christophers, B. (2020) *Rentier Capitalism: Who Owns the Economy, and Who Pays for It?*, London: Verso.

Cini, L. (2023) 'Resisting algorithmic control: understanding the rise and variety of platform worker mobilisations', *New Technology, Work and Employment*, 38(1): 125–44.

Clark, C. and Shankley, W. (2020) 'Ethnic minorities in the labour market in Britain', in B. Byrne, C. Alexander, O. Khan, J. Nazroo and W. Shankley (eds) *Ethnicity, Race and Inequality in the UK: State of the Nation*, Bristol: Policy Press, pp 171–96.

Clark, I. and Colling, T. (2018) 'Work in Britain's informal economy: learning from road-side hand car washes', *British Journal of Industrial Relations*, 56(2): 320–41.

Clark, P. (2018) 'Unions', in A. Wilkinson, T. Dundon, J. Donaghey and A. Colvin (eds) *The Routledge Companion to Employment Relations*, Abingdon: Routledge, pp 175–98.

Clark, T. (ed) (2023) *Broke: Fixing Britain's Poverty Crisis*, London: Biteback Publishing.

Clarke, S. and Gregg, P. (2018) 'Count the pennies: explaining a decade of lost pay growth', London: Resolution Foundation.

Clegg, H., Fox, A. and Thompson, A. (1964) *A History of British Trade Unions since 1889*, vol 1, *1889–1910*, Oxford: Clarendon.

Cock, J. (2021) '"Beware of the crocodile's smile": labour-environmentalism in the struggle to achieve a just transition in South Africa', in N. Räthzel, D. Stevis and D. Uzzell (eds) *The Palgrave Handbook of Environmental Labour Studies*, London: Palgrave Macmillan, pp 177–97.

Codd, F. and Ferguson, D. (2020) 'The COVID-19 outbreak and employment rights', House of Commons Library Debate Pack, Available from: https://researchbriefings.files.parliament.uk/documents/CDP-2020-0140/CDP-2020-0140.pdf

Cohen, J. (2020) *Not Working: Why We Have to Stop*, London: Granta.

Cole, M. (2021) 'The wage theft epidemic', *Tribune*, 20 November, Available from: https://tribunemag.co.uk/2021/11/wage-theft-karl-marx-capitalism-workers-bosses-labour

Colfer, B. and Prosser, T. (2022) 'Introduction: European trade unions in the twenty-first century', in B. Colfer (ed) *European Trade Unions in the 21st Century: The Future of Solidarity and Workplace Democracy*, London: Palgrave Macmillan, pp 1–17.

Collins, L., Fineman, D. and Tsuchida, A. (2017) 'People analytics: recalculating the route', Global Human Capital Trends, Deloitte Insights, Available from: https://theleadershipedge.com/download/human_resources/People-analytics-Recalculating-the-route_Deloitte.pdf

Cominetti, N., Hamdan, N. and Slaughter, H. (2023) 'The Resolution Foundation labour market outlook, Q2, 2023', London: Resolution Foundation.

Commission on Care (2016) 'A new deal for care and carers', Available from: https://www.fawcettsociety.org.uk/Handlers/Download.ashx?IDMF=f9df8aec-9d60-4ba4-bbe3-8d8eeccbac10

Cooke, F.L., Dickmann, M. and Parry, E. (2022) 'Building sustainable societies through human-centred human resource management: emerging issues and research opportunities', *The International Journal of Human Resource Management*, 33(1): 1–15.

Coote, A., Harper, A. and Stirling, A. (2020) *The Case for the Four-Day Week*, Cambridge: Polity.

Corbyn, Z. (2022) '"Bossware is coming for almost every worker": the software you might not realize is watching you', *The Guardian*, 27 April, Available from: https://www.theguardian.com/technology/2022/apr/27/remote-work-software-home-surveillance-computer-monitoring-pandemic

Cornfield, D. (2023) 'The new labor activism: a new labor sociology', *Work and Occupations*, 50(3): 316–34.

Cox, J. (2019) 'PASOKification: fall of the European center left or a transformation of the system', *Governance: The Political Science Journal at UNLV*, 6(5), Available from: https://digitalscholarship.unlv.edu/governance-unlv/vol6/iss2/5

Crawford, K. (2024) 'Generative AI's environmental costs are soaring – and mostly secret', *Nature*, 20 February, Available from: https://www.nature.com/articles/d41586-024-00478-x

Creagh, M. (2023) 'Work intensification: the impact on workers and trade union strategies to tackle work intensification', London: Trades Union Congress.

Crenshaw, K. (1991) 'Mapping the margins: intersectionality, identity politics and violence against women of color', *Stanford Law Review*, 43(6): 1241–99.

Crerar, P. (2023) 'Rachel Reeves rules out wealth tax if Labour wins next election', *The Guardian*, 27 August, Available from: https://www.theguardian.com/politics/2023/aug/27/rachel-reeves-rules-out-wealth-tax-if-labour-wins-next-election

Crewe, I. (2020) 'Authoritarian populism and Brexit in the UK in historical perspective', in I. Crewe and D. Sanders (eds) *Authoritarian Populism and Liberal Democracy*, Cham: Palgrave Macmillan, pp 15–31.

Crouch, C. (2011) *The Strange Non-death of Neoliberalism*, Cambridge: Polity.

Cruddas, J. (2021) *The Dignity of Labour*, Cambridge: Polity.

Cunningham, I. and James, P. (2014) 'Public service outsourcing and its employment implications in an era of austerity: the case of British social care', *Competition and Change*, 18(1): 1–19.

Cushen, J. and Thompson, P. (2012) 'Doing the right thing? HRM and the angry knowledge worker', *New Technology, Work, and Employment*, 27(2): 79–92.

Darlow, J. (2023) 'Strikes are a grim prospect, but a broken NHS is worse', *British Medical Journal*, 380: 588.

Davies, W. (2018) 'The neoliberal state: power against "politics"', in D. Cahill, M. Cooper, M. Konings and D. Primrose (eds) *The SAGE Handbook of Neoliberalism*, London: SAGE, pp 273–83.

Davies, W. (2021) 'The revenge of sovereignty on government? The release of neoliberal politics from economics post-2008', *Theory, Culture and Society*, 38(6): 95–118.

Davies, W. (2023) 'Pain, no gain', *London Review of Books*, 13 July, Available from: https://www.lrb.co.uk/the-paper/v45/n14/william-davies/pain-no-gain

Davies, W. and Gane, N. (2021) 'Post-neoliberalism? An introduction', *Theory, Culture and Society*, 38(6): 3–28.

Davies, W., Dutta, S.J., Taylor, N. and Tazzioli, M. (2022) *Unprecedented? How COVID-19 Revealed the Politics of Our Economy*, London: Goldsmiths Press.

De Beer, P. and Keune, M. (2022) 'COVID-19: a prelude to a revaluation of the public sector?', *Transfer*, 28(1): 135–40.

Deem, R. (2004) 'The knowledge worker, the manager academic and the contemporary UK university: new and old forms of public management', *Financial Accountability and Management*, 20(2): 107–28.

Delfanti, A. (2020) *The Warehouse: Workers and Robots at Amazon*, London: Pluto Press.

Della Porta, D. (2013) *Can Democracy Be Saved?*, Cambridge: Polity.

Della Porta, D., Emilio Chesta, R. and Cini, L. (2023) *Labour Conflicts in the Digital Age: A Comparative Perspective*, Bristol: Bristol University Press.

Dén-Nagy, I. (2014) 'A double-edged sword?: a critical evaluation of the mobile phone in creating work–life balance', *New Technology, Work and Employment*, 29(2): 193–211.

DiTomaso, N. (2001) 'The loose coupling of jobs: the subcontracting of everyone?', in I. Berg and A. Kalleberg (eds) *Sourcebook of Labour Markets*, Boston, MA: Springer, pp 247–70.

Dobbins, T. (2022a) 'COVID illuminates global inequalities in workers' rights and working conditions', Research Perspectives, University of Birmingham, Available from: https://www.birmingham.ac.uk/research/perspective/covid-illuminates-global-inequalities-in-workers-rights.aspx

Dobbins, T. (2022b) 'Good work: policy and research on the quality of work in the UK', London: House of Commons Research Briefing, Available from: https://researchbriefings.files.parliament.uk/documents/CBP-9561/CBP-9561.pdf

Doeringer, P. and Piore, M. (1971) *Internal Labour Markets and Manpower Analysis*, Lexington: Heath and Co.

Donaghey, J. and Reinecke, J. (2018) 'When industrial democracy meets corporate social responsibility: a comparison of the Bangladesh Accord and Alliance as responses to the Rana Plaza disaster', *British Journal of Industrial Relations*, 56(1): 14–42.

Dorling, D. (2015) *All That Is Solid*, London: Penguin.

Dowling, E. (2022) *The Crisis of Care*, London: Verso.

Dubas-Fisher, D. and Clements-Thrower, A. (2023) 'UK's richest and poorest areas reveal North-South divide – check where your town ranks', *Mirror Online*, 13 March, Available from: https://www.mirror.co.uk/news/uk-news/uks-richest-poorest-areas-reveal-29442888

Duggan, J., Sherman, U., Carbery, R. and McDonnell, A. (2020) 'Algorithmic management and app-work in the gig economy: a research agenda for employment relations and HRM', *Human Resource Management Journal*, 30(1): 114–32.

Duncan, J. (2022) 'The death of neoliberalism? UK responses to the pandemic', *The International Journal of Human Rights*, 26(3): 494–517.

Dundon, T. (2019) 'The fracturing of work and employment relations', *Labour and Industry*, 29(1): 6–18.

Dundon, T. and Rafferty, A. (2018) 'The (potential) demise of HRM?', *Human Resource Management Journal*, 28(3): 377–91.

Eatwell, R. and Goodwin, M. (2018) *National Populism: The Revolt against Liberal Democracy*, London: Pelican Books.

Ebbinghaus, B. and Lehner, L. (2022) 'Cui bono: business or labour? Job retention policies during the COVID-19 pandemic in Europe', *Transfer*, 28(1): 47–64.

Econie, A. and Dougherty, M. (2019) 'Contingent work in the US recycling industry: permatemps and precarious green jobs', *Geoforum*, 99: 132–41.

The Economist (2022) 'Almost nothing seems to be working in Britain: it could get worse', 9 August, Available from: https://www.economist.com/britain/2022/08/09/almost-nothing-seems-to-be-working-in-britain-it-could-get-worse

Edwards, P. (1986) *Conflict at Work: A Materialist Analysis of Workplace Relations*, Oxford: Basil Blackwell.

Ehnert, I. (2009) *Sustainable Human Resource Management: A Conceptual and Exploratory Analysis from a Paradox Perspective*, Berlin: Physica-Verlag.

Ehnert, I., Parsa, S., Roper, I., Wagner, M. and Muller-Camen, M. (2016) 'Reporting on sustainability and HRM: a comparative study of sustainability reporting practices by the world's largest companies', *International Journal of Human Resource Management*, 27(1): 88–108.

Ehrenreich, B. and Ehrenreich, J. (1977) 'The professional-managerial class', *Radical America*, 11: 7–32.

Eidelson, J. (2013) 'Alt-labor', *The American Prospect*, 29 January.

Elliott, L. (2016) 'Millennials may be first to earn less than previous generation – study', *The Guardian*, 18 July, Available from: https://www.theguardian.com/society/2016/jul/18/millennials-earn-8000-pounds-less-in-their-20s-than-predecessors

Elliott, L. (2022) '30 million in UK "priced out of decent standard of living by 2024"', *The Guardian*, 12 December, Available from: https://www.theguardian.com/business/2022/dec/12/30-million-in-uk-priced-out-of-decent-standard-of-living-by-2024

Elliott, L. (2023) 'Sickness drags down UK economy as job vacancies go unfilled', *The Guardian*, 18 April, Available from: https://www.theguardian.com/business/2023/apr/18/sickness-uk-economy-job-vacancies-rishi-sunak-ons

Elliott, L. (2024a) 'Buoyant UK labour market data belies rise in long-term sickness', *The Guardian*, 13 February, Available from: https://www.theguardian.com/politics/2024/feb/13/uk-labour-market-long-term-sickness-economy-workers

Elliott, L. (2024b) 'Even a technical recession is a headache for Rishi Sunak', *The Guardian*, 15 February, Available from: https://www.theguardian.com/business/2024/feb/15/technical-recession-headache-rishi-sunak-government-general-election-britain

Elliott, L. and Atkinson, D. (1999) *The Age of Insecurity*, London: Verso.

Elliot Major, L. and Machin, S. (2020) *What Do We Know and What Should We Do about Social Mobility?*, London: SAGE.

Ercan, S. and Gagnon, J.-P. (2014) 'The crisis of democracy: which crisis? Which democracy?', *Democratic Theory*, 1(2): 1–10.

Erickson, C., Fisk, C., Milkman, R., Mitchell, D. and Wong, K. (2002) 'Justice for Janitors in Los Angeles: lessons from three rounds of negotiations', *British Journal of Industrial Relations*, 40(4): 543–67.

Erickson, M. (2016) *Science, Culture and Society: Understanding Science in the Twenty-First Century* (2nd edn), Cambridge: Polity.

Erickson, M., Bradley, H., Stephenson, C. and Williams, S. (2009) *Business in Society*, Cambridge: Polity.

Erickson, M., Hanna, P. and Walker, C. (2021) 'The UK higher education senior management survey: a statactivist response to managerialist governance', *Studies in Higher Education*, 46(11): 2134–51.

Erickson, M., Hanna, P. and Walker, C. (2023) 'Moving to teaching online: moral injury, pandemic and the toxic university', in B. Nayak and K. Appleford (eds) *Beyond the Pandemic Pedagogy of Managerialism: Exploring the Limits of Online Teaching and Learning*, London: Palgrave Macmillan, pp 13–31.

Eurofound (2020) 'Employee monitoring and surveillance: the challenges of digitalisation', Luxembourg: Publications Office of the European Union.

Eurofound (2021) 'Involvement of social partners in policymaking during the COVID-19 outbreak', Luxembourg: Publications Office of the European Union, Available from: https://www.eurofound.europa.eu/en/publications/2021/involvement-social-partners-policymaking-during-covid-19-outbreak#:~:text=It%20is%20clear%20that%20the,strengthening%20social%20dialogue%20going%20forward

European Trade Union Confederation (ETUC) (2018) 'A guide for trade unions: involving trade unions in climate action to build a just transition', Brussels: ETUC.

Evans, D (2023) *A Nation of Shopkeepers: The Unstoppable Rise of the Petty Bourgeoisie*, London: Repeater.

Evans, L. and Kitchin, R. (2018) 'A smart place to work? Big data systems, labour, control and modern retail stores', *New Technology, Work, and Employment*, 33(1): 44–57.

Ewing, K. and Hendy, J. (2010) 'The dramatic implications of Demir and Baykara', *Industrial Law Journal*, 39(1): 2–51.

Ewing, K. and Hendy, J. (2020) 'COVID-19 and the failure of labour law: part 1', *Industrial Law Journal*, 49(4): 497–538.

Farnhill, T. (2018) 'Union renewal and workplace greening: three case studies', *British Journal of Industrial Relations*, 56(4): 716–43.

Farnsworth, K. (2012) *Social versus Corporate Welfare: Competing Needs and Interests within the Welfare State*, Basingstoke: Palgrave Macmillan.

Farrer, B., Doyle, L. and Smith, S. (2023) 'Goals, strategies and tactics: continuity and change in Extinction Rebellion in the United Kingdom', *Contention*, 11(2): 29–56.

Fekete, L. (2020) 'Coercion and compliance: the politics of the "hostile environment"', *Race and Class*, 63(1): 97–109.

Felli, R. (2014) 'An alternative socio-ecological strategy? International trade unions' engagement with climate change', *Review of International Political Economy*, 21(2): 372–98.

Ferlie, E. (2017) 'The New Public Management and public management studies', in R. Aldag (ed.), *Oxford Research Encyclopedia of Business and Management*, Oxford: Oxford University Press, https://doi.org/10.1093/acrefore/9780190224851.013.129.

Fernandez, R., Hofman, A. and Aalbers, M.B. (2016) 'London and New York as a safe deposit box for the transnational wealth elite', *Environment and Planning A: Economy and Space*, 48(12): 2443–61.

Fetzer, T. (2019) 'Did austerity cause Brexit?', *American Economic Review*, 109(11): 3849–86.

Figueres, C. and Rivett-Carnac, T. (2020) *The Future We Choose: The Stubborn Optimist's Guide to the Climate Crisis*, London: Manilla Press.

Fine, J. (2006) *Worker Centers: Organizing Communities at the Edge of the Dream*, Ithaca, NY: ILR Press.

Finney, N., Nazroo, J., Bécares, L., Kapadia, D. and Shlomo, N. (eds) (2023) *Racism and Ethnic Inequality in a Time of Crisis: Findings from the Evidence for Equality National Survey*, Bristol: Policy Press.

Fisher, M. (2009) *Capitalist Realism: Is There no Alternative?*, Ropley: Zero Books.

Fleming, P. (2021) *Dark Academia: How Universities Die*, London: Pluto Press.

Focus on Labour Exploitation (FLEX) (2017) 'Risky business: tackling exploitation in the UK labour market', London: FLEX.

Ford, M. (2015) *The Rise of the Robots: Technology and the Threat of Mass Unemployment*, London: OneWorld.

Ford, M. and Ward, K. (2021) 'COVID-19 in Southeast Asia: implications for workers and unions', *Journal of Industrial Relations*, 63(3): 432–50.

Foroohar, R. (2022) 'The new rules for business in a post-neoliberal world', *Financial Times*, 9 October, Available from: https://www.ft.com/content/e04bc664-04b2-4ef6-90f9-64e9c4c126aa

Fortado, S. (2018) 'Workplace sexual abuse, labor and the #MeToo movement', *Labor Studies Journal*, 43(4): 241–4.

Foster, J., McChesney, R. and Jonna, R. (2011) 'The global reserve army of labour and the new imperialism', *Monthly Review*, 63(6): 1–31.

Frangi, L., Koos, S., and Hadziabdic, S. (2017) 'In unions we trust! Analysing confidence in unions across Europe', *British Journal of Industrial Relations*, 55(4): 831–58.

Frangi, R., Noh, S.-C. and Hebdon, R. (2018) 'A pacified labour? The transformation of labour conflict', in A. Wilkinson, T. Dundon, J. Donaghey and A. Colvin (eds) *The Routledge Companion to Employment Relations*, Abingdon: Routledge, pp 285–303.

Fraser, N. (2016) 'Contradictions of capital and care', *New Left Review*, 100: 99–117.

Frenkel, S. (2018) 'Globalisation and work: processes, practices, and consequences', in A. Wilkinson, T. Dundon, J. Donaghey and A. Colvin (eds) *The Routledge Companion to Employment Relations*, Abingdon: Routledge, pp 321–41.

Friedman, S. and Lauriston, D. (2020) *The Class Ceiling: Why It Pays to Be Privileged*, Bristol: Policy Press.

Friends of the Earth (2021) 'An emergency plan on green jobs for young people', London: Friends of the Earth.

Fudge, J. (2018) 'Illegal working, migrants and labour exploitation in the UK', *Oxford Journal of Legal Studies*, 38(3): 557–84.

Fuller, J. and Kerr, W. (2022) 'The great resignation didn't start with the pandemic', *Harvard Business Review*, 23 March, Available from: https://hbr.org/2022/03/the-great-resignation-didnt-start-with-the-pandemic

Galgóczi, B. (2020) 'Just transition on the ground: challenges and opportunities for social dialogue', *European Journal of Industrial Relations*, 26(4): 367–82.

Gall, G. (2022) 'Rail strike: UK government's plan to limit industrial action is just a recipe for more discontent', *The Conversation*, 25 May, Available from: https://theconversation.com/rail-strike-uk-governments-plan-to-limit-industrial-action-is-just-a-recipe-for-more-discontent-183677

Gall, G. and Harcourt, M. (2019) 'The union default solution to declining union membership', *Capital and Class*, 43(3): 407–15.

Gamble, A. (1988) *The Free Economy and the Strong State: The Politics of Thatcherism*, Basingstoke: Macmillan.

Garratt, K. (2023) 'NHS strike action in England', House of Commons Library Research Briefing, 27 July, Available from: https://commonslibrary.parliament.uk/research-briefings/cbp-9775

Garraty, J. (1976) 'Unemployment during the great depression', *Labor History*, 17(2): 133–59.

Gavin, M. (2022) 'Unions and collective bargaining in Australia in 2021', *Journal of Industrial Relations*, 64(3): 362–79.

Gayle, D. (2022) 'Fridays for Future school climate strikes resume across the world', *The Guardian*, 25 March, Available from: https://www.theguardian.com/environment/2022/mar/25/fridays-for-future-school-climate-strikes-resume

Geelan, T. (2022) 'The combustible mix of coalitional and discursive power: British trade unions, social media and the People's Assembly Against Austerity', *New Technology, Work and Employment*, 37(2): 161–84.

Geoghegan, P. (2020) *Democracy for Sale: Dark Money and Dirty Politics*, London: Head of Zeus.

Geppert, M. and Pastuh, D. (2017) 'Total institutions revisited: what can Goffman's approach tell us about "oppressive" control and "problematic" conditions of work and employment in contemporary business organizations?', *Competition and Change*, 21(4): 253–73.

Gerbaudo, P. (2021) *The Great Recoil: Politics after Populism and Pandemic*, London: Verso.

Gerbaudo, P. (2023) 'From Occupy Wall Street to the Gilets Jaunes: on the populist turn in the protest movements of the 2010s', *Capital and Class*, 47(1): 107–24.

Gibson-Graham, J.K. (1996) *The End of Capitalism as We Knew It: A Feminist Critique of Political Economy*, Oxford: Blackwell.

Gibson-Graham, J.K. (2006) *A Postcapitalist Politics*, Minneapolis: Minnesota University Press.

Gill, R. (2009) 'Breaking the silence: the hidden injuries of neoliberal academia', in R. Ryan-Flood and R. Gill (eds) *Secrecy and Silence in the Research Process: Feminist Reflections*, London: Routledge, pp 228–44.

Glaze, M. (2023) 'Millions of women's jobs paid less than the real living wage, research shows', *Mirror Online*, 3 March, Available from: https://www.mirror.co.uk/news/politics/millions-womens-jobs-paid-less-29355792

Glucksmann, M. (1995) 'Why "work"? Gender and the "total social organization of labour"', *Gender, Work and Organization*, 2(2): 63–75.

GMB (2021) 'More than 350 deaths and 31,000 infections linked to COVID-19 exposure at work', GMB News, 31 March, Available from: https://www.gmb.org.uk/news/more-350-deaths-and-31000-infections-linked-covid-19-exposure-work

Godard, J. (2014) 'The psychologisation of employment relations', *Human Resource Management Journal*, 24(1): 1–18.

Goldthorpe, J. (1982) 'On the service class, its formation and future', in A. Giddens and G. Mckenzie (eds) *Social Class and the Division of Labour*, Cambridge: Cambridge University Press, pp 162–85.

Goldthorpe, J., Llewellyn, C. and Payne, C. (1980) *Social Mobility and the Class Structure in Modern Britain*, Oxford: Oxford University Press.

Goodfellow, M. (2019) *Hostile Environment: How Immigrants Became Scapegoats*, London: Verso.

Goods, C. (2017) 'Climate change and employment relations', *Journal of Industrial Relations*, 59(5): 670–9.

Gorz, A. (1994) *Capitalism, Socialism, Ecology*, London: Verso.

Gouzoulis, G. (2023) 'What do indebted employees do? Financialisation and the decline of industrial action', *Industrial Relations Journal*, 54(1): 71–94.

Grady, J. and Simms, M. (2019) 'Trade unions and the challenge of fostering solidarities in an era of financialisation', *Economic and Industrial Democracy*, 40(3): 490–510.

Graeber, D. (2018) *Bullshit Jobs: A Theory*, London: Allen Lane.

Granter, E. (2009) *Critical Social Theory and the End of Work*, Abingdon: Routledge.

Green, F. (1991) 'The reserve army hypothesis: a survey of empirical applications', in P. Dunne (ed) *Quantitative Marxism*, Cambridge: Polity, pp 123–40.

Green, F. (2001) 'It's been a hard day's night: the concentration and intensification of work in late twentieth-century Britain', *British Journal of Industrial Relations*, 39(1): 53–80.

Green, F., Felstead, A., Gallie, D. and Henseke, G. (2022) 'Working still harder', *ILR Review*, 75(2): 458–87.

Green, J. (2022) 'Greening Keynes? Productivist lineages of the Green New Deal', *The Anthropocene Review*, 9(3): 324–43.

Greenhouse, S. (2020) *Beaten Down, Worked Up: The Past, Present and Future of American Labor*, New York: Penguin Random House.

Greenhouse, S. (2021) 'What can Biden do to reverse Trump's assault on labor rights?', *The Guardian*, 9 January, Available from: https://www.theguardian.com/us-news/2021/jan/09/joe-biden-labor-workers-rights-unions-wages

Greenhouse, S. (2023a) 'US experts warn AI likely to kill off jobs – and widen wealth inequality', *The Guardian*, 8 February, Available from: https://www.theguardian.com/technology/2023/feb/08/ai-chatgpt-jobs-economy-inequality

Greenhouse, S. (2023b) '"It feels like it's strike summer": US unions flex muscles across industries', *The Guardian*, 26 July, Available from: https://www.theguardian.com/us-news/2023/jul/26/strike-summer-us-unions-flex-muscles

Greer, I. and Doellgast, V. (2017) 'Marketization, inequality and institutional change: toward a new framework for comparative employment relations', *Journal of Industrial Relations*, 59(2): 192–208.

Greussing, E. and Boomgaarden, H. (2017) 'Shifting the refugee narrative? An automated frame analysis of Europe's 2015 refugee crisis', *Journal of Ethnic and Migration Studies*, 43(11): 1749–74.

Griffths, M. and Yeo, C. (2021) 'The UK's hostile environment: deputising immigration control', *Critical Social Policy*, 41(4): 521–44.

Gruijters, R., Van Winkle, Z. and Fasang, A. (2023) 'Life course trajectories and wealth accumulation in the United States: comparing late baby boomers and early millennials', *American Journal of Sociology*, 129(2): 530–69.

Guerci, M., Montanari, F., Scapolan, A. and Epifanio, A. (2016) 'Green and nongreen recruitment practices for attracting job applicants: exploring independent and interactive effects', *The International Journal of Human Resource Management*, 27(2): 129–50.

Gueye, M. (2022) 'Climate action is about people, not just numbers', SDG Action blog, United Nations, Available from: https://sdg-action.org/climate-action-is-about-people-not-just-numbers%EF%BF%BC

Gumbrell-McCormick, R. and Hyman, R. (2013) *Trade Unions in Western Europe: Hard Times, Hard Choices*, Oxford: Oxford University Press.

Gunderson, R. (2019) 'Work time reduction and economic democracy as climate change mitigation strategies: or why the climate needs a renewed labor movement', *Journal of Environmental Studies and Sciences*, 9(1): 35–44.

Gunningham, N. (2019) 'Averting climate catastrophe: environmental activism, Extinction Rebellion and coalitions of influence', *King's Law Journal*, 30(2): 194–202.

Gunningham, N. (2020) 'Can climate activism deliver transformative change? Extinction Rebellion, business and people power', *Journal of Human Rights and the Environment*, 11(3): 10–31.

Gustafsson, M. (2020) 'Young workers in the coronavirus crisis: findings from the Resolution Foundation's coronavirus survey', London: Resolution Foundation, Available from: https://www.resolutionfoundation.org/app/uploads/2020/05/Young-workers-in-the-coronavirus-crisis.pdf

Habermas, J. (1975) *Legitimation Crisis*, Boston: Beacon Press.

Habermas, J. (1984) *The Theory of Communicative Action Volume 1: Reason and the Rationalization of Society*, Cambridge: Polity.

Habermas, J. (1987) *Theory of Communicative Action Volume 2: Lifeworld and System; A Critique of Functionalist Reason*, Cambridge: Polity.

Haddock-Millar, J., Sanyal, C. and Müller-Camen, M. (2016) 'Green human resource management: a comparative qualitative case study of a United States multinational corporation', *The International Journal of Human Resource Management*, 27(2): 192–211.

Hadjisolomou, A., Mitsakis, F. and Gary, S. (2022) 'Too scared to go sick: precarious academic work and "presenteeism culture" in the UK higher education sector during the COVID-19 pandemic', *Work, Employment and Society*, 36(3): 569–79.

Haldane, A. (2023) 'Austerity is back, and this time it's monetary', *Financial Times*, 30 June, Available from: https://www.ft.com/content/b70b7a8f-cc1a-4be9-b51a-866f5d0dab23

Halffman, W. and Radder, H. (2015) 'The academic manifesto: from an occupied to a public university', *Minerva*, 53: 165–87.

Hall, S.-M., McIntosh, K., Neitzert, E., Pottinger, L., Kalwinder, S., Stephenson, M.-A. et al (2018) 'Intersecting inequalities: the impact of austerity on Black and minority ethnic women in the UK', Report for Runnymede Trust and Women's Budget Group.

Hammer, A. and Ness, I. (2021) 'Informal and precarious work: insights from the Global South', *Journal of Labor and Society*, 24(1): 1–15.

Hampton, P. (2015) *Workers and Trade Unions for Climate Solidarity: Tackling Climate Change in a Neoliberal World*, London: Routledge.

Hampton. P. (2018) 'Trade unions and climate politics: prisoners of neoliberalism or swords of climate justice?', *Globalizations*, 15(4): 470–86.

Hanley, L. (2022) 'From Thatcher to Johnson: how right to buy has fuelled a 40-year housing crisis', *The Guardian*, 29 June, Available from: https://www.theguardian.com/society/2022/jun/29/how-right-to-buy-ruined-british-housing

Hanna, P., Erickson, M. and Walker, C. (2022) 'UK higher education staff experiences of moral injury during the COVID-19 pandemic', *Higher Education*, Available from: https://doi.org/10.1007/s10734-022-00956-z

Hansen, K. (2022) '2022: the year trade unions came back', *Tribune*, 31 December, Available from: https://tribunemag.co.uk/2022/12/strikes-industrial-action-labour-movement-2022

Hansen, K. (2023) 'Labour turns its back on workers' rights', *Tribune*, 8 August, Available from: https://tribunemag.co.uk/2023/08/labour-turns-its-back-on-workers-rights

Harari, D. (2023) 'GDP: international comparisons; key economic indicators', House of Commons Library Research Briefing, 15 November, Available from: https://commonslibrary.parliament.uk/research-briefings/sn02784

Harari, D., Francis-Devine, B., Bolton, P. and Keep, M. (2023) 'Rising cost of living in the UK', House of Commons Library Research Briefing.

Harney, B., Dundon, T. and Wilkinson, A. (2018) 'Employment relations and human resource management', in A. Wilkinson, T. Dundon, J. Donaghey and A. Colvin (eds) *The Routledge Companion to Employment Relations*, Abingdon: Routledge, pp 108–24.

Harvey, D. (2005) *A Brief History of Neoliberalism*, Oxford: Oxford University Press.

Harvey, F. and Carrington, D. (2022) 'World is on "highway to climate hell" UN chief warns at Cop27 summit', *The Guardian*, 7 November, Available from: https://www.theguardian.com/environment/2022/nov/07/cop27-climate-summit-un-secretary-general-antonio-guterres

Harvey, G., Williams, K. and Probert, J. (2013) 'Greening the airline pilot: HRM and the green performance of airlines in the UK', *The International Journal of Human Resource Management*, 24(1): 152–66.

Harvey, M. (2020) 'Coronavirus exposes Britain's bogus self-employment problem', The Conversation, 14 May, Available from: https://theconversation.com/coronavirus-exposes-britains-bogus-self-employment-problem-138459

Hay, C. (1999) 'Crisis and the structural transformation of the state: interrogating the process of change', *The British Journal of Politics and International Relations*, 1(3): 317–44.

Hay, C. (2013) 'Treating the symptom not the condition: crisis definition, deficit reduction and the search for a new British growth model', *The British Journal of Politics and International Relations*, 15(1): 23–37.

Hayes, L. (2017) *Stories of Care: A Labour of Law; Gender and Class at Work*, Basingstoke: Palgrave.

Hayes, L. and Moore, S. (2017) 'Care in a time of austerity: the electronic monitoring of homecare workers' time', *Gender, Work and Organization*, 24(4): 329–44.

Health and Safety Executive (HSE) (2022) 'Work-related stress, anxiety or depression statistics in Great Britain, 2022', London: HSE.

Heath, A. and Li, Y. (2018) 'Persisting disadvantages: a study of labour market dynamics of ethnic unemployment and earnings in the UK (2009–2015)', *Journal of Ethnic and Migration Studies*, 46(5): 857–78.

Hebson, G., Rubery, J. and Grimshaw, D. (2015) 'Rethinking job satisfaction in care work: looking beyond the care debates', *Work, Employment and Society*, 29(2): 314–30.

Heery, E. and Salmon, J. (eds) (2000) *The Insecure Workforce*, London: Routledge.

Heery, E., Hann, D. and Nash, D. (2018) 'Trade unions and the real living wage: survey evidence from the UK', *Industrial Relations Journal*, 49(4): 319–35.

Heery, E., Hann, D. and Nash, D. (2023) *The Real Living Wage: Civil Regulation and the Employment Relationship*, Oxford: Oxford University Press.

Heller, R.F. (2022) *The Distributed University for Sustainable Higher Education*, Singapore: Springer Briefs in Education.

Helm, T. (2023) 'Labour planning £8bn Biden-style green energy revolution', *The Guardian*, 12 March, Available from: https://www.theguardian.com/environment/2023/mar/12/labour-planning-8bn-green-revolution-for-uk-industry-in-deprived-regions

Helm, T. and Inman, P. (2023) 'Union fury as figures show pay rises among top earners driving inflation', *The Guardian*, 25 June, Available from: https://www.theguardian.com/money/2023/jun/25/union-fury-as-figures-show-pay-rises-among-top-earners-driving-inflation

Hendrikse, R. (2018) 'Neo-illiberalism', *Geoforum*, 95: 169–72.

Hermann, C. (2017) 'Crisis, structural reform and the dismantling of the European social model(s)', *Economic and Industrial Democracy*, 38(1): 51–68.

Hern, A. (2020) 'Shirking from home? Staff feel the heat as bosses ramp up remote surveillance', *The Guardian*, 27 September, Available from: https://www.theguardian.com/world/2020/sep/27/shirking-from-home-staff-feel-the-heat-as-bosses-ramp-up-remote-surveillance

Herod, A. and Lambert, R. (2016) 'Neoliberalism, precarious work and remaking the geography of global capitalism', in R. Lambert and A. Herod (eds) *Neoliberal Capitalism and Precarious Work: Ethnographies of Accommodation and Resistance*, Cheltenham: Edward Elgar Publishing, pp 1–36.

Heyes, J. and Lewis, P. (2015) 'Relied upon for the heavy lifting: can employment protection legislation reforms lead the EU out of the jobs crisis?', *Industrial Relations Journal*, 46(2): 81–99.

Heyes, J., Moore, S., Newsome, K. and Tomlinson, M. (2018) 'Living with uncertain work', *Industrial Relations Journal*, 49(5–6): 420–37.

Hickel, J. (2020) *Less Is More: How Degrowth Will Save the World*, Harmondsworth: Penguin.

Hill, A. and Partington, R. (2023) 'Long-term sickness leaving 1.6m UK adults over 50 unable to work', *The Guardian*, 30 January, Available from: https://www.theguardian.com/business/2023/jan/30/long-term-sickness-leaving-16m-uk-adults-aged-50-or-over-unable-to-work

HM Government (2021) 'Net zero strategy: build back greener', London: HMSO.

Hochschild, A. (2012) *The Second Shift: Working Parents and the Revolution at Home*, London: Penguin.

Hodder, A. (2020) 'New technology, work and employment in the era of COVID-19: reflecting on legacies of research', *New Technology, Work and Employment*, 35(3): 262–75.

Hodder, A. and Kretsos, L. (2015) 'Young workers and unions: context and overview', in A. Hodder and L. Kretsos (eds) *Young Workers and Trade Unions: A Global View*, Basingstoke: Palgrave Macmillan, pp 1–15.

Hodder, A. and Mustchin, S. (2024) 'Examining the recent strike wave in the UK: the problem with official statistics', *The British Journal of Sociology*, 75(2): 239–45, Available from: https://doi.org/10.1111/1468-4446.13069

Hodder, A., Williams, M., Kelly, J. and McCarthy, N. (2017) 'Does strike action stimulate trade union membership growth?', *British Journal of Industrial Relations*, 55(1): 165–86.

Hodkinson, S., Lewis, H., Waite, L. and Dwyer, P. (2021) 'Fighting or fuelling forced labour? The Modern Slavery Act 2015, irregular migrants and the vulnerabilising role of the UK's hostile environment', *Critical Social Policy*, 41(1): 68–90.

Holgate, J. (2015) 'An international study of trade union involvement in community organizing: same model, different outcomes', *British Journal of Industrial Relations*, 53(3): 460–83.

Holgate, J. (2021a) *Arise: Power, Strategy and Union Resurgence*, London: Pluto Press.

Holgate, J. (2021b) 'Trade unions in the community: building broad spaces of solidarity', *Economic and Industrial Democracy*, 42(2): 226–47.

Hopkin, J. (2020) *Anti-system Politics: The Crisis of Market Liberalism in Rich Democracies*, Oxford: Oxford University Press.

Horgan, A. (2021) *Lost in Work: Escaping Capitalism*, London: Pluto Press.

Horton, A. (2022) 'Financialization and non-disposable women: real estate, debt and labour in UK care homes', *Environment and Planning A: Economy and Space*, 54(1): 144–59.

Horvat, S. (2021) *After the Apocalypse*, Cambridge: Polity.

House of Commons Environmental Audit Committee (2018) 'Hand car washes', Tenth Report of Session 2017–19, HC 981, London: House of Commons.

House of Commons Environmental Audit Committee (2019) 'Fixing fashion: clothing consumption and sustainability', 16th Report of Session 2017–19, HC 1952, London: House of Commons.

House of Commons Women and Equalities Committee (2021) 'Unequal impact? Coronavirus and the gendered economic impact', Fifth Report of Session 2019–21, HC 385, London: House of Commons.

House of Commons Work and Pensions Committee (2020) 'DWP's response to the coronavirus outbreak', First Report of Session 2019–21, HC 178, London: House of Commons.

Howell, C. (2005) *Trade Unions and the State*, Princeton: Princeton University Press.

Howell, C. (2016) 'Regulating class in the neoliberal era: the role of the state in the restructuring of work and employment relations', *Work, Employment and Society*, 30(4): 573–89.

Humphrys, E., Goodman, J. and Newman, F. (2022) '"Zonked the hell out": climate change and heat stress at work', *The Economic and Labour Relations Review*, 33(2): 256–71.

Hunt, A. (2023) 'A strategy for the care workforce', London: TUC, Available from: https://www.tuc.org.uk/research-analysis/reports/strategy-care-workforce

Hunt, S. (2005) *The Life Course: A Sociological Introduction*, Basingstoke: Palgrave.

Hunter, D.P. (2018) *Chav Solidarity*, Bristol: Lumpen/Active Distribution.

REFERENCES

Hyman, R. (2001) *Understanding European Trade Unionism: Between Market, Class and Society*, London: Sage.

Hyman, R. (2018) 'What future for industrial relations in Europe?', *Employee Relations*, 40(4): 569–79.

Ibsen, C.L. and Tapia, M. (2017) 'Trade union revitalisation: where are we now? Where to next?', *Journal of Industrial Relations*, 59(2): 170–91.

IndustriALL (2016) 'Global unions demand IKEA respect workers' rights and stop anti-union activities in the USA', IndustriALL Press Release, 23 June, Available from: http://www.industriall-union.org/global-unions-demand-ikea-respect-workers-rights-and-stop-anti-union-activities-in-the-usa

Ingram, N., Bathmaker, A.-M., Abrahams, J., Bentley, L., Bradley, H., Hoare, T. et al (2023) *The Degree Generation: The Making of Unequal Graduate Lives*, Bristol: Bristol University Press.

Inman, P. (2022) 'It's not pay claims that are driving up prices in Britain: it's profits', *The Guardian*, 17 December, Available from: https://www.theguardian.com/business/2022/dec/17/its-not-pay-claims-that-are-driving-up-prices-in-britain-its-profits

Inman, P. (2023a) 'Corporate profits drove up prices last year, says ECB president', *The Guardian*, 27 June, Available from: https://www.theguardian.com/business/2023/jun/27/corporate-profits-driving-up-prices-ecb-president-christine-lagarde

Inman, P. (2023b) 'UK economy flatlines in third quarter amid high interest rates', *The Guardian*, 10 November, Available from: https://www.theguardian.com/business/2023/nov/10/uk-economy-flatlines-interest-rates

International Labour Organization (ILO) (2012) 'Are "green" jobs decent?', *International Journal of Labour Research*, 4(2), Available from: https://webapps.ilo.org/wcmsp5/groups/public/@ed_dialogue/@actrav/documents/publication/wcms_207887.pdf

International Labour Organization (ILO) (2013) 'World of work report 2013', Geneva: ILO.

International Labour Organization (ILO) (2015) 'Guidelines for a just transition towards environmentally sustainable economies and societies for all', Geneva: ILO.

International Labour Organization (ILO) (2017) 'World employment social outlook: trends 2017', Geneva: ILO.

International Labour Organization (ILO) (2018a) 'Greening with jobs: world employment social outlook 2018', Geneva: ILO.

International Labour Organization (ILO) (2018b) 'Just transition towards environmentally sustainable economies and societies for all', Policy Brief, Geneva: International Labour Office, Bureau for Workers' Activities.

International Labour Organization (ILO) (2018c) 'Women and men in the informal economy: a statistical picture', Geneva: ILO.

International Labour Organization (ILO) (2019) 'Working on a warmer planet: the impact of heat stress on labour productivity and decent work', Geneva: ILO.

International Labour Organization (ILO) (2021a) 'A global trend analysis on the role of trade unions in times of COVID-19', Geneva: ILO, Available from: https://www.ilo.org/actrav/pubs/WCMS_767226/lang--en/index.htm

International Labour Organization (ILO) (2021b) 'COVID-19, collective bargaining and social dialogue', Geneva: ILO, Available from: https://www.ilo.org/actrav/pubs/WCMS_828623/lang--en/index.htm

International Labour Organization (ILO) (2021c) 'ILO monitor: COVID-19 and the world of work; seventh edition; updated estimates and analysis', Available from: https://www.ilo.org/wcmsp5/groups/public/---dgreports/---dcomm/documents/briefingnote/wcms_767028.pdf

International Labour Organization (ILO) (2022a) 'Collective agreements contribute to fighting inequality, says ILO', Geneva: ILO, Available from: https://www.ilo.org/global/about-the-ilo/newsroom/news/WCMS_843973/lang--en/index.htm

International Labour Organization (ILO) (2022b) 'Job retention schemes during COVID-19: a review of policy responses', Geneva: ILO.

Involvement and Participation Association (IPA) (2020) 'My boss the algorithm: an ethical look at algorithms in the workplace', Available from: https://www.ipa-involve.com/my-boss-the-algorithm-an-ethical-look-at-algorithms-in-the-workplace

Ioannou, G. and Dukes, R. (2021) 'Anything goes? Exploring the limits of employment law in UK hospitality and catering', *Industrial Relations Journal*, 52(3): 255–69.

ITV News (2020) 'Workers walk out at food plants over coronavirus safety fears', 20 March, Available from: https://www.itv.com/news/utv/2020-03-25/workers-walk-out-at-factories-over-coronavirus-safety-fears

ITV News (2023) 'Oxfam workers agree to new pay offer following strike action', 22 December, Available from: https://www.itv.com/news/meridian/2023-12-22/oxfam-workers-agree-to-new-pay-offer-following-strike-action

Jack, A. (2021) 'Growth of staff monitoring software stokes debate over rights and morals', *Financial Times*, 22 September, Available from: https://www.ft.com/content/ab61541a-b6c1-45cb-b9ad-f338ec08cf61

Jaeggi, R. (2014) *Alienation*, New York: Columbia University Press.

Jaffe, S. (2021) *Work Won't Love You Back: How Devotion to Our Jobs Keeps Us Exploited, Exhausted, and Alone*, London: Hurst & Co.

James, P. (ed) (2021) *HSE and COVID at Work: A Case of Regulatory Failure*, Liverpool: Institute of Employment Rights.

Jamieson, D. (2023) 'Starbucks committed "substantial" legal violations to defeat union, officials say', *Huffington Post*, 18 January, Available from: https://www.huffingtonpost.co.uk/entry/starbucks-union-bargaining-order_n_63c86cf9e4b0c8e3fc74918a

Jayanetti, C. (2022) 'Forty councils in England built no social housing for five years due to cuts', *The Observer*, 13 November, Available from: https://www.theguardian.com/society/2022/nov/13/forty-councils-in-england-built-no-social-housing-for-five-years-due-to-cuts

Jennings, W., McKay, L. and Stoker, G. (2021) 'The politics of levelling up', *The Political Quarterly*, 92(2): 302–11.

Jessop, B. (2014) 'Capitalist diversity and variety: variegation, the world market, compossibility and ecological dominance', *Capital and Class*, 38(1): 45–58.

Johnstone, S. (2015) 'The case for workplace partnership', in S. Johnstone and P. Ackers (eds) *Finding a Voice at Work? New Perspectives on Employment Relations*, Oxford: Oxford University Press, pp 153–74.

Johnstone, S., Saridakis, G. and Wilkinson, A. (2019) 'The global financial crisis, work and employment: ten years on', *Economic and Industrial Democracy*, 40(3): 455–68.

Jones, I. (2024) 'More than five million working days lost since current period of strikes began', *The Independent*, 13 February, Available from: https://www.independent.co.uk/business/more-than-five-million-working-days-lost-since-current-period-of-strikes-began-b2495322.html

Jones, K., Ahmed, A., Madoc-Jones, I., Gibbons, A., Rogers, M. and Wilding, M. (2020) 'Working and homeless: exploring the interaction of housing and labour market insecurity', *Social Policy and Society*, 19(1): 121–32.

Jones, O. (2011) *Chavs: The Demonization of the Working Class*, London: Verso.

Jones, O. (2021) *This Land*, London: Penguin.

Jones, P. (2021) *Work without the Worker: Labour in the Age of Platform Capitalism*, London: Verso.

Joseph Rowntree Foundation (JRF) (2022) 'UK poverty 2022: the essential guide to understanding poverty in the UK', York: JRF, Available from: https://www.jrf.org.uk/report/uk-poverty-2022

Judge, L. and Leslie, J. (2021) 'Stakes and ladders: the costs and benefits of buying a first home over the generations', London: Resolution Foundation, Available from: https://www.resolutionfoundation.org/publications/stakes-and-ladders

Kalleberg, A. (2011) *Good Jobs, Bad Jobs: The Rise of Polarized and Precarious Employment Systems in the United States, 1970s to 2000s*, New York: Russell Sage Foundation.

Kalleberg, A. (2018) *Precarious Lives: Job Insecurity and Well-Being in Rich Democracies*, Cambridge: Polity.

Kalleberg, A., Hewison, K. and Shin, K.-Y. (2021) *Precarious Asia: Global Capitalism and Work in Japan, South Korea, and Indonesia*, Stanford: Stanford University Press.

Kalra, V. (2007 [2000]) *From Textile Mills to Taxi Ranks: Experiences of Migration, Labour and Social Change*, Abingdon: Routledge.

Katsaroumpas, I. (2023) 'Crossing the Rubicon: the Strikes (Minimum Service Levels) Act 2023 as an authoritarian crucible', *Industrial Law Journal*, 52(3): 513–59.

Kaufman, B. (2020) 'The real problem: the deadly combination of psychologisation, scientism, and normative promotionalism takes strategic human resource management down a 30-year dead end', *Human Resource Management Journal*, 30(1): 49–72.

Keating, M. and McCrone, D. (eds) (2013) *The Crisis of Social Democracy in Europe*, Edinburgh: Edinburgh University Press.

Kelley, N., Khan, O. and Sharrock, S. (2017) 'Racial prejudice in Britain today', London: Natcen Social Research.

Kellogg, K., Valentine, M. and Christin, A. (2020) 'Algorithms at work: the new contested terrain of control', *Academy of Management Annals*, 14(1): 366–410.

Kelly, J. (2015) 'Trade union membership and power in comparative perspective', *The Economic and Labour Relations Review*, 26(4): 526–44.

Kenway, E. (2021) *The Truth about Modern Slavery*, London: Pluto Press.

Kerr, S. (2023) 'Yes, the climate crisis is raising your grocery bills', *The Guardian*, 27 April, Available from: https://www.theguardian.com/commentisfree/2023/apr/27/climate-crisis-grocery-bills-food-environment

Keune, M. and Pedaci, M. (2020) 'Trade union strategies against precarious work: common trends and sectoral divergence in the EU', *European Journal of Industrial Relations*, 26(2): 139–55.

Kezar, A.J., DePaola, T. and Scott, D. (2019) *The Gig Academy: Mapping Labor in the Neoliberal University*, Baltimore: Johns Hopkins University Press.

Khan, N. (2020) *Arc of the Journeyman: Afghan Migrants in England*, Minneapolis: University of Minnesota Press.

Kioupkiolis, A. and Katsambekis, G. (2017) 'Radical left populism from the margins to the mainstream: a comparison of Syriza and Podemos', in Ó. García Agustín and M. Briziarelli (eds) *Podemos and the New Political Cycle: Left-Wing Populism and Anti-establishment Politics*, Cham: Palgrave Macmillan, pp 201–26.

Kirton, G. (2018) 'Unions and equality: 50 years on from the fight for fair pay at Dagenham', *Employee Relations*, 41(2): 344–56.

Kirton, G. (2021) 'Union framing of gender equality and the elusive potential of equality bargaining in a difficult climate', *Journal of Industrial Relations*, 63(4): 591–613.

Kirton, G. and Greene, A.-M. (2022) *The Dynamics of Managing Diversity and Inclusion: A Critical Approach* (5th edn), London: Routledge.

Klein, N. (2008) *The Shock Doctrine*, London: Penguin.

Klein, N. (2014) *This Changes Everything: Capitalism vs the Climate*, London: Allen Lane.

Klein, N. (2019) *On Fire: The Burning Case for a Green New Deal*, London: Allen Lane.

Koch, I., Fransham, M., Cant, S., Ebrey, J., Glucksberg, L. and Savage, M. (2021) 'Social polarisation at the local level: a four-town comparative study on the challenge of politicising inequality in Britain', *Sociology*, 55(1): 3–29.

Koumenta, M. and Williams, M. (2019) 'An anatomy of zero-hour contracts in the UK', *Industrial Relations Journal*, 50(1): 20–40.

Kramar, R. (2014) 'Beyond strategic human resource management: is sustainable human resource management the next approach?', *The International Journal of Human Resource Management*, 25(8): 1069–89.

Kramar, R. (2022) 'Sustainable human resource management: six defining characteristics', *Asia-Pacific Journal of Human Resources*, 60(1): 146–70.

Kumar, A. (2020) *Monopsony Capitalism*, Cambridge: Cambridge University Press.

Kuruvilla, S. (2021) *Private Regulation of Labor Standards in Global Supply Chains: Problems, Progress, and Prospects*, Ithaca: Cornell University Press.

Laaser, K. (2016) '"If you are having a go at me, I am going to have a go at you": the changing nature of social relationships of bank work under performance management', *Work, Employment, and Society*, 30(6): 1000–16.

Labour Behind the Label (2020) 'Boohoo and COVID-19: the people behind the profits', Bristol: Labour Behind the Label, Available from: https://labourbehindthelabel.net/wp-content/uploads/2020/06/LBL-Boohoo-WEB.pdf

Labour Force Survey (LFS) (2020) 'Annual report', London: Office for National Statistics.

Labour Party (2022) 'A new deal for working people', London: Labour Party.

Lagios, C., Lagios, N., Stinglhamber, F. and Caesens, G. (2023) 'Predictors and consequences of work alienation in times of crisis: evidence from two longitudinal studies during the COVID-19 pandemic', *Current Psychology*, 42: 22866–80, Available from: https://doi.org/10.1007/s12144-022-03372-9

Langan, D., Sanders, C. and Thompson, D. (2023) 'A culture of care at the police? Crisis specific possibilities and lessons', paper presented at the European Sociological Association Conference, 'Feminist Action: Welfare State, the Labour Market, and Sociological and Ecological Crises', 6 September, UWE Bristol.

Lansley, S. (2022) *The Richer, the Poorer: How Britain Enriched the Few and Failed the Poor*, Bristol: Policy Press.

Lapavitsas, C. (2011) 'Theorizing financialization', *Work, Employment, and Society*, 25(4): 611–26.

Lapavitsas, C., Meadway, J. and Nicholls, D. (2023) *The Cost of Living Crisis (and How to Get Out of it)*, London: Verso.

Lavery, S. (2019) *British Capitalism after the Crisis*, Cham: Palgrave Macmillan.

Lawson, N (2023) 'How Keir Starmer is reshaping the Labour Party in his image', PoliticsJoe, Available from: https://www.youtube.com/watch?v=wveBbqVaKxs

LeBaron, G. (2020) *Combatting Modern Slavery: Why Labour Governance Is Failing and What We Can Do about It*, Cambridge: Polity Press.

Lee, T. and Tapia, M. (2021) 'Confronting race and other social identity erasures: the case for critical industrial relations theory', *ILR Review*, 74(3): 637–62.

Lee, T. and Tapia, M. (2023) 'A critical industrial relations approach to understanding contemporary worker uprising', *Work and Occupations*, 50(3): 393–9.

Leggett, C. (2007) 'From industrial relations to manpower planning: the transformations of Singapore's industrial relations', *The International Journal of Human Resource Management*, 18(4): 642–64.

Lehndorff, S. (2015) 'Europe's divisive integration: an overview', in S. Lehndorff (ed) *Divisive Integration: The Triumph of Failed Ideas in Europe – Revisited*, Brussels: ETUI, pp 7–37.

Lehndorff, S., Dribbusch, H. and Schulten, T. (2018) *Rough Waters: European Trade Unions in a Time of Crises*, Brussels: ETUI.

Levitas, R. (2013) *Utopia as Method: The Imaginary Constitution of Society*, Basingstoke: Palgrave Macmillan.

Lewis, F. (2021) 'Hundreds of DVLA workers on strike after "worst workplace COVID outbreak in the UK"', Wales Online, 2 June, Available from: https://www.walesonline.co.uk/news/wales-news/dvla-coronavirus-covid-strike-swansea-20723100

Livingstone, E. (2021) *Make Bosses Pay: Why We Need Unions*, London: Pluto Press.

Locke, R. (2013) *The Promise and Limits of Private Power: Promoting Labor Standards in a Global Economy*, Cambridge: Cambridge University Press.

Lockwood, M. (2018) 'Right-wing populism and the climate change agenda: exploring the linkages', *Environmental Politics*, 27(4) 712–32.

Logan, J. (2006) 'The union avoidance industry in the United States', *British Journal of Industrial Relations*, 44(4): 651–75.

Logan, J. (2021) 'Crushing unions, by any means necessary: how Amazon's blistering anti-union campaign won in Bessemer, Alabama', *New Labor Forum*, 30(3): 38–45.

Logan, J. (2023) 'A model for labor's renewal? The Starbucks campaign', *New Labor Forum*, 32(1): 87–94.

Loomis, E. (2023) 'Independent unions: the allure of a failing strategy', *New Labor Forum*, 32(2): 5–11.

López-Andreu, M. (2019) 'Neoliberal trends in collective bargaining and employment regulation in Spain, Italy and the UK: from institutional forms to institutional outcomes', *European Journal of Industrial Relations*, 25(4): 309–25.

Lowenstein, A. (2022) 'Biden's climate bill victory was hard won: now, the real battle starts', *The Guardian*, 6 November, Available from: https://www.theguardian.com/global-development/2022/nov/06/inflation-reduction-act-climate-crisis-congress

Lyddon, D. (2015) 'The changing pattern of UK strikes, 1964–2014', *Employee Relations*, 37(6): 733–45.

Macartney, H., Montgomerie, J. and Tepe, D. (2022) *The Fault Lines of Inequality: COVID 19 and the Politics of Financialization*, London: Palgrave Macmillan.

Macy, J. and Johnstone, C. (2012) *Active Hope: How to Face the Mess We're in without Going Crazy*, San Francisco: New World Library.

Maffie, D. (2022) 'The global "hot shop": COVID-19 as a union organising catalyst', *Industrial Relations Journal*, 53(3): 207–19.

Major, K. (2023) 'Millennials are getting older – and their pitiful finances are a timebomb waiting to go off', *The Guardian*, 6 March, Available from: https://www.theguardian.com/commentisfree/2023/mar/06/millennials-older-pensions-save-own-home

Manfredi, S. (2016) 'Equality and diversity at work under the coalition', in S. Williams and P. Scott (eds) *Employment Relations under Coalition Government: The UK Experience, 2010–15*, Abingdon: Routledge, pp 108–26.

Mann, M. (2021) *The New Climate War: The Fight to Take Back Our Planet*, London: Scribe.

Marantz, A. (2021) 'Are we entering a new political era?', *The New Yorker*, 24 May, Available from: https://www.newyorker.com/magazine/2021/05/31/are-we-entering-a-new-political-era

Mariappanadar, S. (2019) *Sustainable Human Resource Management: Strategies, Practices and Challenges*, London: Red Globe Press.

Markey, R. and McIvor, J. (2019) 'Environmental bargaining in Australia', *Journal of Industrial Relations*, 61(1): 79–104.

Markey, R., McIvor, J. and Wright, C. (2016) 'Employee participation and carbon emissions reduction in Australian workplaces', *The International Journal of Human Resource Management*, 27(2): 173–91.

Markova, A. (2021) 'Want to know what a just transition to a green economy looks like? Ask the workers', *The Guardian*, 18 October, Available from: https://www.theguardian.com/commentisfree/2021/oct/18/just-transition-green-economy-workers-resources-empowerment

Marsh, S. (2023) '"It's cheaper to not work": childcare shortage in England puts strain on parents', *The Guardian*, 9 March, Available from: https://www.theguardian.com/money/2023/mar/09/its-cheaper-to-not-work-childcare-shortage-in-england-puts-strain-on-parents

Marshall, M. (2023) 'The four most urgent questions about long COVID', *Nature*, 9 June, Available from: https://www.nature.com/articles/d41586-021-01511-z

Martell, L. (2017) 'Book review: Accelerating Academia: The Changing Structure of Academic Time by Filip Vostal', LSE blog, 18 August, Available from: https://blogs.lse.ac.uk/lsereviewofbooks/2017/08/18/book-review-accelerating-academia-the-changing-structure-of-academic-time-by-filip-vostal

Marx, K. (1954 [1867]) *Capital Volume I*, Moscow: Foreign Languages Publishing House.

Marx, K. (1975) *Early Writings*, Harmondsworth: Penguin.

Mason, R. and Allegretti, A. (2023) 'Labour postpones £28bn green plan as it seeks to be trusted on public finances', *The Guardian*, 9 June, Available from: https://www.theguardian.com/politics/2023/jun/09/labour-government-would-have-to-delay-28bn-green-fund-rachel-reeves-says

Mazzucato, M. (2021) *Mission Economy: A Moonshot Guide to Changing Capitalism*, London: Allen Lane.

McAlevey, J. (2016) *No Shortcuts: Organizing for Power in the New Gilded Age*, Oxford: Oxford University Press.

McAlevey, J. (2020) *A Collective Bargain: Unions, Organizing, and the Fight for Democracy*, New York: Ecco.

McBride, J. and Greenwood, I. (eds) (2009) *Community Unionism: A Comparative Analysis of Concepts and Contexts*, Basingstoke: Palgrave Macmillan.

McBride, J. and Smith, A. (2022) '"I feel like I'm in poverty. I don't do much outside of work other than survive": in-work poverty and multiple employment in the UK', *Economic and Industrial Democracy*, 43(3): 1440–66.

McCulloch, A. (2023) 'Strikes Act consultation aims to establish minimum service levels', *Personnel Today*, 25 August, Available from: https://www.personneltoday.com/hr/strikes-act-consultation

McKenzie, L. (2012) 'The stigmatised and devalued working class: the state of a council estate', in W. Atkinson, S. Roberts and M. Savage (eds) *Class Inequality in Austerity Britain*, Basingstoke: Palgrave Macmillan, pp 128–44.

McKenzie, L. (2015) 'The estate we're in: how working-class people became the problem', *The Guardian*, 21 January, Available from: https://www.theguardian.com/society/2015/jan/21/estate-working-class-problem-st-anns-nottingham

McKinney, C.J. and Sturge, G. (2023) 'Visas for social care workers', House of Commons Library, 3 October, Available from: https://commonslibrary.parliament.uk/visas-for-social-care-workers

McKinney, C.J., Coe, S. and Stewart, I. (2022) 'Seasonal worker visas and UK agriculture', House of Commons Library Research Briefing, 26 June, Available from: https://commonslibrary.parliament.uk/research-briefings/cbp-9665

Meadway, J. (2021) 'Neoliberalism is dying: now we must replace it', Open Democracy, 3 September, Available from: https://www.opendemocracy.net/en/oureconomy/neoliberalism-is-dying-now-we-must-replace-it

Meardi, G. (2014) 'Employment relations under external pressure: Italian and Spanish reforms during the Great Recession', in M. Hauptmeier and M. Vidal (eds) *Comparative Political Economy of Work*, Basingstoke: Palgrave Macmillan, pp 332–50.

Metten, A. (2021) 'Rethinking trade union density: a new index for measuring union strength', *Industrial Relations Journal*, 52(6): 528–49.

Migration Advisory Committee (MAC) (2018) 'EEA migration in the UK: final report', London: Migration Advisory Committee.

Milkman, R. (2020) *Immigrant Labor and the New Precariat*, Cambridge: Polity Press.

Milman, O., Sadiq, M., Swan, L., Clarke, S., Symons, H. and Scruton, P. (2023) 'A visual guide to the Canada wildfires and US smoke pollution', *The Guardian*, 9 June, Available from: https://www.theguardian.com/world/2023/jun/09/canada-wildfires-smoke-new-york-map-pictures

Milmo, D. (2021) 'Algorithmic tracking is "damaging mental health" of UK workers', *The Guardian*, 11 November, Available from: https://www.theguardian.com/technology/2021/nov/11/algorithmic-monitoring-mental-health-uk-employees

Minchin, T. (2021) '"The factory of the future": historical continuity and labor rights at Tesla', *Labor History*, 62(4): 434–53.

Mirowski, P. (2013) *Never Let a Serious Crisis go to Waste*, London: Verso.

Montgomerie, J. (2023) 'COVID Keynesianism: locating inequality in the Anglo-American crisis response', *Cambridge Journal of Regions, Economy and Society*, 16(1): 211–23.

Moore, S. and Hayes, L. (2016) 'Taking worker productivity to a new level? Electronic monitoring in homecare- the (re)production of unpaid labour', *New Technology, Work and Employment*, 32(2): 101–14.

Moore, S. and Newsome, K. (2018) 'Paying for free delivery: dependent self-employment as a measure of precarity in parcel delivery', *Work, Employment and Society*, 32(3): 475–92.

Moore, S., Onaran, O., Guschanski, A., Antunes, A. and Symon, G. (2019) 'The resilience of collective bargaining: a renewed logic for joint regulation?', *Employee Relations*, 41(2): 279–95.

Morrison, R. (2023) 'Hollywood in peril: whose side are you on?', *The Times*, 23 July, Available from: https://www.thetimes.co.uk/article/hollywood-writers-strike-tv-film-on-hold-3nsg087dz

Mould, O., Cole, J., Badger, A. and Brown, P. (2022) 'Solidarity, not charity: learning the lessons of the COVID-19 pandemic to reconceptualise the radicality of mutual aid', *Transactions of the Institute of British Geographers*, 47(4): 866–79.

Müller, T., Schulten, T. and Drahokoupil, J. (2022) 'Job retention schemes in Europe during the COVID-19 pandemic: different shapes and sizes and the role of collective bargaining', *Transfer*, 28(2): 247–65.

Murray, C. (2021) 'The climate for change in UK agriculture', UK Research and Innovation blog, 1 December, Available from: https://www.ukri.org/blog/the-climate-for-change-in-uk-agriculture

Naidoo, R. (2008) 'L'état et le marché dans la réforme de l'enseignement supérieur au royaume-uni (1980–2007)' [The state and the market in higher education reform in the UK (1980–2007)], *Critique Internationale*, 39(2): 47–65.

Natali, D. (2022) 'COVID-19 and the opportunity to change the neoliberal agenda: evidence from socio-employment policy responses across Europe', *Transfer*, 28(1): 15–30.

National Audit Office (NAO) (2018) 'The adult social care workforce in England', Available from: https://www.nao.org.uk/report/the-adult-social-care-workforce-in-england

National Institute of Economic and Social Research (NIESR) (2023) 'UK economic outlook: summer 2023', Available from: https://www.niesr.ac.uk/publications/uk-heading-towards-five-years-lost-economic-growth?type=uk-economic-outlook

NHS For Sale (2019) 'Contract report 2018/2019', Available from: https://www.nhsforsale.info/contract-award-activity-2018-2019

Nichols, T. and Beynon, H. (1977) *Living with Capitalism*, London: Routledge & Kegan Paul.

Niranjan, A. (2023) '"Era of global boiling has arrived", says UN chief as July set to be hottest month on record', *The Guardian*, 27 July, Available from: https://www.theguardian.com/science/2023/jul/27/scientists-july-world-hottest-month-record-climate-temperatures

Norris, P. and Inglehart, R. (2019) *Cultural Backlash: Trump, Brexit and Authoritarian Populism*, Cambridge: Cambridge University Press.

O'Brady, S. (2021) 'Fighting precarious work with institutional power: union inclusion and its limits across spheres of action', *British Journal of Industrial Relations*, 59(4): 1084–107.

O'Connor, S. (2022a) 'The term "quiet quitting" is worse than nonsense', *Financial Times*, 13 September, Available from: https://www.ft.com/content/a09a2ade-4d14-47c2-9cca-599b3c25a33f

O'Connor, S. (2022b) 'Has the pendulum really swung from capital to labour?', *Financial Times*, 20 December, Available from: https://www.ft.com/content/30bfcfdd-c555-4c8b-94ba-97047c56ef5c

REFERENCES

O'Connor, S. (2023) 'How Spain has taken on the problem of precarious work', *Financial Times*, 3 April, Available from: https://www.ft.com/content/293aa201-c63b-4144-86b9-84e7bd892d69

Ofcom (2022) 'Report: equity, diversity and inclusion in TV and radio', Available from: https://www.ofcom.org.uk/tv-radio-and-on-demand/information-for-industry/guidance/diversity/diversity-equal-opportunities-tv-and-radio

Office for AI (2019) 'Understanding artificial intelligence: an introduction to understanding and using artificial intelligence in the public sector', Available from: https://www.gov.uk/government/publications/understanding-artificial-intelligence

Office for Budget Responsibility (OBR) (2023) 'Economic and fiscal outlook', CP 804, Available from: https://obr.uk/docs/dlm_uploads/OBR-EFO-March-2023_Web_Accessible.pdf

Office for National Statistics (ONS) (2019) 'Which occupations are at highest risk of being automated?', 25 March, Available from: https://www.ons.gov.uk/employmentandlabourmarket/peopleinwork/employmentandemployeetypes/articles/whichoccupationsareathighestriskofbeingautomated/2019-03-25

Office for National Statistics (ONS) (2020) 'Parenting in lockdown: coronavirus and the effects on work–life balance', Available from: https://www.ons.gov.uk/releases/parentingunderlockdown

Office for National Statistics (ONS) (2023a) 'Housing affordability in England and Wales: 2022', Available from: https://www.ons.gov.uk/peoplepopulationandcommunity/housing/bulletins/housingaffordabilityinenglandandwales/2022

Office for National Statistics (ONS) (2023b) 'The impact of strikes in the UK, June 2022 to February 2023', Available from: https://www.gov.uk/government/statistics/the-impact-of-strikes-in-the-uk-june-2022-to-february-2023--2

Organisation for Economic Co-operation and Development (OECD) (2020a) 'OECD indicators of employment protection', Paris: OECD, Available from: https://www.oecd.org/employment/emp/oecdindicatorsofemploymentprotection.htm

Organisation for Economic Co-operation and Development (OECD) (2020b) 'Job retention schemes during the COVID-19 lockdown and beyond', Paris: OECD, Available from: https://www.oecd.org/coronavirus/policy-responses/job-retention-schemes-during-the-covid-19-lockdown-and-beyond-0853ba1d

Organisation for Economic Co-operation and Development (OECD) (2023) 'OECD economic outlook', vol 23, issue 1, Paris: OECD.Organisation for Economic Co-operation and Development (OECD) (no date) *Trade Union Dataset*, Available from: https://stats.oecd.org/Index.aspx?DataSetCode=TUD

Osnos, E. (2020) *Joe Biden: American Dreamer*, London: Bloomsbury.

Otte, J. (2024) '"We never got off the treadmill": the Britons who can't afford to retire', *The Guardian*, 8 February, Available from: https://www.theguardian.com/money/2024/feb/08/britons-cant-afford-to-retire-insufficient-pension-pots

Özdemir, Y. (2020) 'AKP's neoliberal populism and contradictions of new social policies in Turkey', *Contemporary Politics*, 26(3): 245–67.

Pakulski, J. and Waters, M. (1996) *The Death of Class*, London: SAGE.

Papadopoulos, O. and Ioannou, G. (2023) 'Working in hospitality and catering in Greece and the UK: do trade union membership and collective bargaining still matter?', *European Journal of Industrial Relations*, 29(2): 105–22.

Partington, R. (2021) '"It's a seller's market for workers": how COVID and Brexit have shaken up UK jobs', *The Guardian*, 16 September, Available from: https://www.theguardian.com/politics/2021/sep/16/workers-covid-brexit-uk-jobs-shortages-unions-pay-conditions

Partington, R. (2022) 'Thousands of British Airways workers to get pay rise of up to 13%', *The Guardian*, 15 August, Available from: https://www.theguardian.com/business/2022/aug/15/thousands-of-british-airways-workers-to-get-pay-rise

Partington, R. (2023) 'Two-thirds of UK women say childcare duties affected career progression', *The Guardian*, 8 March, Available from: https://www.theguardian.com/society/2023/mar/08/two-thirds-of-women-say-childcare-duties-affected-career-progression

Pass, S. (2017) 'Life on the line: exploring high-performance practices from an employee perspective', *Industrial Relations Journal*, 48(5–6): 500–17.

Paulet, R., Holland, P. and Bratton, A. (2021) 'Employee voice: the missing factor in sustainable HRM?', *Sustainability*, 13(17): 1–16.

Peck, J. and Theodore, N. (2019) 'Still neoliberalism?', *South Atlantic Quarterly*, 118(2): 245–65.

Peck, J., Theodore, N. and Brenner, N. (2010) 'Postneoliberalism and its malcontents', *Antipode*, 41: 94–116.

Pellow, D., Sonnenfeld, D. and Smith, T. (eds) (2006) *Challenging the Chip: Labor Rights and Environmental Justice in the Global Electronics Industry*, Philadelphia: Temple University Press.

Pennington, H. (2022) *COVID-19: The Postgenomic Pandemic*, Cambridge: Polity.

Però, D. (2020) 'Indie unions, organizing and labour renewal: learning from precarious migrant workers', *Work, Employment and Society*, 34(5): 900–18.

Pettifor, A. (2019) *The Case for a Green New Deal*, London: Verso.

Pettinger, L. (2017) 'Green collar work: conceptualizing and exploring an emerging field of work', *Sociology Compass*, 11(1): e12443.

Pettinger, L. (2019) *What's Wrong with Work?*, Bristol: Policy Press.

Phillips, T. and Iglesia, F. (2024) 'Argentinians stage nationwide strike against Javier Milei's far-right agenda', *The Guardian*, 24 January, Available from: https://www.theguardian.com/world/2024/jan/24/argentina-strike-protest-javier-milei

Piketty, T. (2014) *Capital in the Twenty-First Century*, Cambridge, MA: Harvard University Press.

Pilkington, E. (2021) 'Sanders urges progressives to stand firm in Democratic battle over Biden agenda', *The Guardian*, 3 October, Available from: https://www.theguardian.com/us-news/2021/oct/03/bernie-sanders-democratic-battle-biden-agenda

Polanyi, K. (1957) *The Great Transformation*, Boston: Beacon Press.

Pollert, A. (1981) *Girls, Wives and Factory Lives*, Basingstoke: Macmillan.

Portes, J. (2022) 'Immigration and the UK economy after Brexit', *Oxford Review of Economic Policy*, 38(1): 82–96.

Portes, J. and Springford, J. (2023) 'Early impacts of the post-Brexit immigration system on the UK labour market', Policy Commons, Centre for European Reform, Available from: https://policycommons.net/artifacts/3371536/insight_js_jp_17123/4170340

Potter, J. (2015) *Crisis at Work: Identity and the End of Career*, Basingstoke: Palgrave Macmillan.

Powell, A., Francis-Devine, B. and Clark, H. (2021) 'Coronavirus Job Retention Scheme: statistics', House of Commons Library Briefing Paper, 9152, London: House of Commons Library.

Prassl, J. (2018) *Humans as a Service: The Promise and Perils of Work in the Gig Economy*, Oxford: Oxford University Press.

Pratt, A. (2023) 'Food banks in the UK', House of Commons Library Briefing, Available from: https://researchbriefings.files.parliament.uk/documents/CBP-8585/CBP-8585.pdf

Preminger, J. (2018) 'Creating a multilayered representational "package" for subcontracted workers: the case of cleaners at Ben-Gurion University', *Industrial Relations Journal*, 49(1): 24–49.

Prosser, T. (2019) *European Labour Movements in Crisis*, Manchester: Manchester University Press.

Purcell, J. (2014) 'Disengaging from engagement', *Human Resource Management Journal*, 24(3): 241–54.

Quiggin, J. (2012) *Zombie Economics: How Dead Ideas Still Walk among Us*, Princeton: Princeton University Press.

Radice, H. (2013) 'How we got here: UK higher education under neoliberalism', *ACME: An International E-Journal for Critical Geographies*, 12(3): 407–18.

Rankin, J. and Walker, S. (2021) 'EU launches legal action over LGBTQ+ rights in Hungary and Poland', *The Guardian*, 15 July, Available from: https://www.theguardian.com/world/2021/jul/15/eu-launches-legal-action-over-lgbtq-rights-in-hungary-and-poland

Rathgeb, P. and Tassinari, A. (2022) 'How the Eurozone disempowers trade unions: the political economy of competitive internal devaluation', *Socio-Economic Review*, 20(1): 323–50.

Räthzel, N. and Uzzell, D. (2011) 'Trade unions and climate change: the jobs versus environment dilemma', *Global Environmental Change*, 21(4): 1215–23.

Räthzel, N. and Uzzell, D. (eds) (2013) *Trade Unions in the Green Economy: Working for the Environment*, Abingdon: Routledge.

Räthzel, N., Stevis, D. and Uzzell, D. (2021) 'Introduction: expanding the boundaries of environmental labour studies', in N. Räthzel, D. Stevis and D. Uzzell (eds) *The Palgrave Handbook of Environmental Labour Studies*, Cham: Springer International, pp 1–31.

Rawlinson, K. (2023) 'UK workers £11,000 worse off after years of wage stagnation – thinktank', *The Guardian*, 20 March, Available from: https://www.theguardian.com/business/2023/mar/20/uuk-workers-wage-stagnation-resolution-foundation-thinktank

Rayton, B., Dodge, T. and D'Analeze, G. (2012) 'The evidence: Employee Engagement Task Force "Nailing the Evidence" workgroup', London: Engage for Success.

Readings, B. (1996) *The University in Ruins*, Cambridge, MA: Harvard University Press.

Redman, T., Hamilton, P., Malloch, H. and Kleymann, B. (2011) 'Working here makes me sick! The consequences of Sick Building Syndrome', *Human Resource Management Journal*, 21(1): 14–27.

Reece, N. (2022) 'Workers say no to increased surveillance since COVID-19', Trades Union Congress blog, 1 March, Available from: https://www.tuc.org.uk/blogs/workers-say-no-increased-surveillance-covid-19

Reich. R. (2023) 'Why aren't Americans happier about the economy?', *The Guardian*, 10 July, Available from: https://www.theguardian.com/commentisfree/2023/jul/10/america-economy-robert-reich

Reid, J. (2020) 'Mothers, COVID-19 and work at home: their account in words and portraits', University of Huddersfield Research Portal, Available from: https://pure.hud.ac.uk/en/publications/mothers-covid-19-and-work-at-home-their-account-in-words-and-port

Renner, M., Sweeney, S. and Kubit, J. (2008) 'Green jobs: towards decent work in a sustainable, low-carbon world', Washington: UNEP, ILO/IOE/ITUC Worldwatch Institute.

Renwick, D. (2018) *Contemporary Developments in Green Human Resource Management Research: Towards Sustainability in Action?*, London: Routledge.

Renwick, D., Redman, T. and Maguire, S. (2008) 'Green HRM: a review, process model and research agenda', Discussion Paper, Management School, University of Sheffield, UK.

Renwick, D., Redman, T. and Maguire, S. (2013) 'Green human resource management: a review and research agenda', *International Journal of Management Reviews*, 15(1): 1–14.

Renwick, D., Jabbour, C., Muller-Camen, M., Redman, T. and Wilkinson, A. (2016) 'Contemporary developments in green (environmental) HRM scholarship', *International Journal of Human Resource Management*, 27(2): 114–28.

Resolution Foundation (2016) 'Millennials facing "generational pay penalty" as their earnings fall £8,000 behind during their 20s', Resolution Foundation Press Release, 18 July, Available from: https://www.resolutionfoundation.org/press-releases/millennials-facing-generational-pay-penalty-as-their-earnings-fall-8000-behind-during-their-20s

Resolution Foundation (2022) 'Stagnation nation: navigating a route to a fairer and more prosperous Britain', London: Resolution Foundation, Available from: https://economy2030.resolutionfoundation.org/wp-content/uploads/2022/07/Stagnation_nation_interim_report.pdf

Resolution Foundation (2024) 'UK falls into recession, and a far deeper living standards downturn', Resolution Foundation Press Release, 15 February, Available from: https://www.resolutionfoundation.org/press-releases/uk-falls-into-recession-and-a-far-deeper-living-standards-downturn

Richards, J. (2022) 'Putting employees at the centre of sustainable HRM: a review, map and research agenda', *Employee Relations*, 44(3): 533–54.

Richards, S. (2018) *The Rise of the Outsiders: How Mainstream Politics Lost Its Way*, London: Atlantic Books.

Richardson, B. (2023) 'The art of disobedience: climate justice activism', in D. Brown, K. Gwiazdon and L. Westra (eds) *The Routledge Handbook of Applied Climate Change Ethics*, Abingdon: Routledge, pp 428–41.

Ringqvist, J. (2022) 'Union membership and the willingness to prioritize environmental protection above growth and jobs: a multi-level analysis covering 22 European countries', *British Journal of Industrial Relations*, 60(3): 662–82.

Roberts, K. (2001) *Class in Modern Britain*, Basingstoke: Palgrave.

Rodríguez-Modroño, P., Agenjo-Calderón, A. and López-Igual, P. (2022) 'Platform work in the domestic and home care sector: new mechanisms of invisibility and exploitation of women migrant workers', *Gender and Development*, 30(3): 619–35.

Royall, F. (2020) 'The Gilets Jaunes protests: mobilisation without third-party support', *Modern and Contemporary France*, 28(1): 99–118.

Royle, T. and Rueckert, Y. (2022) 'McStrike! Framing, (political) opportunity and the development of a collective identity: McDonald's and the UK Fast-Food Rights campaign', *Work, Employment and Society*, 36(3): 407–26.

Rubery, J., Grimshaw, D. and Hebson, G. (2013) 'Exploring the limits to local authority care commissioning: competing pressures, variable practices and unresponsive providers', *Public Administration*, 91(2): 419–37.

Rubery, J., Grimshaw, D., Hebson, G. and Ugarte, S. (2015) '"It's all about time": time as contested terrain in the management and experience of domiciliary care work in England', *Human Resource Management*, 54(5): 753–72.

Rubery, J., Keizer, A. and Grimshaw, D. (2016) 'Flexibility bites back: the multiple and hidden costs of flexible employment policies', *Human Resource Management Journal*, 26(3): 235–51.

Ruhs, M. and Anderson, B. (2010) *Who Needs Migrant Workers? Labour Shortages, Immigration and Social Policy*, Oxford: Oxford University Press.

Runciman, D. (2014) *The Confidence Trap: A History of Democracy in Crisis from World War One to the Present*, Princeton: Princeton University Press.

Rydzik, A. and Bal, P. (2023) 'The age of insecuritisation: insecure young workers in insecure jobs facing an insecure future', *Human Resource Management Journal*, Available from: https://doi.org/10.1111/1748-8583.12490

Ryner, M. (2010) 'An obituary for the Third Way: the financial crisis and social democracy in Europe', *The Political Quarterly*, 81(4): 554–63.

Sainato, M. (2020) 'US employers step up anti-unionization efforts as pandemic spurs activism', *The Guardian*, 18 June, Available from: https://www.theguardian.com/us-news/2020/jun/18/us-employers-unions-pandemic-activism

Sainato, M. (2022) 'New "Striketober" looms as US walkouts increase amid surge in union activity', *The Guardian*, 26 September, Available from: https://www.theguardian.com/us-news/2022/sep/26/striketober-unions-strikes-us-october

Sainato, M. (2023a) 'Joe Biden hails reported UAW deal with General Motors to end strike', *The Guardian*, 30 October, Available from: https://www.theguardian.com/us-news/2023/oct/30/uaw-contract-gm-strike-end-update

Sainato, M. (2023b) '"We can't trust them": workers decry alleged union busting at Amazon air hub', *The Guardian*, 29 November, Available from: https://www.theguardian.com/technology/2023/nov/29/amazon-union-busting-kentucky-air-hub

Saltmarsh, C. (2021) *Burnt: Fighting for Climate Justice*, London: Pluto Press.

Savage, M. (2021) *The Return of Inequality: Social Change and the Weight of the Past*, Cambridge, MA: Harvard University Press.

Savage, M., Cunningham, N., Devine, F., Friedman, S., Laurison, D., Mckenzie, L. et al (2015) *Social Class in the Twenty-First Century*, Harmondsworth: Pelican.

Sayer, A. (2012) 'Facing the challenge of the return of the rich', in W. Atkinson, S. Roberts and M. Savage (eds) *Class and Inequality in Austerity Britain*, Basingstoke: Palgrave Macmillan, pp 163–79.

Scarpetta, S., Pearson, M., Hijzen, A. and Salvatori, A. (2020) 'Job retention schemes during the COVID-19 lockdown and beyond', Paris: OECD.

Scheiber, N. (2022) 'Most "pro-union president" runs into doubts in labor ranks', *New York Times*, 27 December, Available from: https://www.nytimes.com/2022/12/27/business/economy/biden-labor-unions.html

Schmidt, W., Müller, A., Ramos-Vielba, I., Thörnquist, A. and Thörnqvist, C. (2019) 'Austerity and public sector trade union power: before and after the crisis', *European Journal of Industrial Relations*, 25(2): 129–45.

Schor, J. (1993) *The Overworked American: The Unexpected Decline of Leisure*, New York: Basic Books.

Scottish Government (2019) 'Fair work: action plan', Available from: https://www.gov.scot/publications/fair-work-action-plan

Seifert, R. and Wang, W. (2018) 'Race discrimination at work: the moderating role of trade unionism in English local government', *Industrial Relations Journal*, 49(3): 259–77.

Selberg, R. and Mulinari, P. (2022) 'Exit spirals in hospital clinics: conceptualising turnover contagion among nursing staff', *Scandinavian Journal of Public Administration*, 21(1): 107–21.

Selyukh, A. (2020) 'Amazon workers stage new protests over warehouse coronavirus safety', National Public Radio, 21 April, Available from: https://www.npr.org/sections/coronavirus-live-updates/2020/04/21/839888501/amazon-workers-stage-new-protests-over-warehouse-coronavirus-safety?t=1661096653718

Sennett, R. (1998) *The Corrosion of Character: The Personal Consequences of Work in the New Capitalism*, New York: W.W. Norton.

Shankley, W. and Rhodes, J. (2020) 'Racisms in contemporary Britain', in B. Byrne, C. Alexander, O. Khan, J. Nazroo and W. Shankley (eds) *Ethnicity, Race and Inequality in the UK: State of the Nation*, Bristol: Policy Press, pp 264–96.

Sharma, P. (2022) 'Digitalisation and precarious work practices in alternative economies: work organisation and work relations in e-cab services', *Economic and Industrial Democracy*, 43(2): 559–84.

Shay, J. (1994) *Achilles in Vietnam: Combat Trauma and the Undoing of Character*, Oxford: Maxwell Macmillan International.

Shay, J. (2014) 'Moral injury', *Psychoanalytic Psychology*, 31(2): 182–91.

Shenker, J. (2023) '"To them, we are like robots. The things that make us human are ground out of you": the inside story of a strike at Amazon', *The Guardian*, 29 July, Available from: https://www.theguardian.com/technology/2023/jul/29/to-them-we-are-like-robots-inside-story-of-a-strike-at-amazon

Sikwebu, D. and Aroun, W. (2021) 'Energy transitions in the Global South: the precarious location of unions', in N. Räthzel, D. Stevis and D. Uzzell (eds) *The Palgrave Handbook of Environmental Labour Studies*, Cham: Springer International, pp 59–81.

Simmonds, B. (2022) *Ageing and the Crisi in Health and Social Care: Global and National Perspectives*, Bristol: Bristol University Press.

Simms, M. (2015) 'Union organizing as an alternative to partnership: or what to do when employers can't keep their side of the bargain', in S. Johnstone and P. Ackers (eds) *Finding a Voice at Work? New Perspectives on Employment Relations*, Oxford: Oxford University Press, pp 127–52.

Simms, M. (2019) *What Do We Know and What Should We Do about the Future of Work?*, London: SAGE.

Simms, M., Holgate, J. and Heery, E. (2013) *Union Voices: Tactics and Tensions in UK Organizing*, Ithaca, NY: Cornell University Press.

Simms, M., Eversberg, D., Dupuy, C. and Hipp, L. (2018) 'Organizing young workers under precarious conditions: what hinders or facilitates union success?', *Work and Occupations*, 45(4): 420–50.

Skills for Care (2022) 'Vacancies in social care increase by 52% to their highest rates and the workforce shrinks for the first time', Available from: https://www.skillsforcare.org.uk/news-and-events/news/vacancies-in-social-care-increase-by-52-to-their-highest-rates-and-the-workforce-shrinks-for-the-first-time

Skills for Care (2023) 'The state of the adult social care sector and workforce in England', Available from: https://www.skillsforcare.org.uk/Adult-Social-Care-Workforce-Data/Workforce-intelligence/publications/national-information/The-state-of-the-adult-social-care-sector-and-workforce-in-England.aspx

Sky News (2023) 'Strikes: who is taking industrial action in 2023 and when?', 31 March, Available from: https://news.sky.com/story/strikes-who-is-taking-industrial-action-in-2023-and-when-12778841

Sleigh, S. (2022) '"The working class is back and we refuse to be poor anymore" – Mick Lynch tells crowd', *Huffington Post*, 18 August, Available from: https://www.huffingtonpost.co.uk/entry/mick-lynch-tells-enough-is-enough-campaign-working-class-is-back_uk_62fdf347e4b071ea958cdee7

Slobodian, Q. (2021) 'Hayek's bastards: the populist right's neoliberal roots', *Tribune*, 15 June, Available from: https://tribunemag.co.uk/2021/06/hayeks-bastards-the-populist-rights-neoliberal-roots

REFERENCES

Slobodian, Q. (2023) *Crack-up Capitalism*, Harmondsworth: Penguin.

Sloterdijk, P. (2014) *In the World Interior of Capital: For a Philosophical Theory of Globalization*, Cambridge: Polity.

Smale, B. (2020) *Exploring Trade Union Identities: Union Identity, Niche Identity and the Problem of Organizing the Unorganized*, Bristol: Bristol University Press.

Smith, A. (2016) '"The magnificent 7[am]?" Work-life articulation beyond the 9[am] to 5[pm] "norm"', *New Technology, Work, and Employment*, 31(3): 209–22.

Smith, A., Strauss, D. and Fray, K. (2023) 'Are Britain's striking public-sector workers underpaid?', *Financial Times*, 11 January, Available from: https://www.ft.com/content/fac8062a-bd83-486b-ac6f-582f1931750b

Snell, D. and Fairbrother, P. (2010) 'Unions as environmental actors', *Transfer*, 16(3): 411–24.

Snell, D. and Fairbrother, P. (2011) 'Toward a theory of union environmental politics: unions and climate action in Australia', *Labor Studies Journal*, 36(1): 83–103.

Soares, S. and Berg, J. (2023) 'Mortality from COVID-19 in the US: did unions save lives?', ILO Working Paper 98, Geneva: ILO.

Sobolewska, M. and Ford, R. (2020) *Brexitland*, Cambridge: Cambridge University Press.

Social Mobility Commission (SMC) (2019) 'State of the nation 2018–19: social mobility in Great Britain', London: SMC.

Social Mobility Commission (SMC) (2020) 'Monitoring social mobility 2013 to 2020', London: SMC, Available from: https://www.gov.uk/government/publications/monitoring-social-mobility-2013-to-2020

Social Mobility Commission (SMC) (2021) 'State of the nation 2021: social mobility and the pandemic', Available from: https://www.gov.uk/government/publications/state-of-the-nation-2021-social-mobility-and-the-pandemic

Soffia, M., Wood, A. and Burchell, B. (2022) 'Alienation is not "bullshit": an empirical critique of Graeber's theory of BS jobs', *Work, Employment and Society*, 36(5): 816–40.

Solomos, J. (2003) *Race and Racism in Britain*, Basingstoke: Palgrave.

Springer, S. (2021) *Fuck Neoliberalism: Translating Resistance*, Oakland, CA: PM Press.

Srnicek, N. and Williams, A. (2015) *Inventing the Future: Postcapitalism and a World without Work*, London: Verso.

Stacey, K. and Harvey, F. (2024) 'Labour cuts £28bn green investment pledge by half', *The Guardian*, 8 February, Available from: https://www.theguardian.com/politics/2024/feb/08/labour-cuts-28bn-green-investment-pledge-by-half

Stahl, G., Brewster, C., Collings, D. and Hajro, A. (2020) 'Enhancing the role of human resource management in corporate sustainability and social responsibility: a multi-stakeholder, multidimensional approach to HRM', *Human Resource Management Review*, 30(3): 1–16.

Standing, G. (2011) *The Precariat: The New Dangerous Class*, London: Bloomsbury.

Stanley, L. (2022) *Britain Alone: How a Decade of Conflict Remade the Nation*, Manchester: Manchester University Press.

Statista (2023a) 'The UK economy: statistics and facts', April 2023, Available from: https://www.statista.com/topics/6500/the-british-economy

Statista (2023b) 'Youth unemployment rate in EU member states', April 2023, Available from: https://www.statista.com/statistics/613670/youth-unemployment-rates-in-europe/

Stecula, D. and Pickup, M. (2021) 'How populism and conservative media fuel conspiracy beliefs about COVID-19 and what it means for COVID-19 behaviors', *Research and Politics*, 8(1), Available from: https://doi.org/10.1177/2053168021993979

Stevis, D. (2011) 'Unions and the environment: pathways to global labor environmentalism', *WorkingUSA: The Journal of Labor and Society*, 14(2): 145–59.

Stevis, D. (2013) 'Green jobs? Good jobs? Just jobs? USA labour unions confront climate change', in N. Räthzel and D. Uzzell (eds) *Trade Unions in the Green Economy: Working for the Environment*, Abingdon: Routledge, pp 179–95.

Stevis, D. (2018) 'US labour unions and green transitions: depth, breadth, and worker agency', *Globalizations*, 15(4): 454–69.

Stevis, D. and Felli, R. (2015) 'Global labour unions and just transition to a green economy', *International Environmental Agreements*, 15: 29–43.

Stevis, D., Uzzell, D. and Räthzel, N. (2018) 'The labour–nature relationship: varieties of labour environmentalism', *Globalizations*, 15(4): 439–53.

Stewart, H. (2022) 'The long battle to get Britain's lost employees back to work', *The Guardian*, 22 October, Available from: https://www.theguardian.com/business/2022/oct/22/the-long-battle-to-get-britains-lost-employees-back-to-work

Stewart, H. (2023) 'Four-day week: "major breakthrough" as most UK firms in trial extend changes', *The Guardian*, 21 February, Available from: https://www.theguardian.com/money/2023/feb/21/four-day-week-uk-trial-success-pattern

Stiglitz, J. (2019) 'Neoliberalism must be pronounced dead and buried: where next?', *The Guardian*, 30 May, Available from: https://www.theguardian.com/business/2019/may/30/neoliberalism-must-be-pronouced-dead-and-buried-where-next

Stoilova, R. and Ilieva-Trichkova, P. (2023) 'Digitalization and the challenge of intersecting inequalities towards participation in adult education in Europe', Paper presented at European Sociological Association Conference, 'Feminist Action: Welfare State, the Labour Market, and Sociological and Ecological Crises', 6 September, UWE Bristol.

Strangleman, T. (2007) 'The nostalgia for permanence at work? The end of work and its commentators', *The Sociological Review*, 55(1): 81–103.

Strauss, D. and Parker, G. (2022) 'UK unemployment falls to lowest level in nearly 50 years', *Financial Times*, 17 May, https://www.ft.com/content/8015b43f-5cdd-443e-bdcc-3079d4582e48

Streeck, W. (2016) *How Will Capitalism End? Essays on a Failing System*, London: Verso.

Streeck, W. (2017) *Buying Time: The Delayed Crisis of Democratic Capitalism*, London: Verso.

Stuart, M., Spencer, D., McLachlan, C. and Forde, C. (2021) 'COVID-19 and the uncertain future of HRM: furlough, job retention and reform', *Human Resource Management Journal*, 31(4): 904–17.

Stuart, M., Trappmann, V., Bessa, I., Joyce, S., Neumann, D. and Umney, C. (2023) 'Labor unrest and the future of work: global struggles against food delivery platforms', *Labor Studies Journal*, 48(3): 287–97.

Sullivan, R. (2010) 'Labour market or labour movement? The union density bias as barrier to labour renewal', *Work, Employment and Society*, 24(1): 145–56.

Šumonja, M. (2021) 'Neoliberalism is not dead: on political implications of COVID-19', *Capital and Class*, 45(2): 215–27.

Susskind, D. (2020) *A World without Work: Technology, Automation and How We Should Respond*, New York: Metropolitan Books.

Sutton Trust (2019) 'Elitist Britain 2019', Available from: https://www.suttontrust.com/wp-content/uploads/2020/01/Elitist-Britain-2019-Summary-Report.pdf

Sweney, M. (2023) 'Royal Mail boss blames rogue managers for tracking devices on workers', *The Guardian*, 22 February, Available from: https://www.theguardian.com/business/2023/feb/22/royal-mail-boss-blames-rogue-managers-for-tracking-devices-on-workers

Tapia, M. (2013) 'Marching to different tunes: commitment and culture as mobilizing mechanisms of trade unions and community organizations', *British Journal of Industrial Relations*, 51(4): 666–88.

Tapia, M. and Turner, L. (2018) 'Renewed activism for the labor movement: the urgency of young worker engagement', *Work and Occupations*, 45(4): 391–419.

Tapper, J. (2022) 'Quiet quitting: why doing the bare minimum at work has gone global', *The Guardian*, 6 August, Available from: https://www.theguardian.com/money/2022/aug/06/quiet-quitting-why-doing-the-bare-minimum-at-work-has-gone-global

Tassinari, A. and Maccarrone, V. (2020) 'Riders on the storm: workplace solidarity among gig economy couriers in Italy and the UK', *Work, Employment and Society*, 34(1): 35–54.

Tattersall, A. (2010) *Power in Coalition: Strategies for Strong Unions and Social Change*, Ithaca, NY: ILR Press.

Taylor, P. (2013) 'Performance management and the new workplace tyranny', Available from: http://www.stuc.org.uk/files/Document%20download/Workplace%20tyranny/STUC%20Performance%20Management%20Final%20Edit.pdf

Taylor, P. (2019) 'A band aid on a gaping wound: Taylor on modern working practices', *New Technology, Work and Employment*, 34(2): 100–5.

Taylor, P. (2021) '"The petri dish and Russian roulette": working in UK contact centres during the COVID-19 pandemic', *Work in the Global Economy*, 1(1–2): 185–208.

Taylor, P., Baldry, C., Bain, P. and Ellis, V. (2003) '"A unique working environment": health, sickness and absence management in UK call centres', *Work, Employment and Society*, 17(3): 435–58.

Tendayi Achiume, E. (2018) 'End of mission statement of the Special Rapporteur on Contemporary Forms of Racism, Racial Discrimination, Xenophobia and Related Intolerance at the conclusion of her mission to the United Kingdom of Great Britain and Northern Ireland', Available from: https://www.ohchr.org/en/statements/2018/05/end-mission-statement-special-rapporteur-contemporary-forms-racism-racial

Thelen, K. (2014) *Varieties of Liberalization and the New Politics of Social Solidarity*, Cambridge: Cambridge University Press.

Thomas, A. and Doerflinger, N. (2020) 'Trade union strategies on climate change mitigation: between opposition, hedging and support', *European Journal of Industrial Relations*, 26(4): 383–99.

Thompson, E.P. (1968) *The Making of the English Working Class*, Harmondsworth: Penguin.

Thompson, M. (2023) 'July 2023 is hottest month ever recorded on Earth', *Scientific American*, 27 July, Available from: https://www.scientificamerican.com/article/july-2023-is-hottest-month-ever-recorded-on-earth

Thompson, P. (2013) 'Financialisation and the workplace: extending and applying the disconnected capitalism thesis', *Work, Employment and Society*, 27(3): 472–88.

Tollefson, J. (2020) 'Why deforestation and extinctions make pandemics more likely', *Nature*, 584: 175–6.

Tooze, A. (2018) *Crashed: How a Decade of Financial Crises Changed the World*, London: Allen Lane.

Tooze, A. (2021) *Shutdown: How COVID Shook the World Economy*, London: Allen Lane.

Topham, G. (2018) 'Ryanair reaches "historic" deal with UK pilots' union', *The Guardian*, 30 January, Available from: https://www.theguardian.com/business/2018/jan/30/ryanair-deal-uk-pilots-union-balps

Topham, G. (2022) 'P&O Ferries boss admits firm broke law by sacking staff without consultation', *The Guardian*, 24 March, Available from: https://www.theguardian.com/business/2022/mar/24/po-ferries-boss-says-800-staff-were-sacked-because-no-union-would-accepts-its-plans

Topham, G. (2023) 'One year on, has P&O Ferries got away with illegally sacking all its crew?', *The Guardian*, 17 March, Available from: https://www.theguardian.com/business/2023/mar/17/one-year-on-has-po-ferries-got-away-with-illegally-sacking-all-its-crew

Trades Union Congress (TUC) (2019) 'A just transition to a greener, fairer economy', London: TUC, Available from: https://www.tuc.org.uk/research-analysis/reports/just-transition-greener-fairer-economy

Trades Union Congress (TUC) (2021a) 'COVID-19 and insecure work', London: TUC.

Trades Union Congress (TUC) (2021b) 'Technology managing people: the worker experience', London: TUC.

Trades Union Congress (TUC) (2022a) 'Intrusive worker surveillance tech risks "spiralling out of control" without stronger regulation, TUC warns', TUC News, 28 February, Available from: https://www.tuc.org.uk/news/intrusive-worker-surveillance-tech-risks-spiralling-out-control-without-stronger-regulation

Trades Union Congress (TUC) (2022b) 'TUC calls on employers to keep their staff safe as temperatures soar', TUC News, 11 July, Available from: https://www.tuc.org.uk/news/tuc-calls-employers-keep-their-staff-safe-temperatures-soar-0

Trades Union Congress (TUC) (2023a) 'Labour market: 2022 was the worst year for real wage growth since current records began', TUC News, 14 February, Available from: https://www.tuc.org.uk/news/labour-market-2022-was-worst-year-real-wage-growth-current-records-began

Trades Union Congress (TUC) (2023b) 'Workers' experiences of long COVID', London: TUC, Available from: https://www.tuc.org.uk/sites/default/files/2023-03/Long%20Covid%20at%20Work%20report%20-%20FINAL%20COLOUR%202.pdf

Trapmann, V., Umney, C., Neumann, D., Stuart, M., Joyce, S. and Bessa, I. (2022) 'Labour protests during the pandemic: the case of hospital and retail workers in 90 countries', ILO Working Paper 83, Geneva: ILO, Available from: https://www.ilo.org/global/publications/working-papers/WCMS_860587/lang--en/index.htm

Tunstall, B. (2023) *Stay Home: Housing and Home in the UK during the COVID-19 Pandemic*, Bristol: Bristol University Press.

Tyler, I. (2020) *Stigma: The Machinery of Inequality*, London: Zed Books.

Umney, C. (2018) *Class Matters: Inequality and Exploitation in 21st Century Britain*, London: Pluto Press.

UNI Global Union (2018) 'Unions file OECD complaint against IKEA's international pattern of workers' rights abuses', UNI Global Union News, 29 September, Available from: https://uniglobalunion.org/news/unions-file-oecd-complaint-against-ikeas-international-pattern-of-workers-rights-abuses/

Unite (2023) 'Unite secures £400 million in wage deals for workers through disputes', Unite News, 9 July, Available from: https://www.unitetheunion.org/news-events/news/2023/july/unite-secures-400-million-in-wage-deals-for-workers-through-disputesUnited Nations Department of Social and Economic Affairs (no date) *Sustainable Development*, https://sdgs.un.org/goals/goal8

University and College Union (UCU) (2021) 'Precarious work in higher education', Available from: https://www.ucu.org.uk/media/10899/Precarious-work-in-higher-education-Oct-21/pdf/UCU_precarity-in-HE_Oct21_l883c067yz25.pdf

University and College Union (UCU) (2023) 'Stamp out casual contracts', Available from: https://www.ucu.org.uk/stampout

Upchurch, M. and Taylor, G. (2009) *The Crisis of Social Democratic Trade Unionism in Europe: The Search for Alternatives*, London: Routledge.

Vachon, T. (2021) 'The Green New Deal and just transition frames within the American labour movement', in N. Räthzel, D. Stevis and D. Uzzell (eds) *The Palgrave Handbook of Environmental Labour Studies*, London: Palgrave Macmillan, pp 105–26.

Van Doorn, N. (2017) 'Platform labor: on the gendered and racialized exploitation of low-income service work in the "on-demand" economy', *Information, Communication and Society*, 20(6): 898–914.

Van Doorn, N., Ferrari, F. and Graham, M. (2023) 'Migration and migrant labour in the gig economy: an intervention', *Work, Employment and Society*, 37(4): 1099–111.

Vandaele, K. (2019) 'Bleak prospects: mapping trade union membership in Europe since 2000', Brussels: European Trade Union Institute.

Vaughan-Whitehead, D. (2015) 'The European social model in times of crisis: an overview', in D. Vaughan-Whitehead (ed) *The European Social Model in Crisis: Is Europe Losing Its Soul?*, Cheltenham: Edward Elgar Publishing, pp 1–65.

Vermeiren, M. (2021) *Crisis and Inequality: The Political Economy of Advanced Capitalism*, Cambridge: Polity.

Vitols, K., Schütze, K., Mestre, A., Chavanet, S., Marquant, S., Poupard, J.-F. et al (2011) 'Industrial relations and sustainability: the role of social partners in the transition towards a green economy', Dublin: European Foundation for the Improvement of Living and Working Conditions.

Vonnegut, K. (1952) *Player Piano*, New York: Charles Scribner's Sons.

Waddington, J., Müller, T. and Vandaele, K (2019) 'Setting the scene: collective bargaining under neoliberalism', in T. Müller, K. Vandaele and J. Waddington (eds) *Collective Bargaining in Europe: Towards an Endgame, Volume 1*, Brussels: ETUI, pp 1–32.

Wagner, M. (2013) '"Green" human resource benefits: do they matter as determinants of environmental management system implementation?', *Journal of Business Ethics*, 114: 443–56.

Walby, S. (2017) *Crisis*, Cambridge: Polity.

Waldinger, R. (1994) 'The making of an immigrant niche', *International Migration Review*, 28(1): 3–30.

Wallerstein, I. (1989) *The Modern World-System*, London: Academic Press.

Wallerstein, I. (2006) *European Universalism: The Rhetoric of Power*, London: New Press.

Weber, I. (2021) 'Could strategic price controls help fight inflation?', *The Guardian*, 29 December, Available from: https://www.theguardian.com/business/commentisfree/2021/dec/29/inflation-price-controls-time-we-use-it

Weber, I. and Wasner, E. (2023) 'Sellers' inflation, profits and conflict: why can large firms hike prices in an emergency?', *Review of Keynesian Economics*, 11(2): 183–213.

Weber, M. (1922) *Economy and Society* (translated into English 1978), Berkeley: University of California Press.

Weeks, K. (2011) *The Problem with Work: Feminism, Marxism, Antiwork Politics, and Postwork Imaginaries*, Durham, NC: Duke University Press.

Weghmann, V. (2022) 'Theorising practice: independent trade unions in the UK', *Work in the Global Economy*, 2(2): 132–47.

Welsh Government (2021) 'Draft Social Partnership and Public Procurement (Wales) Bill, consultation', Available from: https://gov.wales/draft-social-partnership-and-public-procurement-wales-bill

Wieviorka, M. (2023) 'France protests: Macron's isolation at the top will only fuel more conflict', *The Conversation*, 30 March, Available from: https://theconversation.com/france-protests-macrons-isolation-at-the-top-will-only-fuel-more-conflict-202772

Willetts, D. (2010) *The Pinch: How the Baby Boomers Took Their Children's Future and Why They Should Give It Back*, London: Atlantic Books.

Williams, S. (2024) 'Expanding the boundaries of industrial relations as a field of study: the role of "new actors"', in A. Hodder and S. Mustchin (eds) *The Value of Industrial Relations: Contemporary Work and Employment in Britain*, Bristol: Bristol University Press, pp 65–75.

Williams, S. and Scott, P. (eds) (2016) *Employment Relations under Coalition Government: The UK Experience, 2010–2015*, Abingdon: Routledge.

Williams, S., Bradley, H., Devadason, R. and Erickson, M. (2013) *Globalization and Work*, Cambridge: Polity.

Wolf, M. (2023) *The Crisis of Democratic Capitalism*, London: Allen Lane.

Women's Budget Group (WBG) (2017) 'Intersecting inequalities: the impact of austerity on Black and ethnic minority women in the UK', London: WBG and Runnymede Trust.

Women's Budget Group (WBG) (2020) 'Women, employment and earnings: a pre-budget briefing', London: WBG.

Women's Budget Group (WBG) (2022) 'Women's Budget Group warns against austerity 2.0, a triple whammy for women', Press Release, 14 November, Available from: https://wbg.org.uk/media/wbg-warns-against-austerity-2-0-a-triple-whammy-for-women

Wood, A. (2020) *Despotism on Demand: How Power Operates in the Flexible Workplace*, Ithaca, NY: Cornell University Press.

Wood, A. (2021) 'Algorithmic management consequences for work organisation and working conditions', JRC Working Papers Series on Labour, Education and Technology 2021/07, Seville: European Commission.

Wood, A., Lehdonvirta, V. and Graham, M. (2018) 'Workers of the internet unite? Online freelancer organisation among remote gig economy workers in six Asian and African countries', *New Technology, Work and Employment*, 33(1): 95–112.

Wood, A., Martindale, N. and Lehdonvirta, V. (2023) 'Dynamics of contention in the gig economy: rage against the platform, customer or state?', *New Technology, Work and Employment*, 38(2): 330–50.

Wood, J., Ausserladscheider, V. and Sparkes, M. (2023) 'The manufactured crisis of COVID-Keynesianism in Britain, Germany and the USA', *Cambridge Journal of Regions, Economy and Society*, 16(1): 19–29.

Woolfson, C. (2017) 'The "Singapore scenario": the uncertain prospects for labour standards in post-Brexit Britain', *Industrial Relations Journal*, 4(5–6): 384–402.

Wren-Lewis, S. (2018) *The Lies We Were Told: Politics, Economics, Austerity, and Brexit*, Bristol: Bristol University Press.

Wright, C. and Nyberg, D. (2017) 'An inconvenient truth: how organizations translate climate change into business as usual', *Academy of Management Journal*, 60(5): 1633–61.

Wright, S. and Dwyer, P. (2022) 'In-work Universal Credit: claimant experiences of conditionality mismatches and counterproductive benefit sanctions', *Journal of Social Policy*, 51(1): 20–38.

Index

References to figures are in *italics*.

A

A22 network 166
AB InBev brewery 115
activism 29–30, 46, 72, 138, 153–6
  see also climate activism; labour activism
Adkins, L. et al 85, 97
Africa 5, 37, 38, 99
age-based inequalities 84, 86, 90–2, 95–8, 125
  see also young people
Ainsley, C. 87
algorithmic management (AM) techniques 4, 41, 51–2, 58–63, 66
Allan, S. et al 58
Alper, Liz 161
Alton, Zeke 161
Amazon
  AI technology 39, 160
  inequalities 79, 165
  labour markets 52
  platform economy 40, 41
  trade unions 105, 107, 112, 162
anti-immigration policies 94–5, 99, 139, 140–1, 142
anti-work movement 153–6
Antràs, P. et al 32
Apple 39, 40, 72, 79, 160
ArcelorMittal 104
Argentina 140, 141
Aronowitz, Stanley 43
Aroun, W. 118
artificial intelligence (AI)
  monitoring role 4–5, 60–3
  platform economy 3, 4–5, 39, 41, 61
  replacing workers xii, 3, 4–5, 176
  trade unions 160–1, 170
Ashley, Louise 81
Asia 9, 37, 38, 53, 99, 111, 150–1
asylum seekers *see* refugees and asylum seekers

austerity policies
  Conservative Party (UK) 9, 50, 84, 123, 147, 152
  'cost-of-living crisis' (2021–23) 130, 132, 134
  COVID-19 12, 14, 152
  economic stagnation 9, 123–4, 128, 130, 132, 148
  global financial crisis (2007–8) 22, 59
  inequalities 84, 89, 93, 97
  labour markets 49, 50
  Labour Party (UK) 174
Australia 15, 70, 103, 112, 163
authoritarianism 30, 140, 141–2, 151–2, 159, 176
automation xii, 3–5, 60–3

B

Bell, Torsten 96
Biden, Joe 95–6, 138, 139, 149
Black, Bob 154
Black Lives Matter 99, 165
Blair, Tony 137
Blakeley, Grace xii–xiii
Blauner, R. 18
Blockadia 166
BlueGreen Alliance (BGA) 114
Boohoo 69
BP 167
Bradley, H. 97–8
Brandl, B. 111
Braverman, Harry xii, 18
Brexit 36, 42, 93, 124, 130, 140–2, 150
British Airways 66, 158
British Chambers of Commerce 127
British Gas 66, 167
British Social Attitudes surveys 92
Bulgaria 90
Buller, A. 178–9
Buzogány, A. 167

232

INDEX

C

Calafati, L. et al 129, 132
Cambodia 111
Canada 15, 90
capitalism *see* neoliberal capitalism
carbon emissions 16, 26, 33, 69, 72, 115–19
care sector *see* social care
Care Workers Union (CWU) 50, 52
caring responsibilities 1, 88, 124, 126–8
casualization 11–12, 38, 48, 58, 64, 93–4
Chagnon, C. et al 31
Charlwood, A. 62
ChatGPT 4–5, 60, 176
childcare 1, 42, 88–90, 97, 127, 149
China 32, 53, 70
Clark, C. 92
class 35–9, 78–87, 97
  see also elite (upper class); working class
Clean Clothes Campaign 173
climate activism 17, 99, 165–7, 180
climate emergency
  employment relations 67–76
  interconnectivity of crises xi, 6–7, 15–20, 24–6, 34, 70
  right-wing populism 99, 140
  social democracy 138
  trade unions 17, 113–19, 167, 170–2, 177
  see also 'just transition'
Cohen, Josh 154
collective bargaining
  climate emergency 118, 170–2, 177
  global financial crisis (2007–8) 9, 56, 105, 147
  strengthening of 165, 170–3, 177
  weakening of 8, 9, 56, 102–9, 132–3, 149
colonialism xii, 29, 31–2
Commission on Care 49
commodification 15–16, 30, 43, 49
  see also labour commodification
'community unionism' 110, 164–5, 172–3
Conferences of the Parties (CoPs) 16, 116
Conservative Party (UK)
  austerity policies 9, 50, 84, 123, 147, 152
  inequalities 81, 84, 85, 89, 94
  labour markets 36, 50
  market radical agenda 150
  P&O 'fire and rehire,' response to 67
  right-wing populism 140, 141, 142–3
  trade unions 142, 158–9, 172, 173
Corbyn, Jeremy 138
Cornfield, D. 164
Coronavirus Job Retention Scheme (CJRS) 14, 64, 98, 111, 125
'cost-of-living crisis' (2021–23) 129–35
  inequalities 79, 83–4
  labour markets 38, 42, 52, 129–30
  state intervention 148, 153, 159, 178
  trade unions 114, 132–3, 156–62, 164

Costa Rica 177
COVID-19
  AI/AM technologies 42, 61, 66
  anti-work movement 153–4, 155
  economic stagnation 122, *122*, 124
  employment relations 61, 63–7
  health and social care 12, 50, 52, 65, 125–6
  higher education (HE) 46–8
  inequalities 12, 64, 79, 86, 90–1, 98
  interconnectivity of crises 6–7, 12–14, 19–20, 24, 25, 32–4
  precarity 3, 38, 64
  remote working 4, 12, 46–7, 61, 66–7, 86, 153–4
  state intervention 7, 12–14, 34, 63–5, 140, 148, 152–3
  trade unions 14, 64, 111–13, 157–8, 163
crises of work, definition and history xi, 2–8, 19–20
crisis, definition and types 6, 21–6
critical social theory 18–19, 22, 24, 27
Cushen, J. 60

D

Davies, W. 149
decarbonization 16, 17, 71, 116–19, 148, 167
'decent work' *see* 'good work' agenda
deindustrialization xii, 35–6, 37, 82, 92, 104, 136
Delfanti, Alessandro 41
Deliveroo 11, 39, 40
democracy 17, 19, 22, 24–30, 174, 180
  see also social democracy
Democratic Party (USA) 138, 149
deregulation 8, 9, 13, 56, 146–7, 150–1
digitalization 36, 39–42, 51–2, 59, 160–1, 176
DiTomaso, Nancy 39
Doerflinger, N 117
Doeringer, P. 36
Dougherty, M. 71
Driver and Vehicle Licensing Agency (DVLA) 112

E

Econie, A. 71
economic inactivity 1, 88, 92, 124–8
economic stagnation 18, 22, 122–5, *122*
  see also wage stagnation
education 83, 87, 89–90, 96–7, 119, 128, 161–2
  see also higher education (HE)
Edwards, P. 6
elite (upper class) 42, 78–83, 84–6, 141, 152
employment relations 55–76
  climate emergency 67–76
  COVID-19 61, 63–7

definition 55
see also 'good work' agenda; 'just transition'; labour commodification
'end of work' predictions 3–5, 156
energy companies 39, 134, 166–7, 180
energy prices 130–2, 134, 148, 149, 156, 178
environment degradation 16, 29, 30, 34, 69–72
Equality Act (2010) 77
Erickson, Mark 88
ethnic minorities
  AM monitored jobs 41
  inequalities 10, 78, 82, 87, 89, 91–5, 99
  platform economy 39, 93–4
  right-wing populism 141
  trade unions 107, 164
  workplace exclusion 91, 92–3, 94
Eurofound 40
Europe
  austerity policies 9, 123
  climate emergency 15, 99, 114
  COVID-19 32, 36, 64
  history of 31–3
  social democracy 136, 137
  trade unions 102, 104, 105, 108, 114
  unemployment 11, 97
European Centre for Disease Prevention and Control 32
European Trade Union Confederation (ETUC) 114
European Union 50, 56, 147, 150
  see also Brexit
Evans, D. 82–3
Extinction Rebellion (XR) 17, 166

F

'fair pay agreements' 171, 173
'fast-food rights' campaign 107
Felli, R. 114
Ferlie, E. 45
Figueres, C. 176, 177
financialization
  AI/AM technologies 62
  class-based inequalities 79–80, 84
  economic stagnation 123–5, 130, 132–3
  global financial crisis (2007–8) 10, 22, 56
  neoliberal capitalism xii–xiii, 10–11, 56–60
  social care 10, 49–50, 57, 127
  sustainability 75
Fisher, Mark 176, 179
flexibilization
  climate emergency 71
  COVID-19 66–7
  economic stagnation 124–5, 129
  higher education (HE) 45
  inequalities 94–5, 98
  neoliberal capitalism 9–11, 56–9, 146, 147, 152
  platform economy 40

trade unions 102, 103–4, 105
  see also casualization
food banks 42, 84, 130, 157
food prices 130–2
fossil fuels 39, 117–18, 148, 166–7, 176–8, 180
France 31, 103, 137, 138, 139
Fridays for Future 165
Friedman, M. 136
Friedman, S. 80
fuel prices *see* energy prices
full-time work 40, 42, 44, 46, 89
'furlough' (Coronavirus Job Retention Scheme) 14, 64, 98, 111, 125

G

Galescu, Jonathan 72
Galgóczi, B. 116
Gamble, A. 27
Gane, N. 149
gender 62, 107–8, 164, 165, 177
  see also LGBTQ+; men; women
Germany 10, 14, 32, 63–4, 103–4, 105, 137
Gibson-Graham, J.K. 35
'gig' economy 11, 38, 39, 61, 82
  see also platform economy
Gilets Jaunes protests 138
global financial crisis (2007–8)
  inequalities 33, 79, 96
  job quality 5, 59
  neoliberal intensification 7, 8–11, 56, 105, 146–7
  precarity/unemployment 9–11, 22, 37–8, 41, 96, 147
  right-wing populism 139, 140, 142
  social democracy 137
  stagnation 9, 122–3, *122*, 124, 128–9, 132
global warming 15, 16–17, 18, 68, 70, 99, 166
globalization xii, 2–3, 7–10, 31–3, 136–7, 139
  see also multinational companies
Glucksmann, Miriam 88
Goldthorpe, J. 83
'good work' agenda
  anti-work movement 153–6
  climate emergency/sustainability 7, 16, 69–71, 73–4, 116
  COVID-19 67
  definition 169
  lack of 5–6, 12, 20, 33–4
  trade unions 14, 114, 116
  see also 'just transition'
Google 39, 40, 160
Graeber, David 5, 153, 154
Greece 15, 97, 112, 137
Green, J. 149
'green' HRM 74–5
'green' jobs 71–2, 114, 116, 118–19, 149, 174, 177

INDEX

Green New Deal (GND) 17, 39, 114
'green' workplaces 115, 170
Greenhouse, S. 157
Greenpeace 167
'greenwashing' 75, 178
Guenole, N. 62
Gunningham, N. 167
Guterres, António 98, 166

H

Habermas, J. 24, 27
Haddock-Millar, J. et al 74
Hall, S.-M. et al 91, 93
Hansen, K 159
Hay, Colin 6, 21
Hayes, L. 50–1, 52
HC-One 49
health *see* mental health; sick pay
health and safety
  AM monitored jobs 51
  climate emergency 68–9, 70, 71, 114
  COVID-19 12, 14, 47, 65, 111–13, 125
  housing 85
  'sustainable' HRM 73
  trade unions 111–13, 114, 162–3, 171
Health and Safety Executive 65
health care 12, 113, 128, 134
  see also National Health Service (NHS)
Hebblethwaite, Peter 67
Hebson, G. et al 50, 51–2
Heller, R.F. 45
Hendrikse, R. 151
Herod, A. 37
Hickel, J. 178
higher education (HE) 30, 38, 43–8, 80–1, 159–60
HireVue 61
Hodder, A. 158
home ownership 84, 86, 96, 97, 134
homelessness 42, 86
Horgan, A. 15
Horton, A. 49
Horvat, Srećko 33
hospitality 90, 97, 101, 104, 156
housing
  climate emergency 17, 99
  economic stagnation 129
  future scenarios 178
  inequalities 84–6, 90–1, 93, 96, 99
  precarity 44
human resource management (HRM) 56–7, 60, 73–5
Hungary 140
Hunter, D. 82

I

IKEA 104
immigration *see* migrant workers; refugees and asylum seekers
Immigration Act (2016) 95
income
  employer–employee relationship 1–2
  higher education (HE) 44, 46, 48
  inequalities 42, 79, 83–4, 123
  trade unions 102, 113, 118, 156–8
  see also Coronavirus Job Retention Scheme (CJRS); living wage; low-paid work; minimum wage; sick pay; wage stagnation
Independent Workers' Union of Great Britain (IWGB) 109, 164
Indonesia 111
inequalities *see* age-based inequalities; class; ethnic minorities; gender
inflation
  asset prices 11, 84, 85, 123
  economic stagnation 122–3, 125, 128
  pay rates 42, 85, 128, 130, 133–5, 163, 165
  trade unions 133, 158, 160
Inflation Reduction Act (USA, 2022) 138, 149
informal employment 5, 10, 35, 37–8, 82
Intergovernmental Panel on Climate Change (IPCC) 16, 178
International Labour Organization (ILO) 37, 111, 113, 116
International Monetary Fund (IMF) 134
International Trade Union Confederation (ITUC) 114, 116
Islamophobia 92–3, 142
Italy 15, 97, 103, 137, 138, 140

J

Jameson, Frederic 176
job protection 114, 117–18, 119, 167
job retention schemes 14, 63–5, 98, 111, 125
Johnson, Boris 142, 150
Jones, Owen 81
Jones, Philip 37–8, 41, 54
Just Stop Oil (JSO) 166–7
'just transition'
  climate activism 167
  'cost-of-living crisis' (2021–23) 135
  future scenarios 175–6, 177, 179
  mitigation of crisis of work 17, 71, 149, 153, 171–2, 173
  social democracy 138, 177
  trade unions 114, 115–19, 171–2, 177, 180
Justice for Janitors campaign 108

K

Kalra, V. 91–2
Katsaroumpas, I 142, 159, 168
Kelley, N. et al 92
Keynsianism 148, 149, 150, 152, 177
Kezar, A.J. et al 44
Klein, N. 17, 166–7, 178
Koch, I. et al 38

L

labour activism 156–65
  see also strikes
labour commodification
  COVID-19 63, 65, 67
  economic stagnation 12, 124, 132–3
  environment degradation 69–70
  migrant labour 93–5, 141
  neoliberal capitalism 56–60, 76
  platform economy/AI 4–5, 9–10, 60–3, 93, 147–8, 162
  trade unions 172, 173
Labour Force Survey 40
labour markets 35–54
  conceptualizations of 35, 36–9
  'cost-of-living crisis' (2021–23) 38, 42, 52, 129–30, 132–5
  COVID-19 38, 42, 46–8, 50, 52, 125–6, 155
  deregulation 8, 9, 13, 56, 146–7, 150–1
  economic stagnation 124–5, 128–9, 130
  see also precarity
Labour Party (UK) 136, 137, 138, 170–1, 173–4
labour shortages
  anti-work movement 155
  'cost-of-living crisis' (2021–23) 130, 156
  COVID-19 52–3, 125–6, 156
  health and social care 36, 52–3, 125–8, 163
  right-wing populism 141, 142
Lambert, R. 37
Lansley, S. 79
Lapavitsas, C. 134
Laurison, D. 80
Lawrence, M. 179
Le Pen, Marine 139
left-wing populism 137–8
Leicester 69, 83
Levitas, Ruth 180
LGBTQ+ 107, 140, 141
Liberal Democrat Party (UK) 147
Lidl 105
living wage 50, 73, 89, 110, 170
local authorities (LAs) 49, 50, 52–3
Local Housing Allowances 90
London 83, 150
long COVID 112, 125
low-paid work
  Biden administration 149
  COVID-19 64, 67, 90, 98
  inequalities 86–7, 89–90, 92, 97–8, 127
  labour markets 37–8, 40, 42, 129, 130
  social care 10, 48–53, 58, 86–7, 126–7
  theoretical background 27, 36
  trade unions 108, 109
  women 37, 42, 86–7, 89–90, 127
Lynch, Mick 39, 101

M

Maccarrone, V. 109
Macron, Emmanuel 139
Maffie, D. 113
market radical agenda 150–1, 153
Marx, Karl/Marxist theory 24–5, 37
McDonald's 107, 165
McKenzie, Lisa 82
Meloni, Giorgia 140
men 92–3, 98, 108, 132, 177
mental health 27, 59–60, 90–1, 131, 180
#MeToo movement 165
middle classes 35, 37, 39, 82–3
Middle East 37
migrant workers
  inequalities 87, 91, 93–5, 99
  labour markets 35, 36, 37, 38, 41, 50, 141
  trade unions 108, 109–10, 164, 165
Milei, Javier 141
minimum wage 38, 89, 149, 171, 173
modern slavery 69, 72, 94–5
Moore, S. 50–1, 52
Morrisons 40
mortgages 8, 42, 84, 134
multinational companies 43, 60, 72, 74, 104
Mustchin, S. 158

N

National Health Service (NHS)
  crisis 23, 26, 126, 127–8, 163–4
  inequalities 89
  labour shortages 36, 126, 163–4
  outsourcing 40
  strikes 157, 163–4
neoliberal capitalism
  corrective model proposal 29–30, 34
  crisis of 8–12, 21–6, 146–53
  critical social theory 18–19, 27
  future scenarios 175–80
  history of 31–3
  see also rentier capitalism; shareholder capitalism
'Net Zero Strategy' (UK) 16
net-zero world 102, 115, 148, 153, 172, 180
'New Deal for Working People' agenda 173
new public management (NPM)
  initiatives 43, 44–8
New Zealand 103, 163
Nottingham 82

O

Occupy movement 146
Office for National Statistics (ONS) 42, 83–94
Oldham 92
Organisation for Economic Co-operation and Development (OECD) 134
'organizing unionism' model 108–9
Osnos, E. 96

INDEX

outsourcing 40, 50
Oxfam 42, 158

P

P&O 67
Pacific region 15, 38
pandemics 16, 18, 32–3
  see also COVID-19
Paris Agreement (2015) 16–17
part-time work 1, 36, 40, 44, 88–9, 124
Pettinger, L. 35
Piketty, Thomas 25–6, 31, 33, 79–80, 85
Piore, M. 36
platform economy
  AI/AM technologies 3, 4–5, 39, 41, 61
  inequalities 39, 82, 93–4
  precarity 9, 10, 11, 39–43, 147
  trade unions 109, 162, 173
Poland 117, 140
populism 30, 83, 94–5, 99, 137–43, 151–2, 176
Potter, Jesse 39
poverty 42, 84, 91, 118, 129, 176
precarity
  COVID-19 3, 38, 64
  definition 37–8
  economic stagnation 130, 133
  higher education (HE) 38, 43–8
  inequalities 86, 94–8
  platform economy 9, 10, 11, 39–43, 147
  social care 48–53
  social democracy 138
  trade unions 106, 109, 164, 171, 172, 173
presenteeism 12, 46, 59, 66, 174
privatization xii, 27, 40, 44, 48–50, 161–2, 180
Prodoscore 58
professional work 38–9, 43–4, 48, 58–9, 80, 83
public transport 177–8, 180

R

racism 62, 93–5, 99–100, 139, 140, 164, 165
Rail, Maritime and Transport Union (RMT) 39, 101
Räthzel, N. 113–14
Readings, Bill 43
Red Cross 42
Red Funnel 157
Reddit 154, 155
redundancies 14, 60, 64, 82
refugees and asylum seekers 41, 91, 94–5, 99, 142, 176
regulation *see* state intervention
remote working
  COVID-19 4, 12, 46–7, 61, 66–7, 86, 153–4
  monitoring of 59, 66, 153–4
  presenteeism 12, 59, 66, 174

renewable and clean energy 38, 114, 119, 149, 177
Renner, M. et al 71
rentier capitalism 26, 80, 84–6, 123–5, 132, 135, 172–3
residential social care 10, 49–50, 57
Resolution Foundation 96
retail
  COVID-19 3, 63, 90, 98, 113
  digitalization 41–2, 58, 61
  inequalities 90, 92, 97–8
  jobs quality 40
  supply chain 69
  trade unions 104, 105, 113, 156
Rhodes, J. 93
right-wing populism 83, 94–5, 139–43, 151–2, 176
Rivett-Carnac, T. 176, 177
Roberts, K. 81
Rodríguez-Modroño, P. et al 94
Romania 97
RotaCloud 62
Royal College of Nursing (RCN) 157
Royal Mail 42, 59
Ryanair 106

S

safety *see* health and safety
SAG-AFTRA (Screen Actors' Guild-American Federation of Television and Radio Artists) 160–1
Saltmarsh, C. 17
Sanders, Bernie 138
Savage, Mike 33, 79, 82
Sayer, Andrew 79
Scandinavia 53, 178
Scherhaufer, P. 167
Schröder, Gerhard 137
Scottish National Party 174
self-employment 11, 40, 64, 82, 92, 111, 173
Shankley, W. 92, 93
shareholder capitalism xii, 42, 53–4, 57, 80
Shay, Jonathan 47
Shell 167
Sick Building Syndrome (SBS) 68–9
sick pay 65, 149
Sikweba, D. 118
Singapore 150, 151
Slobodian, Quinn 84, 142, 150–1
Sloterdijk, Peter 33
Smith, A. 59
social care
  COVID-19 12, 50, 52, 65
  economic inactivity 126–8
  financialization 49–50, 57, 127
  low-paid work 10, 48–53, 58, 86–7, 126–7
  social care 10
  women 10, 49–52, 86–7, 88, 94, 97

social democracy 102, 103, 105, 122, 135–9, 177–9
Social Mobility Commission (SMC) 80
South Africa 118
Southern Cross 49
Spain 94, 97, 137, 138
Springer, Simon 146
Standing, Guy xii, 11, 37
Starbucks Workers United (SBWU) 162
Starmer, Keir 138
state intervention
  climate emergency 17, 72, 148
  COVID-19 7, 12–14, 34, 63–5, 140, 148, 152–3
  inequalities 77, 90, 94–5
  neoliberal capitalism 7, 10, 27–9, *28*, *29*, 147–52
  trade unions 105, 158–9, 170–4
  see also authoritarianism; deregulation
Statista 97
Streeck, Wolfgang 18–19, 22–3, 24
strikes
  climate-focused 165
  COVID-19 14, 112–13, 157–8
  history of 2, 104, 157
  surge (2022–24) 14, 42, 156–61, 163
  workers' engagement with 107, 133
Strikes (Minimum Service Levels) Act (UK, 2023) 142, 158–9
subcontracting 39–40, 50
Sure Start 89
sustainability 8, 67–76, 124–5, 148, 178
  see also 'good work' agenda; 'green' jobs; 'just transition'
'sustainable' HRM 73–5
Sweden 137, 163–4

T

Tassinari, A. 109
tax havens 42, 78, 150
taxation 9, 13, 27, 134, 149–52, 172–4, 178
Taylorism 45–6, 62
Tebbit, Norman 36
Teller, Edward 18
temporary work 9, 36, 37–8, 44, 71, 89
Tendayi Achiume, E. 93
Tesla 41, 71–2, 118
Thatcherism xii, 49, 150
Thomas, A. 117
Thompson, P. 60
Tooze xi, 175
trade unions 101–20
  anti-work movement 155
  climate emergency 17, 113–19, 167, 170–2, 177
  COVID-19 14, 64, 111–13, 157–8, 163
  future scenarios 175–6, 177, 180
  health and safety 111–13, 114, 162–3, 171
  higher education (HE) 48, 159–60

inequalities 39, 40, 102–3, 107–10, 165, 177
  'just transition' 114, 115–19, 171–2, 177, 180
  membership levels 102–3, 105, 106–8, 118, 160, 164
  power resources 103–4, 105, 109, 110, 160, 165, 170–1
  right-wing populism 141–2, 152
  social democracy 136, 138
  strike surge (2022–24) 14, 42, 156–61, 163
Trades Union Congress (TUC) 111, 112, 114–15, 116–17, 161–2, 177
Trapmann, V. et al 113
Trump, Donald 105, 139, 141
Trussell Trust 84
Turkey 140, 152

U

Uber 11, 39, 40
Ukraine crisis 23, 42, 130, 156
UN Framework Convention on Climate Change (UNFCCC) 16
underemployment 5, 11, 124, 127
unemployment
  automation 60
  COVID-19 64, 124
  decarbonization 118
  history of 22, 35–6, 37, 149
  inequalities 11, 37, 82–93, 96–8
UNISON 50
Unite 110, 158
United Automobile Workers (UAW) union 118, 158
United Kingdom Independence Party (UKIP) 140
United Kingdom (UK)
  gross domestic product (GDP) 122–3, *122*
  history of xii, 31, 32
United Nations (UN) 16, 71, 93
United States of America (USA)
  climate emergency 15, 16, 113–14, 116, 118, 119, 177
  COVID-19 14, 64, 155, 157
  labour markets/relations 37, 43–4, 54, 64, 155
  neoliberal capitalism xii, 8, 9, 10, 11
  trade union action 110, 112, 116, 118–19, 157, 160, 162, 164–5
  trade union membership 103, 108, 164
  trade unions, opposition to 104–5, 107, 111, 170
  see also Biden, Joe; Trump, Donald
United Steelworkers 114
University and College Union (UCU) 38, 48
unpaid work
  conservation work 38
  higher education (HE) 46
  social care 49, 51–2, 126–7

INDEX

'wage theft' 53–4
women 1, 40, 49, 51–2, 127
Uzzell, D. 113–14

V

Vodafone 61
Vonnegut, Kurt 18

W

wage stagnation
  'cost-of-living crisis' (2021–23) 130–3, *131*
  global financial crisis (2007–8) 9, 124, 128–9, 132
  trade unions 158, 159, 161, 172
Wales 174
Wallerstein, Immanuel 33
wars 16, 100, 176
weather events 15, 24, 68, 176, 178
Weber, Max 36
Weeks, Kathi 155
Weghmann, V. 165
welfare state
  austerity policies 9, 130, 147
  disciplinary use 37
  inequalities 82, 89
  populism 140, 151
  social democracy 102, 137, 177
Willetts, David 96
women
  inequalities 64, 86–90, 92–4, 97, 99
  labour markets 37, 40, 42, 49, 50–2, 88, 127
  low-paid work 37, 42, 86–7, 89–90, 127
  social care 10, 49–52, 86–7, 88, 94, 97, 127
  trade unions 107
  unpaid work 1, 40, 49, 51–2, 127
Women's Budget Group (WBG) 89, 90

work degradation
  automation 3–5
  climate emergency 7, 16, 17, 70
  COVID-19 7, 12, 52–3, 67
  labour activism 163–4
  lack of 'good' jobs 5–6, 12, 20, 33–4
  social care 49, 52–3
  see also precarity
work intensification
  COVID-19 66, 67, 90
  higher education (HE) 46–8
  presenteeism 12, 59, 66, 174
  social care 51–2
  sustainability 75
  trade unions 113, 161–2, 163–4, 170, 172
working class
  inequalities 80–1, 84–7, 89, 95, 97
  labour markets 35, 37, 38–9
  right-wing populism 139
  social democracy 136
  trade unions 102, 156
World Health Organization (WHO) 18
Writers Guild of America (WGA) 160–1

Y

young people
  climate activism 165
  COVID-19 90–1, 98
  housing 84, 91, 96
  labour markets 12, 35, 37–8, 39, 41, 95–8
  mental health 27, 91
  trade unions 102–3, 107, 108, 162
  unemployment 11, 37, 92, 96, 97, 98

Z

zero-hours contracts 11, 38, 50, 58, 89–90, 124, 173
Žižek, Slavoj 176

www.ingramcontent.com/pod-product-compliance
Lightning Source LLC
Chambersburg PA
CBHW051536020426
42333CB00016B/1949